The Eurozone Crisis

Topical and timely, this book offers an economically informed constitutional analysis of European responses to the crisis. It discusses the longer-term proposals on the table including rescue measures and stability mechanisms, as well as the tightening of European economic governance. The authors see the European constitution as a multi-dimensional and multi-temporal process of constitutionalisation. They examine how the crisis has catapulted the economic constitution back to the 'pacemaker' position from where it determines developments in the political and social dimension. However, now the key role is not played by the constitution of 'microeconomics', focusing on free movement and competition law, but by the constitution of 'macroeconomics', introduced in Maastricht.

Kaarlo Tuori is Professor of Jurisprudence and Academy Professor at the University of Helsinki. He is also Vice President of the Venice Commission of the Council of Europe and serves as a consulting expert on the Constitutional Law Committee at the Finnish Parliament.

Klaus Tuori is a researcher of EU constitutional law at Helsinki University. He has worked extensively within the financial market sector, focusing on asset management and sovereign debt markets. Between 1997 and 2000, he worked as a monetary policy economist at the European Central Bank designing the framework of the common monetary policy.

Cambridge Studies in European Law and Policy

This series aims to produce original works which contain a critical analysis of the state of the law in particular areas of European Law and set out different perspectives and suggestions for its future development. It also aims to encourage a range of work on law, legal institutions and legal phenomena in Europe, including 'law in context' approaches. The titles in the series will be of interest to academics; policy makers; policy formers who are interested in European legal, commercial and political affairs; practising lawyers including the judiciary; and advanced law students and researchers.

Books in the series

The Eurozone Crisis
A Constitutional Analysis

Kaarlo Tuori

and

Klaus Tuori

CAMBRIDGE
UNIVERSITY PRESS

University Printing House, Cambridge CB2 8BS, United Kingdom

Published in the United States of America by Cambridge University Press, New York

Cambridge University Press is part of the University of Cambridge.

It furthers the University's mission by disseminating knowledge in the pursuit of education, learning and research at the highest international levels of excellence.

www.cambridge.org
Information on this title: www.cambridge.org/9781107649453

© Kaarlo Tuori and Klaus Tuori 2014

First published 2014

Printing in the United Kingdom by TJ International Ltd, Padstow, Cornwall

A catalogue record for this publication is available from the British Library

Library of Congress Cataloguing in Publication data
Tuori, Kaarlo, 1948– author.
The Eurozone crisis : a constitutional analysis / Kaarlo Tuori, Klaus Tuori.
    pages   cm. – (Cambridge studies in European law and policy)
Includes bibliographical references and index.
ISBN 978-1-107-05655-8 (hardback) – ISBN 978-1-107-64945-3 (paperback)
1. Constitutional law–European Union countries.   2. Financial crises–European
Union countries.   3. Monetary policy–European Union countries.   4. Eurozone.
5. European Union countries–Economic policy.   I. Tuori, Klaus, author.   II. Title.
KJC4445.T86 2013
337.1′42–dc23
2013032793

ISBN 978-1-107-05655-8 Hardback
ISBN 978-1-107-64945-3 Paperback

Contents

Series editors' preface

This new contribution from Kaarlo Tuori and Klaus Tuori, offering an innovative constitutional analysis of the Eurozone crisis, is an important addition to the series *Cambridge Studies in European Law and Policy*. Combining expertise on law, theory and economics, the authors are able to open our eyes to the many aspects of the Eurozone crisis and its ramifications for societies and polities. They want to take us beyond thinking about the crisis merely as a financial crisis, a crisis of the banking sector or a threat to public debt, and to give it a broader public order and constitutional perspective. The Eurozone crisis goes to the very heart of the European constitutional order, understood in a multi-perspectival manner to incorporate both the legal order sustained by the EU treaties, and also the systems of the Member States. The Eurozone crisis thus entreats us to consider also issues of democracy and transparency, as well as issues about the values which underpin our societies in the early twenty-first century including issues around security in its widest sense. Tuori and Tuori, through a historically and conceptually grounded analysis, show how these issues are intimately linked to each other. We warmly welcome this volume to the series.

Jo Shaw
Laurence Gormley

Preface

This is a book about relations: relations between constitutional law and economy, but also between different dimensions of the constitution and different layers of the economic constitution. These relations transfer and transform the effects of shocks introduced by the economic crisis, and, by the same token, testify to the interconnectedness of the constitutional system. Often enough, relations take the form of open-ended dialogues. We hope to make a modest contribution to these dialogues by pointing to some hitherto neglected connections and repercussions.

The German ordoliberal school has pursued the ambitious project of combining legal and economic scholarship; much more ambitious, we would argue, than the law and economics movement of recent decades. Law and economics have mainly been content with buttressing legal reasoning with policy arguments drawn from an economic assessment of alternative readings of law. In contrast, ordoliberals have sought cooperation between law and economics at a deeper, conceptual level. In this cooperation both partners are supposed to learn from each other. Thus, lawyers are not merely at the receiving end, as is their lot in law and economics.

For ordoliberals, the need of a dialogue between lawyers and economists arose from the perceived necessity of an *ordo* – a legal and institutional framework – for the functioning of the economic system. A central means for facilitating dialogue consisted of common concepts which had their place in both law and economics. One of these key concepts – if not the very key concept – was 'economic constitution'.

Adhering to the general dialogical style if not the substantive tenets of ordoliberals, our book is a product of cooperation between legal scholarship and economics. One of us is a constitutional lawyer and legal theorist, the other both an economist and a lawyer with a professional background at the ECB during the years of preparing for introduction of the common currency. To facilitate mutual dialogue and learning, and to guarantee textual coherence, we chose to co-author all the chapters; the reader, though, may, if he or she so wishes, make more or less educated guesses as to who has been responsible for drafting which parts of the manuscript. We present a constitutional scrutiny of the Eurozone crisis which includes economic analyses as well. We justify the place of economic analyses in our constitutional discussion with a theoretical view of constitutions in general and the European constitution in particular. We employ a relational notion of constitution and argue that a constitution must be examined through the interrelation between constitutional law and its object of regulation. Here we find the concept of economic constitution highly relevant.

We acknowledge the ordoliberal origins of this concept, but we do not subscribe to the contents the ordoliberals assigned to it. For ordoliberals the economic constitution signified a fundamental decision in favour of a market economy, based on free competition. We detach the concept from its link to a specific model of the economy and simply define it through the interrelation between constitutional law and economy. In the European economic constitution we distinguish between two layers: the microeconomic constitution, centred around free movement and competition law and introduced by the Treaty of Rome (1958), and the macroeconomic constitution, centred around aggregate economic objectives and economic policies, and introduced by the Treaty of Maastricht (1993). In its constitutional aspect, the Eurozone crisis must be examined primarily as a crisis of the Maastricht macroeconomic constitution. Yet, in our discussion we continually recall the interdependence of the two layers of the European economic constitution.

We follow our programme of mingling economic with legal analysis by, first, reconstructing the economic assumptions which underpinned the Maastricht principles of the macroeconomic constitution; and, second, by examining the economic background of the present crisis, especially how the underlying economic assumptions have stood the test of reality. We conclude that many of the assumptions have been invalidated; that this has led to a teetering of some of the vital principles of the Maastricht macroeconomic constitution; and that this, in turn, has launched a significant constitutional mutation, some aspects of which were consecrated in the *Pringle* ruling of the Court of Justice of the European Union in November 2012. The economic analyses do not constitute an external introduction to but, rather, an integral element of the constitutional discussion.

Our notion of constitution, emphasising the interaction of constitutional law and its societal object of regulation, is an important aspect, but not the only aspect, of the general approach we term 'relational analytic'. We also point to the relationships linking the economic constitution to other dimensions of the European constitution, such as the political and social constitutions. An essential part of the Eurozone crisis as a constitutional crisis consists of its repercussions for democracy and social rights.

Our objective of treating economic analysis as an integral part of constitutional investigation has led us to consult our colleagues not only in law but in economics as well. We have greatly benefited from comments by Joxerramon Bengoetxea, Niilo Jääskinen, Sixten Korkman, Tuomas Ojanen, Allan Rosas, Tuomas Saarenheimo, Suvi Sankari, Jukka Snell, Pedro Teixeira and Vesa Vihriälä. We have learned a lot but, of course, remain solely responsible for the views put forth in this book.

Things in Europe have moved fast, although we have been able to complete our manuscript in a period of relative calm. We have been able to follow developments up to June 2013.

We have received financial support for our work from the Finnish Academy, through the Centre of Excellence 'Foundations of European Law and Polity', and the Wihuri Foundation (Klaus Tuori). The quite rapid production of the manuscript would not have been possible without the invaluable help of our research assistants Anna-Maria Rehbinder and Mikko Hakkarainen, and our linguistic adviser Christopher Goddard. During completion of the manuscript, one of us was sitting on the porch of his summer house in Loppi in Central Finland while the other was sailing in the waters between Finland and Sweden; Anna-Maria was fine-tuning the footnotes and the typography in Mumbai; Christopher was checking the language at his forest home near Riga; and our very helpful editor Helen Frances was waiting for the end result in Cambridge. A wonderful example of positive globalisation!

We dedicate this book to the Helsinki CoE 'Foundations of European Law and Polity' and to all our colleagues there. The Centre, financed by the Finnish Academy, has provided an extremely stimulating environment for our research.

PART I

Setting the scene

1 Introduction: framework of the analysis

The Eurozone crisis possesses many aspects. Most conspicuously, it has manifested itself as an economic, financial and fiscal crisis; as increasing unemployment and laggard economic growth; as bottlenecks in the financial system as well as liquidity and solvency problems of financial institutions; and as mounting public debt and threatening state insolvency. But at issue is also a constitutional crisis. The crisis has shaken the foundations of what we shall term the second, macroeconomic layer of the European economic constitution. The Maastricht principles of the European economic constitution are teetering, with implications reaching out beyond the economic dimension and extending to the national level, too. A constitutional analysis of the crisis must adopt a broad perspective and a comprehensive analytical framework.

Our discussion of the constitutional implications of the Eurozone crisis is based on a specific understanding of what constitutions in general and the European constitution in particular are about. In the nation-state context, especially in the revolutionary French and American traditions, constitutions are seen as unified normative entities which result from the exercise of constituent power – *pouvoir constituant* – by the people – the demos – at a clearly definable constitutional moment. This tripartite conceptual apparatus – 'constituent power' – 'demos' – 'constitutional moment' – is not applicable to the European constitution: there is no unified European constitution to which the European citizenry would have given birth as an expression of its constituent power at a particular constitutional moment. When discussing the European constitution, revolutionary constitutional concepts must be replaced by an evolutionary counterpart; namely constitutionalisation. Characteristic of the European constitution is its process-like nature; it is not a temporarily and sub-stantively clear-cut normative entity but, rather, a continuous process of constitutionalisation. Of course, this process includes such high profile constitutional events – constitutional speech acts, we could also say – as new Treaties and Treaty amendments, such as the Treaty of Rome and the Treaty of Maastricht, which have played a crucial role in the development of the economic constitution. But it also includes much else, speech acts by other constitutional actors, such as the ECJ, the Commission and the Council, the ECB, constitutional scholars, national constitutional courts …

We also maintain that the European process of constitutionalisation contains a number of dimensions which evolve pursuant to diverging temporal paces; at issue is a multi-dimensional and multi-temporal process. We employ a relational concept of law and constitution, which has affinities with the institutional theory of law, with Carl Friedrich Savigny as an early precursor and Neil MacCormick as perhaps the most prominent twentieth-century exponent.[1] We propose examining the constitution through the relation – constitutional relation, we could also say – that constitutional law maintains with its object of regulation, the constitutional object. The relational concept of constitution facilitates distinguishing between diverse dimensions of the European constitution in accordance with the respective constitutional object – the object of constitutional regulation. Our tentative proposal for identifying what we call the many constitutions of Europe is the following:

- the economic constitution (with the economy as the main constitutional object);
- the juridical constitution (the reflexive constitution having the legal system as the constitutional object);
- the political constitution (with the European polity as the constitutional object);
- the security constitution (with security risks as the constitutional object);
- the social constitution (addressing the social welfare of European citizens).

---

[1] See MacCormick's contributions in N. MacCormick and O. Weinberger (1986), as well as N. MacCormick (2007). The French institutional school of the early twentieth century, with León Duguit and Maurice Hauriou as the main representatives, should be kept in mind as well.

A relational and multi-dimensional approach can be fruitful in the nation-state setting, too,[2] although the tacit understanding usually is that all the aspects of constitution go together and that, say, juridical and political constitution emerge and develop in parallel to each other. But at the European level, due to the process character of the constitution, no guarantees exist that the various dimensions develop at a similar pace; on the contrary, temporal diversity has been a key character of European constitutionalisation. So we claim that the European constitution is both an evolutionary and, at the same time, a differentiated process: the putative European constitutions have not emerged simultaneously but, rather, successively, following a certain order; nor have they evolved at the same pace. Typical of European constitutionalisation is – to borrow Ernst Bloch's expression – *Gleichzeitigkeit des Ungleichzeitigen*.[3]

According to our (hypo)thesis, distinct periods can be discerned in European constitutionalisation, which receive their particular colouring from a particular constitution. Reflecting the temporal and functional primacy of economic integration, the first wave, initiated by the Treaty of Rome or even earlier by the Treaty of Paris establishing the European Steel and Coal Community, proceeded under the auspices of economic constitution.[4] The landmark decisions of the ECJ defining the basic principles characterising Community law as an independent legal system manifested the significance of the juridical constitution. The Maastricht Treaty epitomised at least the temporary dominance of the political constitution. The Amsterdam Treaty (1998), with its new provisions on the Area of Freedom, Security and Justice, inaugurated the prominence of the security constitution, which was further reinforced by 9/11.[5] Finally, the Eurozone crisis has again catapulted the economic

---

[2] In fact, as we will make clear below, the concept of economic constitution was first introduced in a nation-state context.

[3] On the multi-dimensional and multi-temporal process of European constitutionalisation, see K. Tuori (2010).

[4] Arguably, though, in the early 1950s, economic integration was at least partly an *ersatz* solution when political integration proved not to be reachable. See, e.g., Chapters 1 and 2 in Gilbert (2012).

[5] Although too much should not be made of the provisions on the values and objectives of the EU, it is worth mentioning that in the present list of objectives in Art. 3 TEU, the provision on the area of freedom, security and justice precedes that on the internal market and other economic (and social) aims. According to Art. 3(2), "the Union shall offer its citizens an area of freedom, security and justice without internal frontiers, in which the free movement of persons is ensured in conjunction with appropriate measures with respect to external border controls, asylum, immigration and the prevention and combating of crime".

constitution back to the pacemaker role.[6] However, if the emphasis in the Rome Treaty and the subsequent case law of the ECJ lay on what we call the microeconomic constitution, the crisis has highlighted the role of the second, macroeconomic layer of the European economic constitution. The pacemaker role of the macroeconomic constitution entails that ongoing 'constitutional mutation'[7] is not restricted to the economic aspect and that, accordingly, the present constitutional crisis should not merely be conceived of in economic terms. It extends to the political and social dimensions; it also affects democracy and transparency, as well as social values and rights. In our constitutional analysis, we shall emphasise the risk that changes in the economic dimension may be allowed to dictate development in the political and social dimensions so that the particular constitutional aspects of the latter are not sufficiently heeded.

According to our understanding, constitutional law as the legal pole of the constitutional relation develops through specific constitutional speech acts, making up constitutional discourse. An important task for EU constitutional scholarship is to identify the relevant constitutional actors and assess the weight of their respective interventions. The two primary actors, whose contributions provide our discussion with the most important institutional support, are the constitutional legislator issuing Treaties and their amendments, and the Court of Justice (ECJ), the constitutional court of the EU, issuing constitutionally relevant case law. Yet, constitutional law should not be conceived of solely in terms of surface-level normative material, such as explicit constitutional provisions and precedents. Constitutional law also comprises a legal cultural level through which individual constitutional provisions or precedents are read and interpreted and which also lends surface-level normative material a certain kind of coherence. This legal cultural level also involves – so we claim – a particular view of the constitutional object: a hidden social theory, as it were. Without such legal-cultural underpinnings, scattered individual

---

[6] Such a *temporal succession* should not be interpreted in the sense of an emerging constitutional aspect replacing or supplanting the previous one; rather, the constitutional dimensions complement each other. Thus, the history of the economic constitution did not end with the first period of constitutionalisation. Emphasis on the juridical constitution should not be taken as signifying a standstill or an eclipse of the economic constitution; the latent and manifest development of the economic constitution continued, and the economic constitution has always retained its functional primacy.

[7] E. Chiti *et al.* (2012), pp. 418 ff.

provisions in the formal constitution or fragmentary constitutional case law would hardly give rise to a distinct constitutional dimension. Constitutional law should be examined, not only in its relation to the constitutional object, but also as an interplay between surface-level normative material and its legal-cultural underpinnings. The relations between the layers of (constitutional) law manifest the second aspect of the relational analytic we try to apply in our discussion. These relations include

- relations of sedimentation – the formation and development of (constitutional) legal culture through individual (constitutional) speech acts by legislators, judges and scholars;
- constitutive relations – (constitutional) legal culture constituting the very possibility of (constitutional) legal speech acts through its normative, conceptual and methodological resources; as well as
- relations of justification, criticism and limitation – (constitutional) legal culture providing the yardsticks and means for both justifying and criticising surface-level normative material, as well as imposing limitations on the contents of (constitutional) legal speech acts.[8]

Making sense of the European economic constitution, too, requires attention to the relationship between, on the one hand, surface-level constitutional law as formulated in, first of all, individual Treaty provisions and constitutionally relevant case law of the ECJ, and, on the other hand, underpinning constitutional principles and implicit economic assumptions – the 'hidden social theory' of the economic constitution. Miguel Poiares Maduro's discussion of the three rival models of the European economic constitution and their manifestations in the case law of the ECJ is a good example of such an approach to the first, microeconomic layer of the European economic constitution.[9] A similar approach must be applied in examining the macroeconomic constitution. Thus, to lay foundations for our treatment of the current crisis as a constitutional crisis, we shall try to reconstruct the central principles underlying the individual provisions of the Maastricht Treaty on EMU – the Maastricht principles – and the economic assumptions on which they rely. Our multi-level view of the macroeconomic constitution

---

[8] Kaarlo Tuori has presented his view on the multilayered nature of law in K. Tuori (2002) and (2011).
[9] M. Poiares Maduro (1998).

leads us to discuss the crisis at two levels. The major part of academic and general public debate has assessed the crisis and the European responses to it in the light of individual Treaty provisions, such as the no-bailout clause in Art. 125(1) and the prohibition of central-bank financing in Art. 123(2) TFEU. Yet, focusing on separate doctrinal issues and discussing them in the context of individual Treaty provisions may entail losing sight of the other level of constitutional analysis: the level of principles. Indeed, although we shall discuss the main individual doctrinal issues which the European rescue measures and efforts to tighten European economic governance raise, the emphasis in our conclusions lies on the fate of the Maastricht principles. We claim that the crisis has invalidated or at least questioned many of the economic assumptions implicit in these principles and that a major aspect of the current constitutional crisis lies in the consequent shaking of many of the central Maastricht principles. In turn, this has – so our analysis continues – had important ramifications within the political and social constitution.

Here we encounter the third relational aspect which an examination of the European constitution as a differentiated process of constitutionalisation should address and which is also relevant for discussion of the present crisis: relations between the various constitutions or constitutional dimensions. A common (internal) market has been the motor of the whole integration process and, correspondingly, the non-economic constitutional dimensions largely owe their emergence to the demands raised or consequences set off by the economic constitution. Thus, juridical constitutionalisation responded to the need to guarantee realisation of the (micro)economic constitution, and the original impetus to the security constitution lay in security concerns deriving from free movement of labour and the opening of internal Community borders. These can be termed relations of implication. Such relations may be specified as relations of support: thus, for instance, development of the juridical constitution has supported realisation of the economic constitution.

The idea of specific periods in the European process of constitutionalisation, characterised by the dominance of a pacemaker constitution, relies on relations of implication, detectable between constitutional dimensions. But the relations between the pacemaker constitution and other constitutional dimensions can also be of a conflictual nature. Though non-economical constitutional dimensions seem to have received their original impetus from the economic constitution, in their further development they may acquire a dynamic of their own. This development may also lead to normative results which contradict the demands of the economic constitution. Before the European Court of Justice, such conflicts often assume the guise of contests between different types of rights: between, on the one hand, rights related to market freedoms and, on the other hand, civil and political or social rights. In conflicts with the economic constitution, the social constitution has usually been the loser: the economic constitution has defined the space for social constitutionalism. The present crisis makes exceptionally clear the potentially conflictual relations between constitutional dimensions. Reactions to the crisis which follow the logic of economic constitutionalisation may have implications which contradict basic political or social constitutional values, and jeopardise democracy and transparency or social rights.

The fourth aspect of our analytic concerns relations between the transnational,[10] European constitution and the Member State constitutions. The transnational constitution cannot be examined without paying due attention to its interaction with the national constitutions of the Member States. An analytical conceptual apparatus, at least partly analogous to the one tailored with a view to the interaction between the various dimensions of the transnational constitution, is also needed for dissecting the relationships between the transnational and national levels of constitution. Relationships of support and conflict may be discernible here, too.[11] In crucial respects, the European (micro)economic constitution relies on support from Member State constitutions. National constitutions, for instance, guarantee the fundamental rights indispensable for the functioning of the market economy, such as the right to property, freedom of contract and freedom of trade. On the other hand, the European economic constitution, e.g. the subjection of healthcare and social security to free market and competition law, has considerably reduced Member States' leeway in designing their welfare regimes.

The current Eurozone crisis has constitutional implications at both the European and national level, and these two-level implications are closely interrelated. To take an example, Member States' national fiscal sovereignty is a principle of both European and national constitutional

---

[10] As a terminological choice, we prefer 'transnational' to 'supranational' when referring to EU law's position beyond the dichotomy of national and international law.

[11] For a succinct exposition of the relational analytic see K. Tuori (2013).

law and encroachments on this sovereignty hint at a crisis of both European and national constitutions. And the social consequences of the austerity programmes should be assessed by both European and national constitutional yardsticks. Our focus lies on the transnational, European level, but, as we have argued, an analysis of the European process of constitutionalisation cannot ignore the interaction with national constitutions. Repercussions of the crisis in Member States vary, depending on, first, the division into assisting and receiving states, and, second, national constitutional particularities. Examples are needed, and as regards assisting states, we highlight German developments, especially the renowned rulings of the German Constitutional Court, and compare them with the Finnish constitutional doctrine, as expressed in the Opinions of the Constitutional Law Committee of Parliament. As the case of the German Constitutional Court makes especially clear, rulings of national constitutional courts are not merely speech acts in national constitutional discourse, but intervene in European discourse, as well.

To summarise the general framework of our constitutional analysis of the Eurozone crisis, we understand the European constitution as a multi-dimensional and multi-temporal process of constitutionalisation, where periods of dominance of a particular pacemaker constitution are distinguishable. In our analysis, we rely on the insight into the relational nature of European constitution(alisation) in its four senses, referring to, first, the constitutional relation between constitutional law and constitutional object; second, the relations prevailing between 'surface-level' constitutional material and its legal-cultural underpinnings; third, relationships among the various constitutional dimensions; and, fourth, relationships between the transnational, European constitution and the national, Member State constitutions.

The Maastricht Treaty opened a split in the economic constitution. The economic constitution of the euro area diverges from that applied to non-euro Member States. In our analysis, we concentrate on the euro area. References will be to the Founding Treaties, that is, the Treaty on the European Union (TEU) and the Treaty on the Functioning of the European Union (TFEU), such as they are after Lisbon. Although some amendments to the Maastricht provisions were introduced in Lisbon, they were not, as a rule, of a decisive character.

Our analysis proceeds through the following steps. In Chapter 2, we reconstruct the pre-crisis process of European economic constitutionalisation employing the distinction between micro- and macroeconomic constitution. Our special focus is on the Maastricht principles of the macroeconomic constitution and the economic assumptions on which they are premised; i.e. the 'hidden social theory' of the European macroeconomic constitution. In Chapter 3, we present a stylised economic narrative of the crisis. Our central claim will be that the crisis has in major respects refuted the economic assumptions of the Maastricht principles; this, in turn, is the economic backdrop to the crisis of the economic constitution. In Chapter 4, we depict European responses to the crisis. These fall into three main categories: first, emergency measures and rescue funds; second, strengthening European economic governance; and, third, unconventional monetary policy action by the European Central Bank (ECB), first to combat the financial crisis and then to support other emergency rescue measures in the sovereign debt crisis.

In Part II, we turn to a constitutional analysis of the European responses. As we have already indicated, the constitutional issues can roughly be divided into two groups. First, the measures undertaken to combat the crisis can be examined in the light of individual Treaty provisions, such as the emergency provision in Art. 122(2) TFEU; the prohibition of central-bank financing in Art. 123 TFEU; the no-bailout clause in Art. 125(1) TFEU; the provisions on multilateral surveillance procedure in Art. 121 TFEU and excessive deficit procedure in Art. 126 TFEU; or the provisions on the mandate of the ESCB (Eurosystem) and the ECB in Art. 127 TFEU. Furthermore, the doctrinal constitutional issues we discuss in Chapter 5 include the constitutionality of the intergovernmental option, relied on both in rescue packages and establishment of stability funds and in – as the Treaty on Stability, Coordination and Governance shows – strengthening European economic governance. We also discuss the significance of the amendment to Art. 136 TFEU, which entered into force on 1 January 2013 and which lays down that "the Member States whose currency is the euro may establish a stability mechanism to be activated if indispensable to safeguard the stability of the euro area as a whole".

After examining individual doctrinal issues, we focus our discussion in Chapter 6 on the Maastricht principles of the European economic constitution. We are especially interested in principles concerning Europeanised monetary policy and its objectives, as well as the fiscal liability and sovereignty of the Member States. The sovereignty principle we also discuss from the perspective of national constitutions. In Chapter 7, we address the repercussions of developments in the field of the economic constitution in other constitutional dimensions, especially the political and the social ones. The main topics in our discussion are problematisation of the democratic legitimacy of both the EU and Member State polities and the fate of social rights in the austerity programmes of the crisis states. Finally, in Part III, we present an overview of the reform plans on the table in European institutions; plans aimed at establishing a banking, fiscal and economic union, as well as mending the democratic deficit.

We end up on a rather pessimistic note. When the worst of the crisis seems to have passed the momentum for reforms appears to have faded, too.

2   Two layers of the European economic constitution

Rome and after: the microeconomic constitution

We shall use 'economic constitution' as a neutral concept, that is, not attached to any specific economic model. But in exploring European economic constitutionalisation, especially in its first decades, due attention must be paid to the ordoliberal school of legal and economic thinking, which introduced constitutional discourse at the European level. This school interpreted – and still interprets – the economic constitution in terms of a comprehensive decision (*Gesamtentscheidung*) or system decision (*Systementscheidung*)[1] in favour of a distinct ideal model of the economy: the market economy, premised on performance-based competition (*Leistungswettbewerb*). Only beginning in the 1990s did the term 'economic constitution' gain wider currency in scholarly discourse outside Germany, and only then did it start to escape from the confines of market-liberal economic thought and receive more neutral connotations.[2]

It may seem natural that constitutional discourse and, by the same token, constitutionalisation started out in the economic dimension. In the first decades of its history, say, up to the Maastricht Treaty, European integration was almost exclusively an economic project. But it was not self-evident that the economic orientation of the Community would be conceptualised with a constitutional vocabulary. The very term 'economic constitution' stems from one particular legal culture – the

---

[1] *Gesamtentscheidung* was the term used by Franz Böhm in his *Wettbewerb und Monopolkampf* (1933). *Systementscheidung*, in turn, is the term preferred by, for instance, Jan-Marco Luczak (2009).
[2] Reference should be made especially to the doctoral theses of M. Poiares Maduro (1998) and J. Baquero Cruz (2002), who both studied at the European University Institute in Florence.

German one – and even there the corresponding concept has been highly contested. Opinions on who, exactly, is to be regarded as the father of the term seem to diverge, but general agreement prevails on the crucial age. This was the Weimar period. Hugo Sinzheimer applied the term to the multi-faceted and multi-tiered corporatist organisation for economic decision-making, set out in the Weimar constitution but never really established.[3] The largely abandoned term was picked up by a Freiburg group of legal scholars, such as Franz Böhm, and economists, such as Walter Eucken, who formed the nucleus of what came to be called the ordoliberal school of legal and economic thinking. The main credit for the renaissance and, by the same token, re-conceptualisation of 'economic constitution' is due to Böhm.[4] In correspondence to Carl Schmitt's concept of the political constitution, Böhm conceived of the economic constitution in terms of a comprehensive decision (*Gesamtenscheidung*) on "the nature (Art) and form of the process of socio-economic cooperation".[5]

In the Third *Reich*, the ordoliberal reading of the economic constitution as a *Gesamtentscheidung* for a competition economy did not have a chance to reassert itself in the face of continuously expanding state intervention and state-induced cartelisation of the economy. The hour of the ordoliberals only came after the war, with the German economy lying in ruins and with the need for explicit decisions on the direction of its restructuring. In the post-war intellectual, economic and political search for new coordinates, ordoliberals not only enjoyed scholarly success but won the ear of key decision-makers as well: the allied administrators and also some leading politicians such as Ludwig Erhard, father of the German *Wirtschaftswunder*, a long-time minister of economy and briefly prime minister.[6] But where ordoliberals did not succeed was in their effort to have their view of the economic constitution confirmed in the case law of the German Constitutional Court; not even the term *Wirtschaftsverfassung* found its way into the rulings of the

---

[3] See S. Hänninen (2010).

[4] Böhm used the concept *Wirtschaftsverfassung* already in his 1928 article 'Das Problem der Privaten Macht'. The major work where he expounds the concept is his doctoral thesis (1933).

[5] F. Böhm (1933), p. 107, where Schmitt's concept is explicitly invoked.

[6] In a speech given in 1961, Erhard famously declared himself to be one of the ordoliberals; M. Wegmann (2002), p. 105. Both Eucken and Böhm were members of the *Wissenschaflicher Beirat*, assisting the Allied administration. Later on, Böhm continued counselling Erhard's Ministry of Economics and was also able to further the realisation of his ideas as a Member of Parliament. D. Gerber (1994), pp. 59–62.

Court.[7] Ordoliberals sensed a danger of the state being imprisoned by the pluralism of rent-seeking particular interests, and, consequently, many of them turned their eyes towards Europe: the *ordo* required for a competition-based market economy was perhaps attainable on the transnational echelon.[8] Indeed, ordoliberals exerted considerable influence on German positions in the preparatory work for the Treaty of Rome. They could also impact post-Rome developments in the field of the economic constitution, as well as implementation of what they considered the crux of this constitution; namely, competition law.

In their eagerness to present the Treaty of Rome in terms of an economic constitution, ordoliberals were not deterred by the setback inflicted on them at the state level when the Constitutional Court refused to read any economic *Gesamtentscheidung* into the Basic Law (*Grundgesetz*). Ernst-Joachim Mestmäcker emphasised that in contrast to the Basic Law, the Constitution of the Community has the economy as its direct object, and that postulating a principle of neutrality for Community economic policy would amount to rejecting the very legal content of the Treaty.[9] In the development of Community/Union constitutional law, ordoliberals' main concern has been the increasing number of Treaty provisions which seem to clash with their perception of the economic constitution.[10] Yet, ordoliberals' claim to provide a doctrinally correct exposition of the Treaty of Rome has been controversial and contested from the very beginning, and not merely after Treaty amendments brought about, in particular, by the Single European Act (SEA) and the Maastricht Treaty. When the term 'economic constitution' found wider resonance from the 1990s onwards, the ordoliberal way of applying it in the European context remained merely one scholarly stance among others. In spite of the prominent influence of German ordoliberals, the Treaty of Rome was a compromise, with

---

[7] In its 1954 *Investitionshilfegesetz* judgment, the Constitutional Court stated that, on the one hand, the Basic Law has not adopted any particular economic model, but, on the other hand, does not require of legislation any neutrality in terms of economic policy, either, in BVerfGE 4, 7, 17/18. The Constitutional Court reaffirmed its standpoint in 1979 in its *Mitbestimmungsgesetz* ruling BVerfGE 59, 290, 337/38.

[8] Support for European economic integration among the market liberals was far from unanimous. Especially in the initial phase of the ECSC and the first years of the EEC, some market liberals feared that European integration would entail market-distorting *dirigisme* and bureaucratic interventionism. See M. Wegmann (2008).

[9] E.-W. Mestmäcker (2003).

[10] This has been the line of argumentation which, for instance, Ernst-Wolfgang Mestmäcker has clung to in his extensive oeuvre. See especially the articles collected in E.-W. Mestmäcker (2003).

France, Italy and the Benelux countries pushing for a more *dirigiste* and socially oriented approach. Constructing the Treaty through the ordoliberal notion of the economic constitution was only possible by way of downplaying Treaty provisions which manifested contradictory ideas of the Community's economic role. Even in the original Treaty, provisions on market freedoms and undistorted competition were balanced by those on common policies, in particular common agricultural policy. As scholars contesting the ordoliberal position argue, there is no textual evidence that the market-oriented elements of the Treaty enjoy a higher (constitutional) status than provisions establishing non-market objectives and corresponding policy competences. Hence – the counter-argument continues – the claim that the Treaty would have given expression to a *Gesamtentscheidung*, defined through the ordoliberal vision, is not defensible.[11]

Whatever view one takes of the constitutional and economic theory underlying the Treaty of Rome and whatever significance one grants the *dirigiste* elements, it is clear that free movement and competition law are an essential part of European economic constitution and that their role was particularly crucial in the decades preceding the SEA and the Maastricht Treaty. It was on the basis of the provisions on fundamental market freedoms and competition law that the Court and the Commission started to implement and further develop the economic constitution. The principles of direct effect and primacy as confirmed by such ECJ landmark cases as *Van Gend en Loos* and *Costa* v. *Enel* ensured that the European economic constitution was respected in national legal systems as well.[12]

Both branches of the economic constitution, that is, free movement and competition law, dealt with the behaviour of individual economic actors; to be more exact, behaviour with cross-border implications. This was the case with free movement rules, too, although their edge was directed against Member States' legislation and other measures interpreted as obstacles to cross-border economic activities and to the establishment of a common market. The economic constitution was seen to

---

[11] This counter-position is forcefully advocated by, e.g., Wolfgang Sauter, who claims that the Treaty of Rome did not impose any specific model of economic policy on either the Member States or the Community itself. There simply was no constitutional *Gesamtentscheidung*, but the Treaty adopted an equally neutral standpoint in economic policy as, according to the German Constitutional Court, did the German Basic Law. W. Sauter (1998).

[12] Case 26/62 *Van Gend en Loos* v. *Administratie der Belastingen* [1963] ECR 1; Case 6/64 *Flaminio Costa* v. *Enel* [1964] ECR 585.

protect the economic freedoms of individual economic actors. By ana-
logy with fundamental liberty rights enshrined in national constitutions, the ECJ in its case law treated these freedoms as justiciable rights
which economic actors could invoke in courts. Free movement law was
constructed as providing protection primarily against state measures,
while competition law mainly addressed private economic power.[13] The
focus on the protection of the freedom of individual economic actors
justifies using the term 'microeconomic constitution' for the first layer
of the European economic constitution.

This focus also explains why the law and the courts could play such
an important role in the first decades of European integration and how
the European Community could be conceptualised as a legal community; a *Rechtsgemeinschaft*. At the national level, too, a specific field of
law, which in Germany was called *Wirtschaftsrecht*, had proven that law
was capable of regulating activities of individual economic actors, even
beyond provision of basic safeguards of the market economy, such
as guaranteeing enforcement of contracts and protection of private
property. In Community law, central parts of *Wirtschaftsrecht* were elevated to constitutional level. This was due to the necessity to ensure its
enforcement in all Member States. This necessity found its legal formulation in the master-principle of efficacy; i.e. the primary justification
for the revolutionary doctrines of primacy and direct effect which the
ECJ adopted in order to guarantee full implementation of free market
and competition law in Member States. The central role of the law with
its focus on individual economic actors facilitated engaging national
courts and private litigants in the implementation of the economic
constitution. Furthermore, it made possible the auto-development of
the European Court of Justice into a constitutional court, also and even
primarily in relation to Member State legislation. Finally, it forms the
backdrop to the vital position of the Court, not only in implementing
the economic constitution and reaffirming its legal force but also in
enriching its contents, through such landmark ruling as, e.g., *Dassonville*
or *Cassis de Dijon*.[14]

Alongside the Court, the other central European institution in implementation of the microeconomic constitution was the Commission,
which acted – and still acts – as the European Anti-Trust Authority,

---

[13] However, state aid provisions were – and are – an integral part of competition law,
which, consequently, is not merely about private power.
[14] Case 8/74 *Procureur du Roi* v. *Benoît and Gustave Dassonville* [1974] ECR 837; Case 120/78
Rewe-Central AG v. *Bundesmonopolverwaltung für Branntwein* [1979] ECR 649.

monitoring compliance with competition law. Both the Court and the Commission – especially in its role as an Anti-Trust Authority – are non-political expert bodies whose claim for legitimacy is warranted by their specific legal or legal-economic expertise. In terms of Fritz Scharpf's well-known distinction between input and output legitimacy,[15] the emphasis lies on the latter: expertise is expected to guarantee legally and economically correct decisions.

Under the shadow of the microeconomic constitution – economic policy competences in the Treaty of Rome

What was the position of macroeconomics, especially monetary and fiscal policy, in the European economic constitution which emerged from the Treaty of Rome under the interpretative dominance of the ordoliberals? Arguably, the microeconomic constitution rested on particular macroeconomic presuppositions. In ordoliberal thinking price stability is part of the *ordo*, the formal foundational framework, which the economic constitution and the *Ordnungspolitik* securing its realisation are supposed to guarantee. A well-functioning price mechanism is considered essential for a free market-based economic system; only a stable price mechanism is capable of accomplishing its informational and incentive functions that provide for rational and efficient allocation of resources under decentralised decision-making by households and companies. Correspondingly, monetary policy aiming at price stability formed a central part of the constitutional framework which was to guarantee the proper functioning of European economy. In his *Grundsätze der Wirtschaftspolitik*, Walter Eucken – the leading ordoliberal economist – elevates a functioning price system to an essential criterion of all measures of economic policy and, by the same token, to the basic principle of economic constitutional law. Furthermore, primacy of monetary policy heads his list of the constitutive principles of the economic system based on competition.[16]

A European economic constitution focusing on fundamental market freedoms and competition law builds on support from Member State constitutions and *Ordnungspolitik*. The fundamental rights indispensable for a market economy are guaranteed by national constitutions

---

[15] F. Scharpf (1999), pp. 6–8.   [16] W. Eucken (1952), pp. 254–5.

and not by European Treaty law. These rights comprise private property and freedom of contract, included in Eucken's constitutive principles, and freedom of trade, which for Franz Böhm – the leading legal scholar among first-generation ordoliberals – is the very foundation of the economic constitution.

In the original European economic constitution, guaranteeing price stability and primacy of monetary policy was also a task, not for the centralised European level, but for the decentralised Member State level. In Germany, the powerful Bundesbank consequently pursued its successful anti-inflationary monetary policy with stability of currency as its overriding objective. Art. 104(1) of the Rome Treaty evoked such aims of exchange-rate and monetary policy as equilibrium of overall balance of payments, maintenance of confidence in the currency and price stability, but these were defined as objectives for the Member States. In pursuing these objectives, Member States benefited from the Bretton Woods system, which mostly managed to support national efforts to keep inflation low and to prevent dramatic exchange-rate fluctuations. Hence, an important part of the *ordo* framing the microeconomic constitution was provided by international agreements and bilateral cooperation with the US. Until the end of Bretton Woods, the US dollar (and, indirectly, gold) was the anchor of European exchange-rate arrangements.[17] Yet, a need existed to complement the Bretton Woods system with arrangements guaranteeing exchange-rate stability among European states. These arrangements were based on agreements between central banks outside the Treaty framework.

Exchange-rate and monetary policy objectives were not the only aims the Treaty expected Member States to heed. Provisions on economic policy were a compromise between ordoliberal and more *dirigiste* views, primarily advocated by French negotiators. As a concession to the latter, ensuring a high level of employment was invoked as well, and even conjunctural policy received a mention.[18]

Monetary and economic policy fell to Member States, but these were supposed to coordinate their policies in order to facilitate attaining

---

[17] H. James (2012), pp. 39–61.

[18] According to Art. 103(1), Member States were supposed to regard their conjunctural policies as a matter of common concern and to consult each other and the Commission on measures to be taken in the light of the prevailing circumstances. The Common Agricultural Policy was, of course, the most conspicuous example in the Treaty of the influence of (French) *dirigiste* views.

the objectives laid down in Art. 104 of the Treaty.[19] The most far-going Community competences concerned Member States' exchange-rate policy and their balance of payments, where the Treaty went beyond soft methods of coordination. Art. 107(2) granted the Commission the power to react and to authorise other Member States to take necessary counter-measures in case a Member State made an alteration in its exchange rate which was inconsistent with the objectives set out in Art. 104 and which seriously distorted conditions of competition. Where a Member State was in difficulty with regard to its balance of payments or was seriously threatened with such difficulties, and these were liable to jeopardise the functioning of the common market or progressive implementation of the common commercial policy, available Community measures comprised granting mutual assistance. Art. 108, providing for such assistance, is a predecessor to present Art. 143 TFEU, which allows for assistance to non-euro Member States facing difficulties in their balance of payments.[20]

In sum, the European economic constitution introduced by the Treaty of Rome implied monetary policy aiming at price stability but, in the division of competences between the Community and the Member States, assigned this task, alongside fiscal and economic policy, to the latter. Community institutions, such as the Commission and the Monetary Committee,[21] were to play a merely coordinating role. Subsequently,

---

[19] The introductory articles of the Treaty contained some vague and largely programmatic provisions on horizontal coordination. Art. 2 referred to progressive approximation of the economic policies of the Member States: "The Community shall have as its task, by establishing a common market and progressively approximating the economic policies of Member States, to promote throughout the Community a harmonious development of economic activities, a continuous and balanced expansion, an increase in stability, an accelerated raising of the standard of living and closer relations between the States belonging to it." In turn, Art. 3 laid down that the activities of the Community included "the application of procedures by which the economic policies of Member States can be coordinated and disequilibria in their balances of payments remedied". Furthermore, Art. 6(1) provided that "Member States shall, in close cooperation with the institutions of the Community, coordinate their respective economic policies to the extent necessary to attain the objectives of this Treaty". Art. 105 provided for a Monetary Committee, composed of representatives of Member States and the Commission, which was expected to fulfil coordinating tasks but which had a merely advisory status.

[20] Unilateral protective measures were also allowed, either as a precaution or, on the Commission's authorisation, where the Council had not granted mutual assistance or it had proven insufficient.

[21] Art. 105(2) of the Rome Treaty established a Monetary Committee with advisory status "in order to promote co-ordination of the policies of Member States in the monetary field to the full extent needed for the functioning of the common

the ECJ assumed a vital role in supervising that Member States exercised their sovereignty in economic policy within the limits of the core principles of the European economic constitution. The Court employed fundamental market freedoms and competition law, furnished with direct effect and primacy, to strike down Member State legislation which contradicted its reading of the economic constitution.

Preparing for EMU: the Werner and Delors Reports

Economic and monetary union was put on the European agenda in the late 1960s, when the Bretton Woods system showed first signs of decline. In The Hague in 1969, the Heads of State or Government agreed that a plan should be drawn up to create an economic and monetary union within the Community. This led to the Werner Report in 1970 setting out a three-stage process to achieve EMU within a ten-year period.[22]

The Werner Group explicitly pointed to the progress already achieved in European integration. It regarded completion of the customs union and definition of a common agricultural policy of its six Member States as the most significant landmarks. However, it also noted that increasing interpenetration of the economies had weakened the autonomy of national economic policies, which had not been compensated by new instruments at the Community level. The Group set out to remedy this deficit and to ensure that free movement, including that of capital and financial services, is not hampered by economic disequilibria in Member States and insufficient coordination of their economic and monetary policies.[23] The Group formulated the benefits of economic and monetary union so as to reflect the primacy of the microeconomic constitution: "Economic and monetary union will make it possible to

market". It was supposed "to keep under review the monetary and financial situation of the Member States and of the Community and the general payments system of the Member States and to report regularly thereon to the Council and to the Commission". In addition, it was expected to deliver opinions to the Council and the Commission at the request of these institutions or on its own initiative. The Member States and the Commission each appointed two members of the Committee.

[22] Werner Committee (1970), Report to the Council and the Commission on the Realization by Stages of Economic and Monetary Union in the Community (Werner Report), 8 October 1970.

[23] "The extension of the liberation of movements of capital and the realization of the right of establishment and of the free rendering of services by banking and financial undertakings have not progressed far enough. The delay has been caused by the absence of sufficient coordination of economic and monetary policies and by local peculiarities of law and fact."

realize an area within which goods and services, people and capital will circulate freely and without competitive distortions, without thereby giving rise to structural or regional disequilibrium."

In the Werner Report, monetary union among the five currencies of the Community would have implied "the total and irreversible convertibility of currencies, the elimination of margins of fluctuation in exchange rates, the irrevocable fixing of parity rates and the complete liberation of movements of capital". Such a monetary union would not necessarily have required abolishing national monetary symbols. However, the Group argued that "considerations of a psychological and political order militate in favour of the adoption of a single currency which would guarantee the irreversibility of the undertaking". In the Report, the creation of monetary union was accompanied by a rather wide-reaching transfer of fiscal and economic policy competences from Member States to the Community. Medium-term objectives for growth, employment, prices and external equilibrium would have been fixed by the Community. It would also have decided on the outlines of short-term economic policy in order to facilitate "normative and economic budgets". Budgetary policy was accorded particular attention. Although the Community budget would play a more important role, its economic significance would still be weaker than that of the national budgets. Annual and medium-term margins for the main budget aggregates – such as variations in the volume of budgets and methods of financing deficits or utilising surpluses – would have been decided at the Community level, "taking account of the economic situation and the particular structural features of each country". In eliminating structural economic differences and pursuing objectives of structural and regional policy, financial support would have been provided not only from national budgets but from the Community budget as well. The Group also evoked transfers of competences in tax and social policy.

The Werner Group was explicit in pointing to the implications for the political constitution ensuing from its proposals. It saw political union as a logical consequence of economic and monetary union. The Group emphasised that the transfers of responsibility from Member States to the Community it proposed "represent a process of fundamental political significance which implies the progressive development of political cooperation". Thus, "economic and monetary union … appears as a leaven for the development of political union, which in the long run it cannot do without". However, the Group considered designing detailed institutional structures as falling outside its mandate. It only indicated the need for two bodies which it regarded as indispensable to control of economic and monetary policy at the Community level: a centre of decision for economic policy and a Community system for central banks. The centre of decision for economic policy would have been politically responsible to the European Parliament.

As the Werner Group explicitly concluded, realising its proposals would have required Treaty amendments. The Report produced a statement by the Heads of State or Government where Member States expressed their political will to establish an economic and monetary union, but no serious effort to implement its proposals was ever made. European reactions to the collapse of the Bretton Woods system in the early 1970s and the accompanying rampant inflation were on a much more modest scale and were decided on without Treaty amendments. Still, on the road from Rome to Maastricht the major results in coordinating Member State policies were achieved in exchange-rate policy as a European continuation of Bretton Woods. After abandoning formally fixed exchange rates in the early 1970s, an effort was made to retain the floating of Member State currencies within the so-called snake. The most important attempts to coordinate exchange rates and achieve monetary stability were the establishment of the European Monetary System (EMS) in 1978, and subsequent introduction of the Exchange Rate Mechanism (ERM) and the European Currency Unit (ECU). In the 1980s, under the leadership of the Bundesbank, the EMS functioned quite successfully and was able to guarantee exchange-rate stability, largely due to improvements in Member States' price stability. Yet, it was not able to prevent the currency crisis which hit several Member States in 1992–3. The EMS functioned outside the framework of Community law: it was based on an agreement between the participating central banks.[24]

After approval of the Single European Act in 1986 and adoption of the objective of realising the single market before the end of 1992, discussion on economic and monetary union resumed. In an atmosphere of widespread integration euphoria and Euro-optimism, Jacques Delors, President of the Commission, was asked to chair a committee

---

[24] Politically, the EMS was launched through a Resolution of the European Council of 5 December 1978 on the establishment of the European Monetary System (EMS) and related matters, Compendium 1979, p. 42; Council Regulation (EEC) No. 3181/78 of 18 December 1978 relating to the European Monetary System; and Council Decision (EEC) 78/1041 of 21 December 1978 amending Decision 71/143/EEC setting up machinery for medium-term financial assistance, [1978] OJ L379/3.

to propose a new timetable with clear, practical, realistic steps for creating an economic and monetary union. In its Report,[25] the Delors Committee not only invoked the single market objective and the SEA but experiences from the EMS as well. It considered the EMS a success but, by the same token, claimed that it had not fully exhausted its potential. This was due, inter alia, to the fact that "the lack of sufficient convergence of fiscal policies as reflected in large and persistent budget deficits in certain countries has remained a source of tensions and has put a disproportionate burden on monetary policy". The Committee anticipated that completion of the single market would deepen economic integration and interdependence within the Community, amplify the cross-border effects of economic developments in each Member State and reduce the leeway for independent policy manoeuvre. This would necessitate more effective policy coordination, as well as Community policies in support of balanced development. More intensive policy coordination would be needed not only in the monetary field but also in areas of national economic management which affect aggregate demand, prices and costs of production; in particular, fiscal policy.

Economic and monetary union would be built on completion of the single market, i.e. complete freedom of movement for persons, goods, services and capital, as well as "irrevocably fixed exchange rates between national currencies and, finally, a single currency". In accordance with the Werner Group, the Delors Committee did not consider a single currency strictly necessary but saw it for economic, psychological and political reasons as "a natural and desirable further development of the monetary union". What permanently fixed exchange rates did require was a common monetary policy for which responsibility should be vested in a new institution. This institution – a European System of Central Banks – would take decisions on the supply of money and credit, as well as on other monetary policy instruments, such as interest rates. The Committee clearly noted that "the permanent fixing of exchange rates would deprive individual countries of an important instrument for the correction of economic imbalances and for independent action in the pursuit of national objectives, especially price stability".

---

[25] Committee for the Study of Economic and Monetary Union (Delors Committee) (1989), 'Report on an Economic and Monetary Union in the European Community', 17 April 1989.

In addition to the requirement of common monetary policy, the Delors Committee pointed to the need for "a high degree of compatibility of economic policies and consistency in a number of other policy areas, particularly in the fiscal field". Economic policies "should be geared to price stability, balanced growth, converging standards of living, high employment and external equilibrium". The Committee emphasised that a need for transfer of decision-making power from Member States to the Community would arise not only in monetary policy but in macroeconomic management, too. In economic policy, a wide range of decisions would remain the preserve of national and regional authorities. This would include wage negotiations and other economic decisions in the fields of production, savings and investment. Because of their external effects and implications for the conduct of common monetary policy, these decisions "would have to be placed within an agreed macroeconomic framework and be subject to binding procedures and rules". As the Community budget was likely to remain a very small part of public-sector spending, Community-wide fiscal policy would have to be performed through coordination of national budgetary policies.

Interestingly enough, the Committee was quite mistrustful of the disciplinary effect of market forces on Member States' fiscal policy. According to its Report, "experience shows that market perceptions do not necessarily provide strong and compelling signals and that access to a large capital market may for some time even facilitate the financing of economic imbalances". In light of recent events, the following assessment sounds almost prophetic: "Rather than leading to a gradual adaptation of borrowing costs, market views about the creditworthiness of official borrowers tend to change abruptly and result in the closure of access to market." The constraints imposed by market forces may be too slow and weak or too sudden and disruptive. Hence, binding policy constrictions are needed. In budgetary policy, binding rules should, first, define upper limits on the budget deficits of individual Member States; in setting these limits, though, the situation of each country was to be taken into consideration. Second, access to direct central bank credit and other forms of monetary financing should be excluded while, however, allowing for open market operations in government securities. Third, recourse to external borrowing in non-Community currencies should be limited. As regards the general macroeconomic field, a common overall assessment of short- and medium-term developments in the Community would be periodically agreed on. This would constitute the basis for country-specific assessments and policy guidelines.

The Delors Committee treated economic union and monetary union as "two integral parts of a single whole", which should be implemented in parallel. In the Committee's view, contrary to monetary policy, in non-monetary fields formulation and implementation of common policies or coordination of national policies would not necessarily require a new institution. A revision and possible restructuring of the existing institutional structure would suffice. Here the Delors Committee departed from the conclusions of the Werner Group, which included a proposal for establishing a specific centre of decision for economic policy, politically responsible to the European Parliament. The Delors Committee also refrained from explicitly commenting on economic and monetary union's relationship to political union.

In the end, however, the introduction of the macroeconomic layer of the European economic constitution can be seen as resulting from the pacemaker role which the political constitution achieved in the pre-Maastricht years. The central backdrop to the rise of the political constitution lies in the revolutionary events of 1989 and German reunification taking effect on 3 October 1990. Before the *Wende*, the representatives of Germany, with some notable exceptions, had taken a rather hesitant view of monetary and economic union which would entail giving up the *Deutsche Mark* – a powerful symbol of the rise of post-war Germany – as well as sovereign monetary policy, so successfully conducted by the Bundesbank. The most eager proponents of economic and monetary union were to be found in France, where the leading role of Germany in the EMS was cause for national resentment. After 1989, the major political objective of France was to deepen European integration and to direct its course towards a political union. This was seen to be necessary in order, through European ties, to curb the power of a reinforced Germany.[26]

Both the Werner Group and the Delors Committee had argued for economic and monetary union starting from the implications and needs of the microeconomic constitution; economic and monetary union would complement the single market and address its consequences, such as the growing interdependence of national economies. Yet in the end, EMU was established as a central part of the Maastricht package whose aim was to further political rather than economic

[26] M. Gilbert (2012), pp. 143 ff.; D. Marsh (2011), pp. 139 ff.

integration. France held a strong negotiating position as one of the Four Powers and could decisively influence not only establishment of EMU, but even the shape it received. Thus, the combination of centralised monetary policy with mainly national fiscal and economy policy was largely due to French misgivings while Germany had pushed for more extensive centralisation of fiscal and economy policy as a precondition for successful common monetary policy. In a somewhat paradoxical way, economic and monetary union was subordinated to political objectives but its implications in the dimension of a political union were more modest than the Werner Group, in particular, would have preferred.

The Maastricht principles of the European economic constitution

With its provisions on Economic and Monetary Union (EMU), the Treaty of Maastricht added a new layer to the European economic constitution, while leaving intact the constitutional foundation of fundamental market freedoms and competition law. Where the first layer of the European economic constitution focuses on the basic principles of microeconomics – free movement and competition law – the second layer addresses issues of macroeconomics. As a backdrop to our constitutional analysis of the Eurozone crisis we try to distil the major Maastricht principles of the European economic constitution. In our reconstruction, we pay due attention to the Stability and Growth Pact, concluded in 1997 in anticipation of the approaching third stage in implementing EMU. The Pact consists of a legally non-binding, political Resolution of the European Council and two Regulations, translating the political guidelines into legal language.[27] The Pact does not possess any formal constitutional status, but it is based on the Maastricht principles and acts out some of their implications, particularly with regard to the excessive deficit procedure.

---

[27] On the negotiations leading to the Pact see M. Heipertz and A. Verdun (2010), pp. 19–41. The term 'Stability and Growth Pact' is misleading in the sense that no legal intergovernmental agreement exists. Resolution on the Stability and Growth Pact of Amsterdam, [1997] OJ C236/1; Council Regulation (EC) No. 1466/97 of 7 July 1997 on the strengthening of the surveillance of budgetary positions and the surveillance and coordination of economic policies and Council Regulation (EC) No. 1467/97 of 7 July 1997 on speeding up and clarifying the implementation of the excessive deficit procedure, [1997] OJ L209/1.

The Maastricht Treaty still manifested the principle of the unity of the European Union. The provisions on EMU were premised on the assumption that Member States would join as soon as they fulfilled the convergence criteria. Indeed, this was considered a legal obligation, except for the UK and Denmark who had negotiated opt-outs confirmed in separate Protocols attached to the Maastricht Treaty. Moreover, in Maastricht the general expectation was that the opt-outs would be merely temporary and that the UK and Denmark, too, would enter sooner or later. Yet, though still sticking to the principle of unity, the Maastricht Treaty also launched a bifurcation of the economic constitution which shows no signs of being dissolved, indeed, rather the contrary: the economic constitution of the euro area is not identical to that applicable to non-euro Member States. In the following, we shall maintain our focus on the euro area.

The major change brought about by the Maastricht Treaty was the introduction of a common monetary policy: Europeanisation of monetary policy, which had been the central item on the agenda of both the Werner Group and the Delors Committee. Art. 3(1)(c) TFEU lays down that the Union has exclusive competence in monetary policy for Member States whose currency is the euro. Initially, scepticism about EMU and the common currency was quite common among German economists and officials, many of them leaning towards ordoliberalism. Their doubts were shared by many other adherents to the market-liberal monetarist trend, who since the late 1970s seemed to have gained the upper hand over their Keynesian rivals. However, the German perception had a clear impact on the definition of monetary-policy objectives and the institutional position of the European Central Bank (ECB) and the national central banks, forming the European System of Central Banks (ESCB). Even initially recalcitrant German ordoliberals gradually made their peace with the loss of the *Deutsche Mark* and the independent Bundesbank as the guarantor of its stability. In accordance with the monetarist tenet, Arts. 119(2) and 127(1) TFEU elevate price stability to the primary objective of monetary and exchange-rate policy. General economic policies may only be supported if this can be done without prejudice to price stability. Arts. 119(2) and 127(1) also relate monetary policy to the basic principles of the first layer of the European economic constitution: open market economy and free competition. Invoking these principles testifies to the continuing primacy of the microeconomic constitution and recalls price stability as a vital element of the *ordo* which ordoliberals called for to frame and secure free market economy based on undistorted competition.

Institutional provisions on monetary union, in turn, aim to secure the enhanced independence of both the ECB and national central banks, not only in euro states but in other Member States, too. Most importantly, pursuant to Art. 130 TFEU neither the ECB nor national central banks "shall seek or take instructions from Union institutions, bodies, offices or agencies, from any government of a Member State or from any other body". Correspondingly, Union institutions and Member States shall "respect this principle and not ... seek to influence the members of the decision-making bodies of the European Central Bank or of the national central banks in the performance of their tasks". In addition, several other provisions of the TFEU and the Statute of the ECB, which also enjoys constitutional status, are meant to enhance independence. These include provisions on special audit procedure, as well as the terms of office of the Executive Board and members of the Governing Council of the ECB.

In the 1980s, central-bank independence, a vital tenet of ordoliberalism and an essential feature of the Bundesbank model, had gained more general support among economists and central bankers themselves. Yet politically it was far from a self-evident premise. Here Germany managed to drive through its standpoint against the hesitation of, primarily, France. On the other hand, central-bank independence and the concomitant special status of monetary policy in economic policy-making facilitated transfer of monetary-policy competences to the Union. After the short experimental period of the Mitterrand Presidency, even France had been forced to grant its central bank increased independence in order to facilitate balanced economic development. For national political decision-makers, monetary policy was largely lost territory even before its transferral to European level.

Still, to a certain extent, the alleged adoption of the Bundesbank model must be considered one of the myths surrounding the origins of EMU. The independence of the Bundesbank was never constitutionally enshrined. By contrast, it was supported by and embedded in a wide political and social consensus, which also by and large guaranteed the consistency of the monetary policy of the Bundesbank with the fiscal and economic policy of the government, and even an accommodating wage policy by the social partners. The ECB functions in a wholly different environment and no corresponding guarantees exist for the mutual harmony of monetary, fiscal and macroeconomic policy.

Division of competences between the Union and Member States is governed by the principle of conferral. Under this principle, "the Union shall act only within the limits of the competences conferred upon it by the Member States in the Treaties to attain the objectives set out therein" while the Member States retain all the competences not conferred upon the Union in the Treaties (Art. 5(2) TFEU).[28] The regulation of ECB competences in the Treaties and in the Statute gives expression to the principle of a strict definition of its mandate, that is, its objectives, tasks and competences. The crucial provisions are now in Art. 127 TFEU. Art. 127(1) defines the objectives of monetary policy, prioritising price stability and invoking the basic principles of the microeconomic constitution. In turn, Art. 127(2) enumerates the basic tasks of the ECB: defining and implementing the monetary policy of the Union; conducting foreign-exchange operations; holding and managing the official foreign reserves of the Member States; and promoting smooth operation of payment systems. What is interesting from the point of view of the recent financial crisis and plans for a future banking union is the way in which the ESCB's role in supervising financial institutions is defined. Art. 127(5) lays down that "the ESCB shall contribute to the smooth conduct of policies pursued by the competent authorities relating to the prudential supervision of credit institutions and the stability of the financial system". The wording intimates that the main responsibility for prudential supervision remains with national authorities. However, Art. 127(6) facilitates conferring on the ECB specific tasks in the prudential supervision of credit institutions and other financial institutions with the exception of insurance undertakings.

National responsibility for financial-stability issues, particularly banking supervision, was based on the principles of home-country supervision and European passport.[29] Only minimum requirements were set in directives, concerning for example deposit insurance and own funds. National responsibility also implied national sovereignty on issues such as bank rescues or investor liability.

Box 2.1: Monetary policy, fiscal policy and other economic policies

Monetary policy refers to a policy conducted by a monetary authority and related to its typically monopolised right to issue the legal

---

[28] The premise was only explicitly enshrined in the Lisbon Treaty, but had been recognised as a general principle even earlier.
[29] It allows banks legally established in one Member State to establish or provide services in other Member States without further authorisation.

tender of a state. Traditionally monetary policy has been conducted through controlling the supply of currency (legal tender). Modern central banks operate primarily through the banking sector by influencing short-term interest rates. Higher interest rates should repress growth and asset prices and thereby indirectly control inflation, and vice versa. Typical objectives for monetary policy are price stability, financial stability and stable economic growth.

Fiscal policy focuses particularly on revenues and expenditures of a state which are typically defined in national budgets and approved by parliaments. Currently, a major part of 'active' fiscal policy takes place through automatic stabilisers. For example, progressive income taxes and company taxes tend to increase in economic upturns and decline in recessions. The opposite is true of unemployment benefits and many other social security expenditures. In developed countries, public revenues and expenditures often represent approximately half of GDP. However, active discretional fiscal policies can only influence a small proportion of this amount.

Economic policy is a comprehensive, second-order concept. In addition to monetary and fiscal policy, it may include various structural policies, such as *industrial and regional policies* which are motivated mainly by economic considerations. Furthermore, many other policies are closely linked to economic policies, particularly to fiscal policy, even if they primarily serve other than economic objectives. Thus, to the extent that *social and educational policies* are publicly provided or funded, they are integral parts of fiscal policy as well.

Contrary to monetary policy, the Maastricht Treaty in principle retained Member State sovereignty in fiscal and economic policy. In effect, due to loss of control over monetary policy instruments, the significance of national fiscal policy in, for instance, reacting to asymmetric, country-specific economic shocks grew. However, Member State sovereignty in fiscal and economic policy is not absolute but conditioned by specific constraints. A latent tension inhered in the Maastricht principles which defined the position of national fiscal policy. On the one hand, its importance increased, which required sufficient leeway for Member State decision-makers. On the other hand, its potential spillover effects, especially with regard to common monetary policy, were seen to require European constraints.

The Founding Treaties now as before presuppose that Member States heed the viewpoints of other Member States and the Union as a whole in their economic policies; in other words, internalise the externalities of their policies. Member States are supposed to "conduct their economic policies with a view to contributing to the achievement of the objectives of the Union" and to regard their economic policies as a matter of common concern. Furthermore, they are supposed to coordinate their policies within the Council (Art. 121(1)).[30] Instead of legal rules and formal sanctions, the multilateral surveillance procedure provided for by Art. 121 TFEU adheres to what is now called the open method of coordination: legally non-binding broad guidelines; peer review through the Council; and likewise legally non-binding country-specific recommendations.

In principle, the multilateral surveillance procedure covers Member States' economic policy as a whole. Yet the Stability and Growth Pact clearly defined fiscal policy as the main target of the procedure. Thus, it must be placed in the context of the other means by which the Maastricht macroeconomic constitution purports to guarantee that Member States pursue the objective of sound public finances, explicitly enshrined in Art. 119(3) TFEU, and obey the fiscal discipline which European monetary policy prioritising price stability presupposes.

The 'basic safeguards against fiscal profligacy'[31] introduced by the Maastricht Treaty include the no-bailout clause precluding shared liability for government debt across Member States or by the Union (Art. 125(1) TFEU). The no-bailout clause addresses the issue of moral hazard. It was intended to function as a barrier to reckless borrowing by sovereigns and reckless lending by credit markets, to which the expectation of a bailout by the Union or other Member States in case of default could induce. The no-bailout clause gives expression to Member States' fiscal responsibility, i.e. their exclusive liability for their fiscal commitments; a constitutional principle which is the reverse of Member States' fiscal sovereignty. The prohibition of central-bank financing in Art. 123(1)

---

[30] The basic provision is in Art. 2(3) TFEU: "The Member States shall coordinate their economic and employment policies within arrangements as determined by this Treaty, which the Union shall have competence to provide." Art. 5(1) TFEU repeats Member States' obligation to coordinate their economic policies within the Union and adds that "to this end, the Council shall adopt measures, in particular broad guidelines for these policies". It also lays down that "specific provisions shall apply to those Member States whose currency is the euro".

[31] L. Schuknecht *et al.* (2011).

TFEU serves the purpose of sound public finances, but can – in line with the bailout prohibition – be read as a manifestation of Member States' fiscal liability, too. It also belongs to the package which was designed to ward off moral hazard in government spending and borrowing. The convergence criteria which have to be met before a Member State is eligible for the euro were designed with a view to securing sound public finances as well. The criteria refer to price stability, general government deficit and debt, stability of exchange rate and the long-term interest rate level (Art. 140(2) TFEU).

Finally, Treaty provisions (Arts. 121 and 126 TFEU) on continuous monitoring by the Commission and the Council were expected to curb and – in case of failure – keep track of and put a stop to Member State deviation from the path of prudent fiscal policy. These provisions were added new thrust through the Stability and Growth Pact. The Resolution of the European Council as the political basis of the Pact made clear the prevalence of Europeanised monetary policy, aiming at price stability, over national fiscal policy. The European Council underlined "the importance of safeguarding sound government finances as a means to strengthen the conditions for price stability and for strong sustainable growth conducive to employment creation", and declared it "necessary to ensure that national budgetary policies support stability oriented monetary policies". The multilateral surveillance procedure, set out in Art. 121 TFEU and further specified by Regulation 1466/97, constitutes the preventive arm of the Stability and Growth Pact. The corrective arm, which is supposed to take over if preventive measures do not lead to expected results, is centred round the excessive deficit procedure.

The Treaty basis for the excessive deficit procedure lies in Art. 126 TFEU and the complementary Protocol. In line with the multilateral surveillance procedure, the emphasis in the excessive deficit procedure, in its original shape, was on peer review and soft-law instruments. Yet, formal sanctions, too, have been available against delinquent states. Art. 126 TFEU assigns the Commission the task of monitoring development of the budgetary situation and the stock of government debt in the Member States. In particular, the Commission is expected to examine compliance with budgetary discipline, employing criteria based on the reference values of government deficit and debt, which the Protocol has fixed at 3% and 60% of gross domestic product, respectively. Subsequent measures laid down in Art. 126 TFEU target budgetary deficits. The decision on the existence of an excessive deficit is taken by the Council. As an ultimate recourse, the Council can impose a non-interest-bearing deposit and fines of appropriate size on a Member State which does not comply with its recommendations concerning deficit-reducing measures.[32]

To sum up, the Maastricht premises of European economic constitution include the following principles:

- exclusive competence of the EU in monetary policy in the euro area;
- price stability as the primary objective of Europeanised monetary policy;
- independence of the ECB and national central banks;
- strict definition of the mandate of the ECB;
- Member States' primary responsibility for the prudential supervision of financial institutions and the stability of the financial system;
- Member State sovereignty in fiscal and economic policy with the Union facilitating coordination of national policies;
- Member State obligation to consider their economic policy as a common concern and, thus, to heed the externalities of their economic policy;
- primacy of price stability pursued by Europeanised monetary-policy over national fiscal-policy objectives;
- sound public finances and fiscal discipline as a major objective of Member State fiscal policy;
- Member State fiscal liability and prohibition of shared liability for government debt;
- the unity of the European Union.

Subsequent Treaty amendments, including those introduced in Lisbon, have not touched upon the central Maastricht principles. The major novelties brought by the Lisbon Treaty concern the specific regime of the euro area. The expectation of all Member States joining EMU after fulfilling the convergence criteria has not been realised. The UK and Denmark have stuck to their formal derogations and Sweden has refused

---

[32] Council Regulation (EC) 1467/97 of July 1997 on speeding up and clarifying the implementation of the excessive deficit procedure, [1997] OJ L209/6, did not introduce new measures but complemented the already quite detailed provisions in the Treaty and the Protocol by regulating the timetable for the diverse phases and measures of the procedure and by further specifying the deposits and fines which can be imposed on a Member State failing to correct its excessive deficit. For a discussion of the Stability and Growth Pact in its original form see F. Amtenbrink and J. de Haan (2003).

to enter, obtaining a 'political', de facto derogation. Furthermore, not all of the Member States accepted in the eastern enlargement are likely to hurry to join. The Lisbon Chapter on the euro area[33] reflects resignation in front of a lingering bifurcation of the Union into the euro area and non-euro Member States. The Chapter constitutionalises a separate legal and institutional framework for the euro area. It facilitates particular secondary legislation on the preventive and corrective arm of the Stability and Growth Pact, and formalises the Euro Group; i.e. the euro-area composition the Ecofin Council, consisting of the Member State economics and finance ministers, as well as budget ministers when budgetary issues are discussed. The Chapter signifies retreat from the principle of European unity which the Maastricht provisions still manifested.[34]

The two layers of the economic constitution in comparison

The European economic constitution consists of two layers: the micro-economic one, introduced by the Treaty of Rome and subsequently rein-forced and developed by the ECJ, and the macroeconomic one, intro-duced by the Maastricht Treaty. They both display their peculiarities, but they are also closely interrelated and should also be examined as a constitutional whole. They share common constitutional themes and objectives, as well as economic presuppositions and assumed causali-ties. The microeconomic constitution of the Treaty of Rome relied on macroeconomic presumptions, such as price stability, which was to be achieved at the Member State level. It also exhorted Member States to heed the externalities of their economic policies: Member States were to consider their economic policies as a matter of common concern. Yet, no specific instruments for coordinating economic policies, com-parable to present multilateral surveillance or excessive deficit proce-dures, were made available.

The Maastricht economic constitution testifies to the continuing sig-nificance of the objectives of the microeconomic constitution for the macroeconomic layer. In Treaty provisions, the main principles of the microeconomic constitution have been made obligatory for monetary

---

[33] Ch. 4 of Title VIII TFEU (Provisions specific to member states whose currency is the euro).
[34] E. Chiti et al. (2012), pp. 423–4.

and economic policy, too. Art. 119(1) TFEU lays down that the economic policy of the Member States and the Union is to be conducted in accordance with the principle of an open market economy with free competition, and Arts. 119(2) and 127(1) impose a similar side-constraint on Europeanised monetary policy. So a formal link between the two layers of the European economic constitution was forged at the level of constitutionally defined policy objectives. This corresponds to the ordoliberal conception of the economic constitution. For ordoliberals, the microeconomic constitution was in a key position for realising broader societal aims, as well as ethical values related to a free society and individual liberty. Macroeconomic principles, such as price stability and stable economic policy, served implementation of the microeconomic constitution.[35]

The prehistory of the Maastricht Treaty shows that the step from micro- to macroeconomic constitution was seen as a consequent sequence of economic development. Both the Werner Group and the Delors Committee evoked the progress that had already been made under the microeconomic constitution and saw economic and monetary union as a natural further stage in economic integration. Economic and monetary union was needed because the common market had deepened interdependencies between national economies and economic policies. But on the other hand, completing the single market, especially promoting free movement of services and capital, was seen to require integration at the macroeconomic level. When Bretton Woods still functioned and could guarantee relative monetary stability, and when the post-war economic boom still continued, macroeconomic constitutionalisation could remain outside the European agenda. The collapse of Bretton Woods stability and the growing divergence of national macroeconomic approaches were increasingly perceived as a threat to market integration and the broader objectives of the Community. The inherent tension between the treatment of micro- and macroeconomics in the economic constitution of the Treaty of Rome became visible. Growing awareness existed that macroeconomic problems could undermine the success of the microeconomic constitution, too.

The interdependence between the micro- and macroeconomic constitutions has always been a two-way relation. Not only was realisation of the microeconomic constitution perceived to depend on

---

[35] This potentially also reflected the recognition that macroeconomic causalities were uncertain and that the most important macroeconomic contribution was stability, which allowed microeconomic factors to have their influence on the economy and society.

macroeconomic presuppositions, but the Maastricht macroeconomic constitution was premised on full implementation of the microeconomic one. Economists have considered labour mobility and wage flexibility an important prerequisite for common monetary policy under remaining Member State sovereignty in fiscal and economic policy. Common monetary policy was not only expected to reward full implementation of market freedoms and performance-based competition but also to punish economies for institutional and economic inefficiencies, for example in national labour and product markets.

Thus, significant interrelations exist between the European micro- and macroeconomic constitutions, with regard to both explicit Treaty provisions and their underlying economic assumptions and presuppositions. Yet the two layers also demonstrate significant differences which are important for a constitutional analysis, too. These differences start from the economic premises of the basic constitutional principles.

Basic microeconomic concepts and paradigms have remained quite stable over time. In addition, the data used in microeconomic analyses of the behaviour of individual consumers, companies and industries are relatively reliable and drawn from direct observation: quantities of output, prices and other outcomes of individuals' and companies' economic operations. Macroeconomics, in turn, focuses on the aggregate level of economy and studies phenomena such as changes in unemployment, national income, rate of growth, gross domestic product, inflation and price levels. In contrast to microeconomics, very few macroeconomic theories have remained unchanged let alone uncontested. While theoretical development in microeconomics appears to be incremental and evolutionary, macroeconomics has witnessed several revolutions and minor revolts, which have had significant consequences for economic policy, too. Consequently, the economic paradigm implicit in the microeconomic constitution is much more robust and stable – though by no means wholly uncontested – than the assumed causalities and links between macroeconomic variables and outcomes. Moreover, while competition policy, for instance, mostly employs temporally and spatially determined data on individual economic behaviour, macroeconomic policy-making relies on aggregate level data, based on statistical estimations with a varying degree of reliability.[36]

---

[36] A case in point is that even the GDP figures of the US and Japan have regularly been subject to large revisions that have changed perceptions of growth patterns considerably. See for example, J. Faust *et al.* (2005).

Compared to constitutionalism at the national level, the extent of constitutional regulation of both micro- and macroeconomic issues in the EU is exceptional. The microeconomic constitution, as it came to be interpreted by the ECJ, constitutionalised a particular, and by no means uncontroversial or value-free, economic model. In constitutional nation-state democracies, such choices are not usually frozen in constitutional provisions but are left to democratic political procedures. The definition of the microeconomic constitution through the principles of free market and undistorted competition has given European integration its liberalist orientation, which also fully accords with its at least initial legal emphasis.

Provisions on macroeconomic objectives, aggregate values and policies are even less frequently found in nation-state constitutions, although recent provisions on balanced budgets, for instance in the German Basic Law, have partly altered the general picture.[37] Still, the starting-point at the state level has been constitutional neutrality in economic policy. The principle of neutrality is based on the recognition that economic policy involves value choices, that policy decisions cannot be derived in an uncontroversial way from generally accepted, objective economic truths and that rival economic theories may lead to different policy conclusions. Hence, controversial policy choices, based on controversial economic theories, should not be fixed at constitutional level but should be left to democratic political decision-making. Constitutional enshrinement would grant economic policy a privileged position vis-à-vis, for instance, social policy.

Both the micro- and macroeconomic layers of the European economic constitution diverge from the standard nation-state template. Macroeconomic objectives, including the primacy of the monetary-policy objective of price stability, the entry criteria for EMU or exactly defined reference values for national fiscal policy are not unequivocally determined economic truths, either; arguably, they reflect a similar market economy (liberalist) bias as the basic principles of the microeconomic constitution. The asymmetry between constitutional protection of economic and, say, social policy, labels both the micro- and macroeconomic constitution. In the meanwhile, though, social values have received constitutional support from inclusion of the Solidarity

---

[37] In Germany the amendment was adopted in 2009. Other European countries with a constitutional debt brake include Austria, Italy, Poland, Spain and Switzerland. See the overview in F. Fabbrini (2013).

Chapter in the European Charter of Fundamental Rights. However, as we shall show in Chapter 7, social rights have not been able to counterweigh the primacy of economic policy measures, backed up by the reinterpreted European macroeconomic constitution.

On the other hand, the fact that in Member States neither micro- nor macroeconomic issues are usually regulated at constitutional level has probably facilitated economic constitutionalisation in the EU. Absence of national constitutional provisions has prevented frictions between the European economic constitution and its Member State counterparts. If conflicts between the transnational and the national level have emerged, they have not been conceptualised in constitutional terms.

Though after Maastricht, both micro- and macroeconomics share a constitutional foundation, the role of the law and the courts varies. As we have argued, the microeconomic constitution deals with the behaviour of individual economic actors, which has enabled the central role of the law and the courts. The field of the macroeconomic constitution, with its focus on objectives, aggregate economic values and policies, is much less susceptible to juridification. Objectives and aggregate values may be fixed in at least seemingly exact terms, such as the upper limits for government deficit or debt, defined in the Protocol on the excessive deficit procedure, or convergence criteria as the test for membership in EMU. However, the attainment or non-attainment of these objectives depends on a great number of individual policy decisions and external factors which simply cannot be exhaustively regulated by law. Hence even exactly defined objectives and values must leave room for exceptions in order to allow for unpredictable and uncontrollable external factors and to facilitate decision-makers' timely reactions to them.

Procedures lend themselves more easily to legal regulation than substantive policies, but the practical impact of mere procedural regulation may be rather weak. This is especially the case if the procedures adhere to the open method of coordination. Much of the Treaty law on, especially, fiscal and economic policy can be characterised as constitutional soft law. Correspondingly, the courts, both the ECJ and national courts, have hardly played any role in implementing or further elaborating the European macroeconomic constitution. Before the *Pringle* case,[38] the only ruling of the Court explicitly pertaining to the macroeconomic

---

[38] Case C-370/12 *Thomas Pringle v. Government of Ireland*, judgment of 27 November 2012 (not yet reported).

constitution was *Commission* v. *Council* in 2004, which dealt with the sanction regime of the excessive deficit procedure.[39] In *Pringle* the Court discussed some of the main doctrinal constitutional issues raised by the European management of the crisis, such as interpretation of the Treaty prohibition on bailouts and the availability of the intergovernmental option in crisis resolution (see below, Chapter 5). Undoubtedly, *Pringle* is the single most important constitutional speech act which the Eurozone crisis has produced. Yet, it mainly confirms the constitutional mutation which had already occurred, while landmark rulings in the field of the microeconomic constitution, such as *Dassonville* or *Cassis de Dijon*, really created new constitutional law. *Pringle* is essentially reactive and, in this sense, backward looking, while the latter rulings focused on the future.

At Member State level, the activity of Constitutional Courts and other institutions responsible for national constitutional review varies. The variance derives from, first, differences in national constitutional doctrine on, for instance, parliamentary budgetary sovereignty and social rights; and, second, the particularities of the national systems of constitutional review, such as the extent to which they allow supervision of European measures.

Reliance on expert bodies is a common characteristic of both layers of the European economic constitution. Within the microeconomic constitution, the key players are the courts – the ECJ and national courts feeding it with their references – and the Commission as the European Anti-Trust Authority. In the field of the macroeconomic constitution, the position of the Court has been rather peripheral, but here the Maastricht Treaty introduced another body relying on expert knowledge and output legitimacy, and insulated from democratic political pressures: the European Central Bank. The Commission also holds a vital position in the coordination and monitoring of Member State economic and fiscal policies. Macroeconomic constitutionalisation has especially strengthened the standing of the Commissioner for Economic and Monetary Affairs and the Directorate-General subordinated to that office.

In both the micro- and macroeconomic fields basic principles and objectives have been regulated at constitutional (Treaty) level, while their operationalisation has been left to independent experts. This combination impacts the way the system can adjust to new and unforeseen

---

[39] Case C-27/04 *Commission* v. *Council* [2004] ECR I-6649.

situations. Questions which at the national level are tackled through ordinary political decision-making may at the Union level be converted into constitutional issues.

Meeting unpredicted problems may require legal or institutional experimentalism. In the microeconomic field, the ECJ has assumed the task of elaborating constitutional principles and filling in the blanks. Relying on its mandate to create and maintain an effective rule of law, the ECJ has been able to provide the necessary legal experimentalism with regard to unforeseen situations; hence the slogan 'integration through law'.[40] Through mounting case law, what started as legal experimentalism has been incrementally reinforced to become an established doctrine. The ECJ has been able to introduce its doctrinal innovations in unspectacular cases and free from political pressure or media attention. In contrast, in the macroeconomic field, the contribution of the ECJ has been very limited. Here hardly any doctrinal tradition exists, and judicial decision-making cannot be based on undisputed, verifiable facts, either. Assessing the consequences of alternative readings of Treaty provisions would presuppose an economic expert knowledge which the ECJ simply does not possess. In divergence from free market and competition law, but few cases touching upon the macroeconomic constitution come before the ECJ, and those which do tend to be politically heavily loaded. In these circumstances, the ECJ cannot assume responsibility for the necessary experimentalism.

In the macroeconomic field, responsibility for experimentalism has rested with other independent experts, such as the ECB and the Commission, and political decision-makers. The ECJ has only been able to exercise restricted *ex post* control. Indeed, perhaps the main burden of legal scrutiny has fallen to Member State level; in particular, to constitutional review in countries where it is exercised by influential bodies. This again reflects the interplay between the transnational and national level, so typical of European constitutionalism.

The economic assumptions of the Maastricht macroeconomic constitution

Like constitutional principles in general, the Maastricht principles of the European economic constitution should be read through their underlying rationale: basic factual and normative assumptions concerning the

---

[40] Probably first used by M. Cappelletti *et al.* (1985).

functioning of the social field they are supposed to organise; the 'hidden social theory of constitutional law', as one could also put it. We have already referred to the continuing impact of ordoliberal thinking on German positions, which, in many respects, were an important influence on the EMU provisions of the Maastricht Treaty. Still, German ordoliberals held no monopoly over the economic views impacting the Maastricht principles.[41] Reconstructing economic theoretical premises is not an easy task, not least because a multi-state currency union is mostly uncharted territory for economics. In addition, the underlying assumptions must be reconstructed from a variety of views and opinions, often enough reflecting conflicting ideologies and interpretations of the aims of EMU.

In the aftermath of the Werner Report, two main approaches to monetary integration distinguished themselves, soon enough labelled Monetarist and Economist.[42] The Monetarist camp, not to be confused with monetarism as a school of thought in economics, argued that monetary union would facilitate deeper integration. As both a necessary and a sufficient condition for the EU's functioning as a single market and, by the same token, approaching what was called an optimal currency area, monetary union would precede and induce further political and economic integration. The Monetarist view was widespread among French politicians, who were keen to end Bundesbank domination in the European economy. It appears that, paradoxically enough, the Monetarists failed to grasp the position of monetary policy in the wider context of economic management.

By contrast, the Economists conceived of monetary union as a potential result of precedent political and economic integration; a final step on the long road of integration. Otmar Issing, subsequently one of the main architects of the ECB's operationalisation, was only one among the prominent economists who pointed out that "there is no example in history of a lasting monetary union that was not linked to one state".[43] The Economist position was common particularly among German economists, as well as officials at the Bundesbank and the Ministry of Finance. They emphasised the significance of monetary policy for economic policy in general and saw in monetary stability a major building block of the economic framework as a whole.

---

[41] Economic theorists, often lumped together as neo-liberals, may, though, display important variance in their views. Thus, the emphasis on the *ordo*, guaranteed by public institutions – such as courts, a competition authority and a central bank – was foreign to neo-liberals of the Hayekian or Chicago brand.

[42] T. Mayer (2012), p. 20, and G. Majone (2012).

[43] T. Mayer (2012), p. 43.

The result consecrated in Maastricht was a compromise between the two camps. As a main victory for the Monetarists, the Maastricht Treaty stipulated an ultimate deadline – 1999 – for the start of the final stage of EMU. In turn, the mainly German Economists managed to include a list of economic criteria to be fulfilled before a country can accede to EMU and to introduce a Bundesbank type of central banking model with an overriding emphasis on price stability.[44]

In the following, we try to highlight how EMU was supposed to function according to the views which found their reflection in the Maastricht Treaty and which impacted the operationalisation of the Treaty provisions during the 1990s. In addition, we shall discuss some issues whose importance was grasped only subsequently. In particular, we shall briefly comment on the implications of different stability concepts. 'Stability' has been a key term in debates on EMU, but it possesses a variety of connotations, all with different constitutional implications.

We start our more detailed reconstruction of the economic theory of the Maastricht macroeconomic constitution from the views supporting the conception of monetary policy as a non-political policy field, which pursues the objective of price stability and which should be left to the care of independent experts.

A wide variety of conceptions of monetary policy have existed over the years, ranging from views advocating the gold standard to those subordinating monetary policy to fiscal policy. The model of independent and inflation-alert central banking only began to gain wider currency from the late 1970s onwards, when monetary economics and central-banking practices largely developed in parallel. With a hint of sarcasm, one could say that Anglo-Saxon academic economics invented the Bundesbank decades after it was founded.

The theoretical and empirical perception of inflation underwent a radical change in the course of the 1970s. After the Great Depression of the 1930s and with the triumph of Keynesianism, inflation was treated as an instrument in the cyclical balancing of the economy. Criticism of inflationary Keynesian economic and monetary policy was raised already in the 1950s by for example, Milton Friedman.[45] Yet, outside Germany inflation was long considered the smallest of economic evils, and the anti-inflationary approach did not obtain much resonance. In addition, the quasi gold-standard system of Bretton Woods actually

---

[44] O. Issing (2008), pp. 6–12.   [45] M. Friedman (1956), pp. 51–67.

managed to keep inflation moderate until the end of the 1960s. Towards the late 1960s, inflationary tendencies of the major economies became harder to cope with, and the system of quasi-fixed exchange rates was increasingly difficult to sustain. The abolition of Bretton Woods in the early 1970s coincided with the oil price shock. As a result, the major economies suffered from both high unemployment and high inflation, which questioned the very foundations of Keynesianism. The exception was Germany where the Bundesbank attempted to check inflation, even defying the political will of the Government.

The experience of the 1970s spawned a flux of empirical analyses of inflation and its impact on economic development. A consensus existed that at least in the long run, inflation is a monetary phenomenon.[46] Evidence of the shorter-term effects of inflation and inflationary policies was more ambiguous. The 1970s high inflation shifted the focus of empirical analyses towards negative short- or medium-term economic and social effects, particularly on employment and growth. In the early 1980s, several countries adopted an anti-inflationary policy, sometimes with considerable social costs. A case in point was the appointment in 1979 of Paul Volcker by President Carter to head the Federal Reserve Board with an explicit mandate to focus on fighting inflation. Institutional economics appeared to support and complement the conclusions of empirical and theoretical monetarism. It argued that in the absence of an independent central bank, the incentive structure of political decision-makers leads them to stimulate the economy excessively, which causes higher inflation but does not increase output. The economy will suffer from an inflation bias if politicians with their typical short-term orientation are free to implement their belief in the positive effects of inflationary policy. Moreover, research had shown that, assuming rational expectations among economic agents, inducing effective inflation shocks to the economy would be difficult for policy-makers.[47]

In the 1980s, a broad consensus on the role of inflation and central banking emerged, conspicuous also in discussions among European central bankers.[48] The trade-off between inflation and employment was shown to be less clear than had been assumed, and, therefore, it was argued that inflation should no longer be used for the purpose of reducing unemployment. The possibility of fine-tuning economic

[46] O. Issing *et al.* (2004), pp. 10–12.   [47] R. Barro (1976).
[48] H. James (2012), pp. 181–323.

development with policy instruments was questioned in more general terms, too, not least because of the short-term orientation of policy-makers. By contrast, structural elements received more emphasis. Under the broad title of supply-side economics, designing the economic framework on the basis of microeconomic behaviour gained momentum at the expense of Keynesian counter-cyclical economic policy.

The shift in economics facilitated common European monetary policy in two important respects. First, the gap was closed between German monetary policy and the prevailing view among economists. Bundesbank monetary policy was highly valued among the German political elite and general public.[49] The trust and respect which the Bundesbank enjoyed was quite unique in Europe. For Germany, stability-oriented monetary policy was non-negotiable. Due to convergence in the 1980s, differences among Member States' monetary policy orientations narrowed. This was reflected in the relatively smooth functioning of the EMS. Second, the new economic consensus covered the requirement of leaving the conduct of monetary policy to an independent central bank. And, as we have already explained, an independent expert function was a suitable candidate for Europeanisation. As it also happened to match the Bundesbank model, it was acceptable to Germany, too.

German Economists had emphasised that monetary union required far-reaching economic and political integration among the participating Member States. However, they had to settle for a few key areas of economic convergence. Both what the Maastricht list of convergence criteria does and does not include is important in reconstructing the underlying economic assumptions of the macroeconomic constitution.[50]

The convergence criteria set only two major preconditions for a common currency. Eligible members were expected to have their public finances in reasonable shape and to have reached a certain level of monetary stability. Strictly speaking only the latter prerequisite required economic convergence. Convergence in the area of monetary stability was checked from three angles. First, the annual inflation rate should not exceed by more than 1.5 percentage points the average of the three Member States with the lowest inflation. In 1990, inflation differentials among EC countries were substantial. In Germany and the Netherlands inflation was below 3%, in Spain and Italy above 6% and in Greece it

---

[49] O. Issing (2008), p. 58.   [50] Ibid., pp. 13–20.

exceeded 20%. In the 1990s inflation rates converged significantly, due not only to anti-inflationary measures in countries with high rates but also to Germany's post-reunification inflationary development, as well as the disinflationary impact of Chinese exports and lower oil prices. By 1998, when the first EMU states were selected, the reference value for inflation was 2.7%, with all EU countries except Greece meeting the convergence criterion.[51]

Second, the exchange-rate criterion presupposed that future EMU members would participate in the ERM for two years without major realignments. The criterion was expected to test the credibility of monetary stability from an external perspective. Yet, the time span was insufficient for checking how prepared countries were to adjust to internal or external shocks. In effect, as soon as currency markets started to anticipate that EMU would become reality and that a given state would join it, there was hardly any pressure on its ERM-parity. The third criterion for monetary stability set out that the long-term interest rate should not exceed by more than 2% the average interest rate of the three countries with the lowest inflation rate. The prospect of EMU membership as such contributed to lower interest rates, turning them in effect into a self-fulfilling objective. The reference value in 1998 stood at 7.8%, which all Member States except Greece passed with relative ease.[52]

In sum, initial monetary stability was checked from both internal and external perspectives and by using both statistical means and perceptions of financial markets. Undoubtedly, the criteria did induce prospective EMU members to monetary stability and facilitate launching EMU by eliminating the largest elements of initial shocks: exchange rates and interest rates. When currency conversion was performed at the ERM parity rate and longer-term interest rates had to be converged before EMU, no major change occurred in either on 1 January 1999. Still, the criteria did not effectively measure the economic integration of the members or test their ability to adjust to asymmetric shocks in the framework of monetary union.

The criteria for public finances contained ceilings for general government deficit and debt. By contrast they did not presuppose rapprochement of national fiscal policies. No convergence of deficit or debt levels was required, but meeting the reference values sufficed. In

---

[51] EMI (1998) Convergence Report of March 1998, p. 6.
[52] Ibid.

addition, the criteria did not cover the content, relative size or cyclicality of public finances. Government deficit was not to exceed 3% of GDP, and debt was to remain under 60% of GDP. All 11 countries which joined EMU at its launch in 1999 fulfilled the deficit criterion based on 1998 figures. Although a relatively good cyclical situation and a certain amount of creative accounting played a role, substantial improvement was achieved in fiscal balances. Greece failed with deficit criterion in 1998, but two years later reported an acceptable figure, which was subsequently revealed to be falsified. Meeting the debt criterion proved to be more difficult. In 1998, not only did Italy and Belgium have debt levels well above the 60% reference value, but its strict interpretation would have excluded Germany, Spain, Netherlands and Austria, too. Hence a more flexible interpretation was adopted, which heeded not only demonstrated but even foreseeable reduction in the debt level. Implicitly, this also reflected the confidence that the excessive deficit procedure of the Maastricht Treaty would bring down debt over time.

Considerations in the Member States that in the end decided to stay outside EMU contain important information about what the Maastricht criteria did not comprise. Particularly interesting are the five economic test questions which the UK Government tried to answer when pondering whether or not to join EMU: 1) Are business cycles and economic structures sufficiently compatible so that Member States can live comfortably with euro interest rates on a permanent basis? 2) If problems emerge, does sufficient flexibility exist to deal with them? 3) Would joining EMU create better conditions for long-term investments in Britain? 4) What impact would entry into EMU have on the competitive position of the UK financial services industry? 5) In sum, would joining EMU promote higher growth, stability and a lasting increase in jobs?[53] The Swedish Government, in turn, commissioned a report from an independent expert group chaired by Professor Lars Calmfors. The extensive report discussed the role of exchange rates, impact on growth, macroeconomic disturbances and monetary policy, inflation and the credibility problem of monetary policy, the role of fiscal policy, as well as labour markets and EMU.[54] Both the UK and Swedish reports concluded that economic grounds did not support EMU membership for the respective country.

[53] HM Treasury Cm 5776, June 2003. The first version was published in 1997.
[54] Calmfors *et al.* (1997). Also published in English.

The fact that economic convergence was not included among the Maastricht criteria reflects the Monetarist view that a single currency would over time lead to necessary economic rapprochement. Moreover, contemporary research seemed to point to increasing parallelism of economic cycles due to a growing share of intra-EU trade. This fed Monetarists' optimism that before long the euro area would constitute a large and relatively homogeneous economy, similar to that of the US. The progress made in the 1990s seemed to lend credence to this optimism.

In an optimal currency area, mobility and flexibility of means of production facilitate adjusting to internal and external shocks. With regard to both labour mobility and wage flexibility, the Union was far from an optimal currency area. However, neither of them was set as a membership criterion in Maastricht. In the UK assessment in 2003, flexibility of labour markets, although much higher than in most euro-area states, was still deemed insufficient in light of the potentially increased national volatility. In turn, the Calmfors report emphasised the fact that losing exchange-rate and monetary-policy instruments for national adjustment purposes would require enhanced flexibility from the Swedish labour market. The report also cautioned against belief in enhanced flexibility – especially increased labour mobility – as a quasi-automatic consequence of monetary union.[55]

Many Eurozone states possess key industries of particular importance which are potential sources of country-specific shocks. It is probably impossible to set EU-level criteria on Member States' ability to cope with vulnerabilities to idiosyncratic shocks. Still, it is striking that in preparing for EMU such risks were not discussed at greater length, also considering that EMU and economic integration in general were expected to increase specialisation among Member States and, hence, even their vulnerability to asymmetric shocks.

For monetary stability, fiscal policy is the crucial non-monetary field of economic policy. The Maastricht model opted for national responsibility for fiscal policy, with certain safeguards against negative externalities and moral hazard. Because of their different locus, little room was reserved for a dialogue between fiscal and monetary policy. Three main considerations determined the place of fiscal policy within EMU. First, fiscal policy – more precisely budgetary imbalances – was deemed to be

[55] *Ibid.*, pp. 229–30.

a major potential source of instability for the common economic framework. To prevent imprudent fiscal policy, market-induced discipline was complemented by institutional, Union-level means. Second, fiscal policy was seen as a crucial national instrument for adjusting to asymmetric internal and external shocks. Third, fiscal policy's redistributive effects were understood to entail a need for democratic legitimacy, which could only be obtained through Member State fiscal sovereignty and national democratic procedures.

Treaty provisions on fiscal policy, complemented by the Stability and Growth Pact, aimed to ward off risks for monetary stability. In economic history, the major risk had arisen from monetising of government debt, and, consequently, an explicit prohibition of central-bank financing was included in the Maastricht Treaty (present Art. 123(1) TFEU). Furthermore, it was realised that in EMU governments could have means for and incentives to deficit financing well beyond the previous situation. Generally, government deficit financing is constrained by the availability and cost of funding. If mounting government deficit and debt casts doubts on sustainability, interest rates on government debt go up. At some point, the costs of funding will outweigh the benefits of further deficit expenditure. In the EMU context, benefits are mostly felt nationally while the cost in terms of higher long-term interest rates is shared by all EMU states. The no-bailout clause of the Treaty (present Art. 125(1)), as well as the Stability and Growth Pact, aim to combat this moral hazard.[56]

Given the importance of fiscal policy as a national adjustment mechanism, this aspect was accorded surprisingly little attention in the run-up to the Maastricht Treaty. In 1999, i.e. at the start of the final phase of EMU, public expenditure accounted for nearly half of the GDP of the Member States.[57] Nevertheless its role varied considerably, as did that of the so-called automatic stabilisers; that is, counter-cyclically altering revenues and expenditures, such as taxes and welfare spending. In Member States with large automatic stabilisers, the fiscal balance should be sufficiently in surplus in good times to allow for them to work without corrective measures in downturn. As the Calmfors report pointed out, the need for fiscal adjustment mechanisms was likely to grow in EMU where exchange-rate and monetary-policy instruments would no longer be available for national adjustment purposes.

---

[56] O. Issing (2008), pp. 193–5.   [57] *Ibid.*, p. 44.

The third major issue determining the position of fiscal policy in the Maastricht architecture concerned redistribution. A broad consensus prevailed over the very restricted role of redistribution between Member States; the EU in general or EMU in particular was not to be developed into a 'transfer Union'. For historical and cultural reasons, internal redistributive mechanisms and welfare regimes varied greatly in Member States. Welfare policy was also at the very heart of national political debates, concentrated around the annual budgetary process. Redistribution is the meeting point of fiscal and social policy, as well as democratic self-assertion. In Maastricht, no attempt was made to harmonise national redistributive systems or to create Union-level redistributive functions. Member States retained their sovereignty over provision of public goods and services as well as social security benefits. Some discussants, among them Karl Otto Pöhl, Bundesbank President and member of the Delors Committee, argued that EMU would require substantial convergence in national fiscal, regional and social policy.[58] Yet this type of argument, while not altogether groundless, was perhaps treated as a tactical manoeuvre to postpone EMU rather than a genuine suggestion worthy of inclusion in the Delors Report and Maastricht Treaty.

The disciplining effect of financial markets on Member States was a thoroughly discussed topic in the long hatching process of EMU. Market discipline works through risks that investors perceive and seek compensation for. Along with the Bundesbank model, EMU inherited the credibility in maintaining monetary stability. This reduced the investment risk which in countries with a shaky fiscal record had been related to possible devaluation. The risk of inflation diminished, too. Furthermore, wider and more integrated EMU bond markets were likely to reduce liquidity risks. By contrast, one would have expected default risk to increase when individual Member States had lost control over the currency. Yet, in total, risk-compensation on bonds and, consequently, the interest rate on sovereign debt were expected to decline.[59]

The emerging consensus appeared to be that the discipline imposed by the financial markets was a necessary condition for Member States' prudent fiscal policy. But it was also well known in European central banks and explicitly stated in the Delors Report that market discipline would not suffice. This was due, first, to the general disaster myopia of

---

[58] H. James (2012), p. 229.
[59] See, e.g., L. Codogno *et al.* (2003); K. Bernoth *et al.* (2004); L. Mosley (2004).

the markets, which are not very good at pricing low-probability events, such as sovereign defaults; this is related to the well-known fat-tail problem. Moreover, suspicions existed that markets might not concede full credence to the no-bailout clause before it was tested in practice. It was also reckoned that when market pressure still had a chance to affect Member State policy, it was likely to be too mild, and when a Member State had already lost control over its finances, market discipline in terms of a high interest rate for sovereign debt was likely to be excessive.

The designers of the fiscal policy bulwark acknowledged the moral hazard related to Member States' incentives to debt-financed consumption and the insufficiency of market discipline. Much hope was laid on the excessive deficit procedure, which was designed as the institutional vehicle to impose prudent fiscal policy. If public deficit was not to exceed 3%, unless in exceptional circumstances, this would basically demand close-to-balanced budgets over the economic cycle and lead to a rapid reduction in government debt, assuming a reasonable GDP growth rate.

In addition, the Treaty framework for ECB monetary policy, which included an explicit prohibition on financing governments, was supposed to enhance market discipline and to prevent unsustainable public expenditure. Moreover, government debt was not supposed to receive any special treatment in ECB monetary policy operations. The Bundesbank would have preferred to oblige the ECB to rely mainly on private credit instruments, but this policy could not be adopted due to differences in Member States' financial market structures and traditions. Hence, for instance, the ECB was free to take government bonds as collateral and use them in open market operations, but subject to the same quality criteria as other credit instruments.

In total, the drafters of the Maastricht (macro)economic constitution took the possibility of reckless public finances very seriously and defined it as a major risk for stability and balanced growth. The artillery of the Treaty provisions on economic and especially fiscal policy was directed against national governments' irresponsible short-term behaviour which would ultimately be detrimental to the longer-term interests of their own constituencies, as well.

Did the Maastricht EMU framework suffer from a fatal asymmetry between common, Europeanised monetary policy and national fiscal policy? Was this asymmetry irresponsibly neglected in pre-Maastricht discussions and negotiations? These questions have provoked heated debates. Yet, beyond a general reference to the division of competences between the European and national levels, the exact meaning and manifestations of the alleged asymmetry tend to remain unclear.

For monetary policy, asymmetry would mainly mean that fiscal policy, in particular deficit-financed consumption, may induce inflation and inflation expectations. If fiscal policy is loose, monetary policy needs to take coercive measures that do not yield optimal outcomes. For example, after German reunification, massive fiscal transfers to East Germany were realised and extensive rebuilding launched. The Bundesbank perceived major risks to price stability and reacted with an aggressive interest-rate policy. In normal times, the government in a state with an independent and credible central bank would refrain from excessively expansionary fiscal policy in anticipation of an adverse central-bank reaction. In the EMU setting, by contrast, no single member state can expect a direct central-bank reaction to its fiscal-policy measures. Unless constrained by other means, governments can end up with an expansionary fiscal policy. Here the Maastricht constraints on national fiscal policy, supplemented by the Stability and Growth Pact, were intended to protect the balanced conduct of monetary policy. Furthermore, Member States were not only expected to pursue prudent fiscal policy but to "regard their economic policies as a matter of common concern", i.e. to heed the externalities of their policies. The architects of the Maastricht macroeconomic constitution put much faith in national incentives for a prudent fiscal policy, too. If domestic inflation and wage trends started to diverge from the euro-area averages, negative patterns would emerge. Fiscally induced unsustainable inflationary development would necessitate adjustment through nominal-wage reductions or a restrictive fiscal policy, or both.

Another but related asymmetry concerns the consequences of uniform nominal interest rates: the one-size-for-all monetary policy. In catch-up countries prices, particularly in non-tradable sectors, tend to increase more than in economically more advanced countries. Hence, in the former countries real interest rates could be lower and monetary policy more expansionary than in the latter ones. Catch-up countries' fiscal policy, in turn, should be alert to inflationary developments and favour restrictions, which could contribute to budgetary balance as well. Were national policies to fail, large adjustment needs would be stored up which could no longer be managed by means of national exchange-rate or monetary policy. Except for measures aiming at fiscal discipline, the Maastricht economic constitution provided but few warning signals or instruments to combat such negative patterns, as they were considered purely national responsibilities.

Another topical pre- and post-Maastricht issue concerns EMU as an optimal currency area: does EMU constitute an optimal currency area or would completion of the single market at least push it on a path in that direction? In 1961, Robert Mundell presented the idea of optimal currency areas as follows: "If the world can be divided into regions within each of which there is factor mobility and between which there is factor immobility, then each of these regions should have a separate currency that fluctuates relative to all other currencies."[60] Within a currency area, factor (labour and capital) mobility is the main mechanism for adjusting to various forms of shocks. Subsequent theoretical developments have loosened the conditions for a currency area by including complementary adjustment mechanisms, such as wage flexibility and inter-region fiscal transfers. Furthermore, economic integration and coinciding cyclical movements are seen to reduce the need for country- or region-specific adjustment mechanisms. Intra-area trade would link the countries at issue more closely together and unify their business cycles. Yet, economists have also acknowledged that to a substantial extent, economic cyclicality can result from an economic policy geared towards short-term electoral needs rather than structural issues or external shocks.

It was clear at the outset that none of the possible member combinations would make EMU into an optimal currency area. What was less clear were the grounds on which the Monetarist optimists based their confidence that EMU would in due time approach such an area. Labour mobility, facilitated by the free movement of labour guaranteed by the Treaty, was deemed important. Still, nobody suggested that EMU could at any reasonable time adjust to economic shocks through labour mobility. German Economists continuously made the case that some level of fiscal and political integration would be needed for monetary union to work. Whether German talk about extending fiscal union to social policy was a genuine proposal, or just a way to curb French enthusiasm for monetary union, remains an open question. In any case, no serious attempt was made to facilitate major fiscal transfers in EMU or to introduce EU-level social policy measures with similar

[60] R. Mundel (1961).

effect, optimally financed by cyclically driven EU-wide taxes. The Delors Report proposed increasing structural funds but more as a measure to alleviate structural problems rather than a policy tool for managing cyclical asymmetries.

So it appears that the optimistic expectation of EMU developing into an optimal currency area was based on assumptions of increased flexibility and simultaneous easing of asymmetric, country-specific shocks. The ECB has hardly held a press conference where it would not have stressed the need for structural reforms improving flexibility. In circumstances of price stability, promoted in Maastricht to a constitutional obligation, even nominal wage flexibility would necessarily be vital for adjustment. In this regard, the pre-history of EMU was not particularly promising. Most adjustments of national exchanges rates in EMS and ERM had their background in a loss of competitiveness occasioned by wage increases, while the list of successful wage adjustments to correct the situation was considerably shorter. Still, the mainly French Monetarist optimists presumed that the price stability achieved by monetary union would facilitate wage adjustments.

Before EMU, financial markets in most EU countries were largely national. The main cross-border link was the international interbank market based on illiquid wholesale bank deposits and securities markets. Globalisation, together with technological progress, was a main theme in banking from the 1980s onwards. The anticipated changes caused by liberalisation of Community/Union capital markets and EMU were thoroughly analysed. Yet, although it was generally acknowledged that financial markets faced pivotal changes, due partly to EMU but to many other factors as well, financial-market issues did not play a major role in designing EMU. The main question was whether institutional reforms were needed in banking supervision and, if they were, whether the ECB should be assigned centralised functions. The Bundesbank opposed central-bank supervision invoking the moral hazard risk which could ensue from banks' expectation that the central bank would not only exert supervision but also employ monetary policy instruments to rescue them.[61] The resulting conclusion was to continue with the existing decentralised framework, with amplified emphasis on cooperation between national supervisors. Responsibility for the financial sector remained at national level with only minimum

---

[61] H. James (2012), p. 291.

harmonisation in some critical areas. By and large, national discretion as to whether and how to rescue failing institutions remained in place as well. Contentment with the existing framework is also explained by the fact that the probability of a major banking crisis was held to be low. EMU was presumed to enhance financial stability. Financial markets would become more synchronised, and integration would produce larger and more liquid markets, which are less prone to failures and less affected by the default of single institutions and which make for better risk diversification.

With hindsight, the scarce attention crisis management received in preparing for EMU and drafting the Maastricht macroeconomic constitution might seem astonishing. We have already tackled the reasons for inattention to fiscal crises. A danger of fiscal crisis was not really discerned on the horizon but was supposed to be excluded by the preventive mechanisms included in the Treaty and the Stability and Growth Pact. In economic theory, a self-fulfilling sovereign debt crisis is conceived of as follows. In good times the subjective risk premium that should cover uncertain negative developments approaches zero. In normal circumstances, preventive mechanisms complemented by the state's taxing power make state default so improbable that it is not priced in by market participants. Once signs appear of the improbability becoming reality, the consequent increase in interest rate would need to be so substantial that it would actually dramatically raise the default risk. Hence no interest rate is able to match the investors' risk perception, and they refuse further financing to the sovereign.[62] In EMU, the very function of the Stability and Growth Pact was to prevent such a situation from arising. Should a fiscal crisis still erupt, the Maastricht framework allowed for but two ways out: an IMF programme with or without state default (debt restructuring). Arguably, default was deemed not only a possible but also to some extent necessary resolution of fiscal crises; necessary for enhancing the credibility of the no-bailout clause of the Treaty.

Turning to financial crises, the inter-linkage between financial instability and macroeconomic developments was already common knowledge in the 1980s. Why, then, was it not addressed in designing EMU? We suggest four partly overlapping explanations.

First, the enhanced stability of the EMU macroeconomic set-up was assumed to reduce the likelihood of adverse financial-market shocks.

---

[62] P. Davis (1992), pp. 136–41.

Price stability was considered the most efficient medicine against financial instability that a central bank can offer. As inflation shocks affect all asset prices, they are a major cause of financial stress. In the same vein, deflationary developments, too, cause financial stress and even spawn negative spirals. Second, the fiscal policy framework was expected to improve the stability of financial markets by eliminating shocks emanating from reckless fiscal policy. Prudent fiscal policy also contributes to macroeconomic stability through automatic stabilisers which prevent self-reinforcing negative patterns of unemployment, reduced income, mounting debt problems and declining asset prices.

Third, most of the targeted regulatory and supervisory measures to thwart financial instability were considered to be national responsibilities. Supervisory functions of the common central bank were rejected because of moral hazard concerns. Other reasons also existed for opting for the Member State level. In economic terms, a correct balance needs to be struck between the benefits of financial freedom and the risks it entails to the economy and taxpayers. In most cases the appropriate level for this decision is the national one, although in some areas international cooperation is needed for regulation and supervision to be effective. Furthermore, there simply was not sufficient political capital to prepare for a more uniform approach to financial stability and supervision at the launch of EMU.

Fourth, the function of the lender of last resort vis-à-vis banks was intentionally left obscure. Central banks in general regard guaranteeing liquidity for the banking sector as part of their responsibility. Even in modern financial intermediation bank runs can occur and affect even wholly solvent and well-managed banks. Deposit insurance systems have been created to cope with bank runs. Yet, occasional needs for emergency liquidity assistance may emerge, whereby central banks may finance solvent but illiquid banks, compromising on collateral requirements. How such liquidity crises would be handled in the EMU context was left open by the drafters of the Maastricht provisions. It is, though, fair to assume that in EMU, too, national central banks would play some role. They would possess the necessary information on the solvency of the bank in crisis and on the quality of its collateral. Moreover, through the national budget national central banks are related to national taxpayers, and, arguably, if liquidity support turned into solvency support, it would be paid for by the appropriate taxpayers.

To conclude, various types of financial crisis were discussed in preparing for EMU. Yet, in the end the German central-banking model prevailed here, too. In this model, the central bank keeps a distance from financial markets and institutions in order to avoid moral hazard. Financial institutions should not be led to expect that the central bank would come to their rescue with monetary policy means. Pursuant to the underlying economic thinking, this would compromise price stability and augment the risk of financial instability as well. Accordingly, the Maastricht macroeconomic constitution retained national responsibility for financial institutions and their solvency.

Foray: stability concepts

'Stability' is a key concept in German ordoliberal thinking and plays a crucial role in the European economic constitution, too. It is one of the hinge concepts linking economic and constitutional language; Niklas Luhmann would perhaps speak of a structural coupling between economy and law.[63] For ordoliberals, the economic constitution provides the economy with a stable framework, which is complemented by a stability-oriented economic policy and price stability. In its rulings, the German Constitutional Court has transformed stability as a characteristic of the European macroeconomic constitution into a requirement of national constitutional law (see Chapter 6). In recent European crisis management, stability has been elevated to the primary objective. Yet, numerous stability concepts exist, and their definitions and interrelations are not always clear. 'Price stability', 'economic stability', 'stability of economic policy', 'financial stability', 'banking stability', 'euro-area stability' and 'euro-area financial stability' are only some of the stability concepts which have abounded in the context of the European macroeconomic constitution and euro-area crisis management. In the following, we attempt to provide preliminary definitions of central stability concepts with a particular view to their use in economics and crisis management.

The most comprehensive aggregate stability concept is *stability of the euro area as a whole*. This concept is explicitly employed in the amendment to Art. 136 TFEU which allows Member States to "establish a stability mechanism to be activated if indispensable to safeguard the stability of the euro area as a whole". European Council Decision 2011/199, which adopted the amendment, invokes both the financial stability of the euro area as a whole and the stability of the euro area

---

[63] On the concept of structural coupling, see N. Luhmann (2004), pp. 381 ff.

as a whole. Furthermore, the Decision relates dealing with risks to the financial stability of the euro area as a whole to preserving the economic and financial stability of the Union itself. Stability of the euro area as a whole is also invoked in the Preamble to the Treaty on Stability, Coordination and Governance (TSCG), where it is indicated as the higher-level objective which Member States' prudent fiscal policy is supposed to pursue.[64]

It appears that in contemporary EU language, the stability of the euro area as a whole consists of economic and financial stability. *Economic stability* can be defined as stable economic growth without major disruptions or excessive fluctuations. Such stability is implicit in the Union objective of "sustainable development of Europe, based on balanced economic growth and price stability, a highly competitive social market economy, aiming at full employment and social progress" (TEU Art. 3(3)).

Financial stability has been a widely used concept during the Eurozone crisis. Although the Founding Treaties do not explicitly mention it, financial stability of the euro area or the Union as a whole has been the objective most often invoked to justify rescue packages and stability mechanisms. The objective seems to encompass an increasing number of elements, which makes it difficult to pin down an unambiguous definition. At a very general level, 'financial stability' refers to a situation where the distinct parts of the financial system are able to perform their functions without major disruptions in the financial system or the economy in general. Basically, at issue is the ability of direct financing through markets and indirect financing through intermediaries to channel funds between suppliers and demanders in a rational manner. In the traditional sense, financial stability is a broader concept for *banking stability*. 'Banking stability' refers to the capacity of the banking sector to fulfil its role in the economy even in deeper downturns. As long as the banking sector holds the key position in financial intermediation between savers and investors, banking stability, maintained through regulation and supervision, is sufficient to guarantee financial stability in general. Banking stability is assumed to be maintained by regulating the banking sector and imposing supervision on individual banks. In addition, amounts and interest rates of banking loans constitute the main pass-through of monetary policy. In the contemporary

---

[64] The Contracting Parties declare to bear in mind that "the need for governments to maintain sound and sustainable public finances and to prevent a general government deficit becoming excessive is of essential importance to safeguard the stability of the euro area as a whole".

financial system, banking channels and financing through markets work in parallel, complementing each other. Consequently, financial stability must cover both aspects.

Monetary stability is the main policy objective most central banks subscribe to. It can be defined either internally through *price stability* or externally through *exchange-rate stability*. In pre-EMU Europe, the German Bundesbank put the clear emphasis on internal price stability, while in many other European countries monetary stability was defined primarily through the exchange rate, first vis-à-vis the US dollar in the Bretton Woods system and then vis-à-vis the D-mark in the European exchange-rate mechanism. EMU – i.e. the European macroeconomic constitution – has inherited the German definition of monetary stability mainly in terms of price stability.

Under the macroeconomic constitution, the ECB is the main guardian of price stability, although, as Art. 3(3) TEU makes clear, the objective is set for the Union as a whole. In qualitative terms, the ECB simply defines price stability as avoidance of both prolonged inflation and deflation. In quantitative terms, the target is "a year-on-year increase in the Harmonised Index of Consumer Prices (HICP) for the euro area of below 2%". The ECB further clarifies that "it aims to maintain inflation rates below, but close to, 2% over the medium term".[65] The ECB definition refers to the relatively narrow concept of consumer prices and explicitly excludes all asset prices. Furthermore, it focuses on average rates in the euro area, while country-specific variation plays no specific role. Thus, it allows for a situation where some euro-area countries have prolonged inflation as long as other countries balance this with deflation. In addition, the ECB definition targets changes and ignores levels. Temporary bursts of inflation do not need to be compensated by deflation. It suffices to stabilise the rate of price increases below the average of 2 per cent.

These features of the ECB definition are understandable and perhaps even unavoidable. Yet, they have important implications for the concept of price stability as it is applied in the euro area. The major reason for not including asset prices in the definition is their complex nature. Asset prices reflect a broad set of variables. This makes it very difficult for a central bank to assess whether price increases are based on fundamental improvements and, hence, are sustainable or whether they constitute an asset price bubble that will burst in due time with

---

[65] ECB website, 'The Definition of Price Stability'.

considerable economic and social costs. In addition, the limited set of tools the ECB has at its disposal for the conduct of monetary policy – basically EMU-wide short-term interest rates and related liquidity management – is hardly sufficient for managing asset prices, were these to behave differently to consumer prices.

Country-specific inflationary or deflationary tendencies are only reflected in the prism of the ECB price-stability concept to the extent that they influence euro-area averages. Unless the still available national policy tools are employed, price stability in small and relatively closed euro-area economies with important domestic service sectors does not have a guardian. Instead of one comprehensive price stability, one should actually speak of many price stabilities. Only euro-area price stability as defined by the change in consumer prices falls under the responsibility of the ECB. Of course, euro-area price stability is expected to support price stability in Member States and provide it with an anchor, but ultimately the responsibility remains at the national level and with national actors. Fiscal and tariff policy, together with wage formation, occupy a crucial position.

Stability of economic policy, in turn, refers to economic policy which is geared towards avoiding policy shocks to the functioning of the economy and towards combating economic instabilities. In ordoliberal thinking, stability of economic policy advises against activist or interventionist economic policies, which are perceived to be destabilising and counterproductive, and subject to the influence of corporatist interests. In a more neutral perspective, 'stability of economic policy' refers to consequent, medium-term-oriented conduct of economic, particularly fiscal policy, with the focus on structural measures. Perhaps due to limited EU competences in economic policy, the concept has not been explicitly used in Union contexts. Arguably, the constraints on national fiscal policy which were included in the Maastricht macroeconomic constitution and, subsequently, complemented by the Stability and Growth Pact, reflect stability-oriented economic policy. *Fiscal-policy stability* was considered necessary in order to prevent externalities with regard to other euro states or common monetary policy. Budget-deficit and sovereign-debt constraints effectively excluded Keynesian discretionary fiscal policy for the purposes of demand management, except in Member States with a large fiscal surplus.

3 Towards the crisis: an economic narrative

Three secular trends

The sovereign debt crisis was the most dramatic manifestation of the Eurozone crisis. It also led to the most profound changes in the European macroeconomic constitution, with important spillover effects in the fields of the political and social constitution. Yet, it was only the last phase in a series of predicaments which hit most of the developed economies beginning in late 2007. The Eurozone crisis was a result of manifold economic factors, which include both long-term secular trends[1] and more recent developments. Together the long- and short-term factors explain why so many of the underlying economic assumptions of the Maastricht macroeconomic constitution proved to be mistaken and why the Eurozone responded to the crisis in the manner it did.

Three secular trends in the global economy, which were more or less neglected in drafting the European macroeconomic constitution, need to be recognised in order to understand the root causes of the crisis: a constant increase of private and public debt in the developed economies since the beginning of the 1980s; inclusion of the emerging economies (EME), particularly those in Asia, in the global economy; and the trend-wise decline in the volatility of GDP growth and inflation which came to be known as the Great Moderation[2] but which could in effect have been a change in the nature of economic cycles from shorter-term traditional cycles to medium-term financial cycles.

---

[1] 'Secular' refers to long-standing trends, i.e. trends that last from more than a decade to multiple decades and do not have a cyclical nature.
[2] A fourth trend could be added: ageing of the population, which already has a profound impact on Japan and is becoming a major force in EU countries as well.

Designations such as 'sub-prime crisis', 'financial crisis' and 'sovereign debt crisis' hint at the importance of debt for the recent economic turmoil. Yet, the role of debt should be approached from a longer-term perspective. The level of debt has risen throughout the developed world over the last three decades. In 1980, the total non-financial debt of the OECD countries was on average 167% of GDP. By 2010, it had reached 314% of GDP. Of this rise, the share of public debt was 49, household debt 56 and corporate debt the remaining 42 percentage points.[3] Debt related to financial markets has grown even more, standing in 2010 at more than 1000% of GDP. This does not necessarily increase the role of debt in the economy, but it certainly makes the financial system more interconnected.

How can such a massive increase be explained? Debt still possesses its traditional welfare-enhancing function. First, it works as a smoothing device: it allows households to smooth their consumption in the face of varying income, corporations to smooth investments and production, and governments to smooth taxes. Second, debt facilitates efficient capital allocation among those who have capital and those who are able to handle it and bear the risks. Third, through public debt inter-generational consumption can be balanced.[4] Still, tentative research results seem to suggest that the welfare-enhancing properties only apply up to a limit and that in many countries this limit may have been exceeded.[5] The main negative impact of debt on macroeconomic performance derives from its property to transmit and amplify shocks, and to reduce an economy's capacity to dampen them. If households, companies and governments have high levels of debt, their ability to respond to negative shocks is constrained by available resources.[6] Countries with a high debt level tend to have long and intensive phases of economic expansion, which most likely end in recession. Once in downturn, high-debt countries face considerably longer negative developments in both private consumption and investments than low-debt ones.[7]

---

[3] S. Cecchetti *et al.* (2011), pp. 5–6.   [4] *Ibid.*, p. 3.

[5] For example, S. Cecchetti *et al.* (2011) found that public debt seems to become negative for growth at 85% of GDP. Similar results have been obtained by Reinhart and Rogoff (2010), although their claim of a 90% limit beyond which debt starts to exert a negative influence on growth has been disputed. It is plausible that the effects of debt depend very much on the precise characteristics of the economy; in particular, the extent to which debt has been used to finance investments in productive capacity instead of current consumption.

[6] OECD (2013), 'Debt and Macroeconomic Stability', pp. 2–3.

[7] *Ibid.*, pp. 4–6.

Welfare-enhancing can thus provide but a partial explanation for the general rise in the level of debt. The fact that the rising trend was not halted by policy means may be due to uncertainty of the exact level where private or public debt starts producing negative structural effects in a given economy. Responsibility for preventing excessive debt and the consequent negative repercussions for growth was not always clearly defined, either. Central banks increasingly focused on combating inflation, and fiscal policy was either considered ineffective or even contributed to high indebtedness. Financial innovations, deregulation and incentive structures of financial-market actors have played their part, too. In particular, the securitisation of financial obligations, i.e. various forms of packaging and reselling them, prompted mounting indebtedness. Incentives to take risks were not in balance with liability for them, and a considerable proportion of risks was actually covered by implicit governmental guarantees; that is, taxpayers' money. Financial regulation and supervision failed to an unprecedented degree on both sides of the Atlantic.[8]

A further explanation for the increased role of private debt in particular is offered by what is often labelled as private Keynesianism. Through management of interest rates, tax incentives – especially for housing loans – and deregulation of credit markets, households were encouraged to take over debt and the related risk, partly in order to facilitate demand management and to replace the traditional Keynesian instruments of public expenditure and debt.[9] In the UK, for example, in accordance with a conscious policy of the Thatcher Government, owner-occupied and privately rented housing started to replace socially based renting in the 1980s, which led to increased housing debt by households.[10] In the US, home ownership started to increase after 1995, most pronouncedly among ethnic minorities and lower income groups.[11]

The development in EU Member States in general and the Eurozone in particular was broadly in line with other OECD countries. Non-financial private debt grew steadily until 2009. During EMU, non-financial corporate debt increased in the euro area from 60% of GDP in 1999 to

---

[8] Many analyses exist of the underlying causes of the financial crisis related to financial innovations, deregulation etc. See, e.g., C. Bean (2010), pp. 10–16.

[9] C. Crouch (2009).   [10] B. Pattison *et al.* (2010), p. 11.

[11] C. Garriga *et al.* (2006). The paper explains the increase by the tax code which favours homeownership, the government agencies which promote homeownership and the Clinton and George W. Bush administrations' programmes to help young and low-income homebuyers, at p. 399.

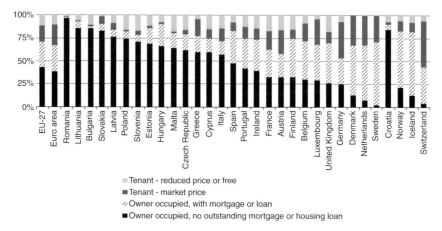

Figure 3.1 Distribution of population by tenure status, type of household and income group
Source: Eurostat (online data code: ilc_lvhc02)

more than 80% by 2009. For households, the respective figures were less than 50% in 1999 and 67% in 2009. These figures mask significant differences between Member States, particularly with regard to corporate and household debt. For instance, in Germany owner-occupied housing is not very common, which reduces the euro-area average for household debt (see Figure 3.1). Similarly, in non-financial corporate debt Germany posted considerably lower ratios with regard to GDP than other large euro-area countries. In contrast, Spanish corporate debt increased dramatically during the euro era and reached unprecedented levels just before the crisis.

The only component of debt which was addressed in the Maastricht Treaty was government debt. The rate of government debt was included in the entry criteria of EMU and further controlled through the excessive deficit procedure. General government debt in the euro area followed a somewhat different pattern from private debt. The debt ratio declined from 74% of GDP in 1996 with only a small cyclical variation until 2007, when it reached 66% of GDP. From thereon, debt increased dramatically to reach nearly 91% of GDP in 2012. Country variation was relatively small in 1999, when EMU started, with most countries close to the 60% threshold, with the notable exceptions of Belgium, Italy and Greece where public debt reached more than 100% of GDP. By 2007, considerable improvements were recorded in Belgium and Spain, with debt ratios declining more than 20 percentage points. This was counterweighed by a worsening debt situation in Portugal and to some extent Greece, even before the outbreak of the crisis. Since 2008, debt patterns have showed great variation. Ireland and Spain, which initially had low debt levels, recorded a major jump. Portugal accelerated its depressive path, and Greece broke new records with its government debt reaching 170% of GDP in 2011. Traditional high debt countries Belgium and Italy showed relative stability, with their debt increasing at more or less the same pace as in Germany and France.

In sum, in most euro-area countries, with the important exception of Germany, private debt had risen to a level which made them vulnerable to changes in economic conditions. The same holds for public debt, but more clearly only after the crisis. The importance and complexity of the financial sector had grown as well, with considerable differences between countries. Private debt and sustainability of financial-market practices remained primarily a national responsibility.

It is possible that the Maastricht debt criteria have created incentives to replace public with private debt, especially when combined with targeted measures such as tax breaks and increased supply of housing debt. If anything, introduction of the euro accelerated not only the accumulation of private debt but also diverging trends within the euro area. Country-specific divergence is particularly problematic as a common Europeanised monetary policy can only address EMU-wide developments. When debt levels were lower, private debt accumulation in some Member States was not yet fully understood as a potential structural weakness. The structural weakness is related to parallel and mutually reinforcing increases in private debt and asset – most often real estate – prices. Debt increase leads to higher asset prices, which in turn encourages and even forces households to take on more debt. Under conditions of stable or falling consumer prices, common monetary policy fuels local asset price bubbles with low or even negative real interest rates. Somewhat simplified, this is more or less what happened in Spain, Portugal and Ireland in the first ten years of EMU.

Debt accumulation was most likely enhanced by the changed risk perception of investors and banks particularly with regard to countries which had traditionally had higher interest rates. EMU was deemed to bring about economic stability which would reduce credit risks for companies and households. This perception was confirmed by economic reality, once the rise of real estate prices and debt accumulation got under way. Something similar probably happened for public debt, too. As longer-term interest rates declined due to the credibility of the ECB's inflation fighting and benign inflation environment, the interest expenses of the high-debt states eased as well. Lower interest expenses improved the fiscal balance and made debt seem more sustainable. It is also possible that the decline in interest rate differentials between euro-area countries reflected the markets' expectation that the no-bail-out clause would yield if a Member State were faced with default. Yet the claim that creditors perceived a substantial risk of Greek default but continued lending at low cost in anticipation of an EU rescue can hardly be substantiated.

Another specific euro-area aspect concerns the relation of debt accumulation to the external position of the respective country. If a country has a large current account deficit,[12] this must be financed with matching financial inflows, which usually take the shape of public or private debt. In the euro area, Greece and Portugal had extensive current account deficits from the start, and the situation deteriorated further in the pre-crisis years. In addition, Spain, and to a lesser extent Ireland, began to accumulate current account deficits during the euro era. In most of these countries, net foreign asset positions reached more than 100% of GDP. In Greece, household savings declined to a very low level while household debt witnessed a corresponding upsurge. In Portugal, debt was accumulated by government and companies. In Spain, the deterioration manifested itself primarily by increased investment, accompanied by growing household and corporate debt. In contrast, household net assets augmented in France and Germany.[13] The result was a peculiar constellation where investors from outside the Eurozone invested in Member States with high creditworthiness, which in turn financed the private and public sector of countries with low creditworthiness.

The dramatic rise of emerging Asian economies – in particular China – is perhaps the single most notable development in the global economy over the last three decades. China's share of global exports increased from a mere 1.2% in 1980[14] to 13.8% in 2010 (17.2% with

[12] A current account is the difference between, on the one hand, a country's exports of goods and services as well as the transfers it receives and which generate external revenues for it and, on the other hand, imports of goods and services as well as the transfers it pays. A current account deficit shows that a country is "earning less than it is consuming" vis-à-vis the rest of the world.
[13] R. Chen *et al.* (2012), p. 30.
[14] European Commission (2004), 'External and Intra-European Union Trade', *Statistical Yearbook 2004*, p. 18.

Hong Kong).[15] Similar although slightly less spectacular upturns have been displayed by a number of other Asian countries (including South Korea, Singapore, Taiwan, India, Malaysia, Thailand, Indonesia and Vietnam), which raised their combined global-export share from less than 6% to nearly 15% in the course of the last three decades. In addition to Asia, EME countries in Latin America and Eastern Europe, too, have asserted themselves in the global economy. The main losers in relative terms have been the early industrialisers, such as the US and Japan. The EU belongs to the losers, too, despite its enlargement from the EU9 to the EU28.[16] EME countries largely account for the expansion of global trade during recent decades. Three main background factors have contributed to this major structural change: liberalisation of trade, vertical specialisation in production and convergence of income levels.

The shift in global production patterns has had a profound impact on the economy and society in general. Living standards in many EME countries have seen a dramatic rise. During the last three decades, hundreds of millions of people have moved from unemployment or non-productive activities and from poverty to productive labour. At the same time, demand for raw materials has exploded, resulting in not only enlarged production but in many cases significant price increases as well.

The euro area has not been spared from the effects of these global changes. At the start of EMU, differences between the trade balances of the Member States were considerable and have, if anything, grown in the euro era. Some euro states, such as Greece and Portugal, already had a large negative trade balance in the 1990s. In most other euro countries, trade balances were converging towards the launch of EMU in 1999, but have subsequently again shown divergent developments, with Spain and Germany occupying opposite extremes. The changes are mainly due to trade with non-euro-area countries: although euro-area trade increased in absolute terms, its share of the total trade of euro states decreased from more than 50% in 1999 to 46% in 2011.[17] Factors explaining divergent developments in euro-area countries include a

---

[15] European Commission (2011), 'External and Intra-European Union Trade', *Statistical Yearbook 2011*, p. 14.

[16] Trade statistics in different sources vary somewhat. All the numbers here are from publications European Commission (2004, 2011), 'External and Intra-European Union Trade', *Statistical Yearbooks 2004* and *2011*.

[17] ECB (2013a), 'Intra-Euro Area Trade Linkages and External Adjustment', *Monthly Bulletin* 1, pp. 60–1.

country's ability to respond to growing demand in EME countries and the extent to which EME (Chinese) products can supersede its staple exports. Traditionally strong exporting Member States – in particular Germany, Belgium and the Netherlands – have been able to benefit from the expansion of global trade, while Greece, Portugal, Spain and, with some qualifications, Italy, belong to the losers.[18] Countries which in the EU context had benefited from low production costs saw their position eroded by superior EME cost competition. This led to a major disruption in economic convergence within the euro area.

Some evidence exists that the structural shift in global production has made economies more sensitive to changes in the real exchange rate,[19] so that loss of price competiveness would have bigger and quicker effects on exports and imports. For euro-area countries, three basic sources of change in the real exchange rate exist: the nominal exchange rate; wage developments, particularly in relation to productivity (unit labour cost); and inflation (or relative prices of tradable goods). According to a recent study by the IMF, all these factors were involved in the deterioration of the real exchange rate in the five Member States which have been worst hit by the Eurozone crisis.[20] Both wages and consumer prices augmented too rapidly compared to productivity gains and trade position in general. However, the appreciation of the euro after 2000 was the major single cause of deterioration.[21] While Germany and other northern Member State countries were able to adjust to the appreciation of the euro, countries subsequently struck by the crisis were not.

External imbalance is linked to increased debt. Persistent current account deficit tends to lead to a corrosion of net asset position,[22] which in turn tends to result in mounting private or public debt. Member States confronted by such development largely neglected reacting to the worsening of their competitive position. In some cases, they even seemed to endorse the idea of consuming their way out of lost

---

[18] IMF (2011), 'Changing Patterns of Global Trade', pp. 27–8.
[19] The real exchange rate is the purchasing power of a currency compared to other currencies. The real exchange rate is calculated by taking into account the importance of trading partners and relative inflation rates.
[20] R. Chen *et al.* (2012).
[21] The euro-area real exchange rate is estimated to have appreciated from 2000 to 2004. Since then, it has been quite stable at a level close to the average of the 1990s.
[22] 'Net asset position' refers to the balance of a country's assets and liabilities vis-à-vis other countries. For example, net assets increase when debts remain the same and the country accumulates assets in other countries or when debt decreases even if assets do not grow.

competitiveness, hoping that loss of external demand could be eter-
nally compensated by domestic demand even if financed by debt. All
in all, the exchange rate appears to be more important for the competitive position of euro-area countries than was assumed at the time
of the Maastricht Treaty. When the macroeconomic constitution and
the adjustment mechanisms it provided for were discussed, neither the
rapidity nor the profundity of changes in global trade and production
patterns were fully grasped. Consequently, the severity of the shocks
which could stem from exchange-rate changes was underestimated.

The 'Great Moderation' refers to reduced volatility in inflation and
GDP growth since the early 1980s. Indeed, until the explosion of the
crisis macroeconomic stability improved substantially, with positive
consequences for employment and price stability.[23] After the inflationary 1970s, inflation dynamics reversed, with global inflation
rates declining until the mid 1990s, and remaining stable and low
thereafter.[24]

Three factors are usually invoked to account for the Great Moderation:
structural economic changes, improved macroeconomic policy and
positive shocks. According to the structural explanation, improvements
in economic policy instruments, technology and business management
have made the economy more resilient to shocks. As traditional economic cycles have been closely related to investment and inventory
cycles, new technology, together with financial innovations and just-
in-time business models, has allegedly enhanced macroeconomic flexibility and stability.[25] Furthermore, structural development in financial
markets is claimed to have made inventory and investment decisions
less dependent on the cyclical availability of credit.[26] Such structural
changes affect the trade-off between inflation and growth: due to the
new flexibility of the economy and better ability of households and
companies to anticipate policy changes, policy-induced inflationary
shocks are less productive in terms of growth. As regards improved

[23] For example, Ben Bernanke, Governor of the Federal Reserve Board, noted in a
speech in 2004 that quarterly variation of growth had halved and quarterly variation
in inflation had declined by two-thirds since the mid 1980s. (Bernanke 2004,
'Remarks by Governor Ben S. Bernanke: Great Moderation', 20 February 2004).

[24] In Japan, there has been a more or less constant threat of deflation since the bursting
of the bubble in the early 1990s.

[25] B. Bernanke's speech (n. 22).

[26] L. González Cabanillas and E. Ruscher (2008).

macroeconomic management,[27] independence and inflation targeting have allegedly made central banks more efficient in fighting economic downturns. Finally, the list of positive shocks includes the dramatic geo-political transformations since the early 1980s, such as the termination of Chinese isolation and the fall of communism in Europe, which have provided a continuous stream of productive and, later on, consumptive capacity to the global economy, and dampened inflationary tendencies.

In the euro area, the Great Moderation was clearly visible as a substantive decline in inflation and growth volatility from the 1980s onwards. The respective role of positive shocks and changes in monetary policy, though, is a disputed issue but can be bypassed here. What, however, is noteworthy is that in the euro area the Great Moderation was to a certain extent a self-fulfilling development. When the future expectations of the general public and financial markets are premised on a stable growth and inflation environment, they contribute to their own realisation. Inflation expectations are important determinants of wage demands, and low inflation expectations tend to keep wage-inflation under control. Correspondingly, low inflation expectations help to maintain long-term interest rates low, as both inflation and the inflation-risk component of interest rates remain moderate.[28]

The theory of Great Moderation has been contested by analyses which see the benign economic environment as a result of medium-term financial cycles replacing or repressing traditional economic cycles. Characteristic of financial cycles would be simultaneous medium-term movement of credit and housing prices, the duration of which would on average be as long as nearly 20 years. The Great Moderation and financial-cycle theories differ considerably in their policy implications. While Great Moderation promises sustained improvements in the economic environment, peaks in financial cycles are associated with financial (banking) crises. Downturns of financial cycles are typically linked to or cause general economic downturns, which are much more

---

[27] Somewhat ironically, both the EU Commission and the ECB published working papers in 2008 highlighting improved macroeconomic management as a major underlying cause of the Great Moderation. See L. González Cabanillas and E. Ruscher (2008); D. Giannone *et al.* (2008); L. Benati and P. Surico (2008).

[28] Generally speaking, long-term interest rates are seen to consist of four components: real interest rate, inflation expectation, inflation risk premia and default risk premia. The risk premia decribe the assumed compensation for the risk that investors demand. In more detailed analyses, other types of risk could play a role as well.

severe than traditional recessions.[29] Hence, avoiding the adverse consequences of the financial cycle would require policy measures which restrict asset price booms fuelled by debt accumulation.

Short-term economics of the crisis

The secular trends summarised above – increase of debt, the impact of emergent economies and the Great Moderation – provide a backdrop to the Eurozone crisis, but its actual eruption is due to shorter-term events. We shall focus on factors which are most relevant for our constitutional analysis.

The crisis set off as a financial crisis, when losses from excessive housing debt granted in the US started to pile up and undermine confidence in financial markets. In 2007, the first signs of mounting losses from sub-prime market debt in the US and mortgage debt in Europe became visible. In late 2007 and early 2008, the deep financial distress of, in particular, US-based investment banks and mortgage institutions was conspicuous.[30] The financial crisis exploded with the collapse of Lehman Brothers and the forced rescues of AIG and German Hypo Real Estate in September 2008, which effectively suspended the mutual trust necessary for the functioning of the financial markets. Central banks throughout the world reacted quickly to the failure of the interbank and capital markets. Indeed, central banks largely replaced financial markets in the provision of bank funding. This was effected through a variety of measures: broadening the list of possible collateral; providing liquidity to banks on unprecedented terms and in unprecedented quantities; as well as purchasing directly debt securities issued by banks and governments. Together with implicit or explicit government guarantees, these measures prevented liquidity-based collapses of banks, but they were slow in restoring mutual confidence in the interbank market.

Losses incurred in many areas, such as the US sub-prime market, were understood to be permanent. At issue were not only market prices, which would recover in due time, but also non-recoverable losses which were not even fully disclosed. The OECD has estimated that the banking sector of the euro area lacks 400 billion euro to reach the target

---

[29] M. Drehmann *et al.* (2012).
[30] See for example BIS 79th *Annual Report* (2009), pp. 16–18. In 2008 the Bear Stearns takeover by JP Morgan Chase was government-facilitated. Fannie Mae and Freddie Mac were taken under direct government control. See BIS 79th *Annual Report* (2009), p. 18.

level for own capital.[31] However, supervisory estimates of capital deficit produced by the euro area itself have continuously remained considerably lower. The first stress test by the Committee of European Banking Supervisors in October 2009 concluded that the capital position of the largest European banks was sufficient even under negative scenarios. As explained below, this was not credible and could actually have worsened distrust among banks.

The initial phase of financial market havoc was quite similar in all OECD countries, although countries with the most exposed and, in relative terms largest, financial sectors were most severely hit. These included the US, the UK, the Netherlands and Ireland. When losses of financial institutions began to influence the global economy, country-specific differences made themselves visible. These were due to divergences in economic structures and underlying vulnerabilities, adjustment mechanisms as well as public- and private-sector reactions to the crisis.

The first channel of transmission from financial crisis to economic slowdown consisted of reduced availability of credit and forced sale of assets. A massive inventory correction and decline in spending by households and companies was a direct implication of the crisis. As banks were reluctant or even unable to finance their clients, companies were forced to shrink inventories and spending even below the level that was needed to maintain production. This led to a steep decline in global industrial production. Yet the inventory shock was only transitory, and by and large inventories were rebuilt in the course of 2009 and 2010. The global economic slowdown in 2008 and 2009 was relatively steep but brief.

Figure 3.2 shows that the slowdown most hit the developed OECD economies which used to be called the industrial economies. The fact that the crisis had a minor impact on emerging economies probably tells something about the underlying causes, which include the structural problems of the developed world. However, even among OECD countries or G20, variation is large. Figure 3.3 demonstrates that the euro area has not been able to recover from the steep slowdown of 2008–9. By 2010, the rest of the world was more or less ready to close the books on the crisis, while the euro area took another turn for the worse.[32] The big issue, of course, is whether the *Sonderweg* of the Eurozone can be explained by the economic structure of the euro states or whether the blame lies in the Maastricht constitutional construction.

---

[31] OECD, 'Strengthening Euro Area Banks'.
[32] The moderately acceptable growth in 2010 was probably due to the refilling of inventories rather than anything more sustainable.

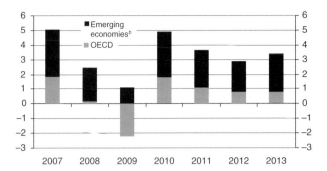

Figure 3.2 Contribution to annual world[a] real GDP growth
Source: OECD Main Economic Indicators and Economic Outlook 92.
Note: Calculated using moving nominal GDP weights, based on national GDP at purchasing power parity 2013 reflects OECD projections from Economic Outlook 92.
a. World GDP is proxied by the sum of OECD and the large non-OECD emerging economies.
b. Emerging economies are here Brazil, China, India, Indonesia, Russia and South Africa.

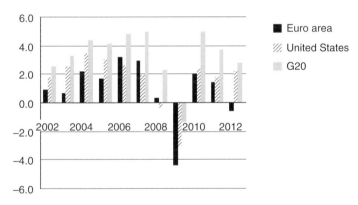

Figure 3.3 GDP growth in euro area, US and G20
Source: IMF Databank.

Additional light on the underlying causes might be provided by differences between the euro-area countries. Of the large euro states, Germany recovered quickly, while Italy and particularly Spain have not been able to regain their former growth (Figure 3.4). Of the smaller countries, Portugal and Ireland were severely hit, whereas Greece was a special case with its idiosyncratic self-induced problems. It is evident that structural features played a large role in conversion of the financial

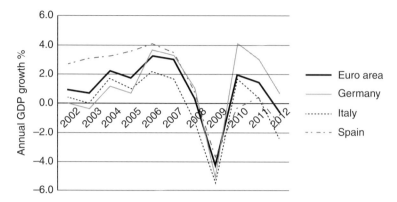

Figure 3.4 GDP growth in euro area, Germany, Italy and Spain
Source: IMF Databank

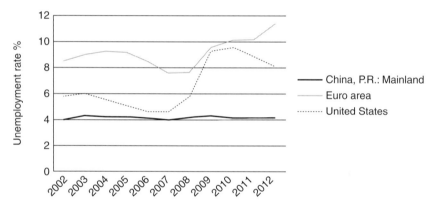

Figure 3.5 Unemployment
Source: IMF Databank

crisis into an economic and fiscal one. After the initial shock, it was clear that at issue was not a traditional economic cycle but first and foremost a structural crisis. Thus, the euro area was unable to recover jobs lost in the initial shock in 2010–11, before employment again deteriorated dramatically in 2012 (Figure 3.5).

For the purposes of our constitutional analysis, of particular interest are the causes of the euro-area economic crisis which cannot be reduced to global financial turmoil and the ensuing economic slowdown. We must take a new look at the economic premises of the Maastricht framework, to assess not only their validity but also their possible contribution to the prolonged economic and social misery in the euro area.

The financial crisis cancelled the most pronounced excesses of the secular trends. In particular, the consumption and investment boom which was boosted by a constant increase in both private debt and house prices came to an end in countries such as the US, the UK, Spain, Portugal, Ireland and Greece. The negative economic impact was heightened by declining activity in the construction sector. The bursting of the housing and credit boom also entailed a general waning of economic optimism. The Great Moderation appeared to be an exaggeration if not a misperception. Consumption and investment decisions could no longer be premised on the assumption of a stable and foreseeable macroeconomic environment.

Indeed, what was called the Great Moderation turned out to be the outcome of a combination of a few mutually self-enforcing assumptions which can no longer be upheld. First, the financial crisis refuted the idea that monetary stability – or more specifically price stability – is a sufficient condition for financial stability. By contrast, the German fear that monetary-policy involvement of a central bank would create moral hazard in the financial markets has gained more understanding. Here the finger points at the US Federal Reserve, which reacted actively to financial-market problems. In the Eurozone, the Maastricht macroeconomic constitution had not conferred on the ECB any responsibility over financial markets, at least partly in order to avoid expectations of central-bank rescue of financial institutions. In practice, though, the ECB reacted more or less similarly to the US Federal Reserve to, for example, the bursting of the tech bubble in 2000 or the 9/11 shock in 2001.

Yet, what was the primary failure in the Eurozone was national institutions' neglect of their responsibility to protect the integrity of financial institutions. In countries with a prolonged increase of housing debt and rise in real estate prices, banks and supervisors should have been more alert to the growing vulnerability of the sector. Debt generation was funded by the financial institutions of other euro-area countries, such as Germany, France and the Netherlands, under approval by local regulators and supervisors. The extreme epitome of imprudent financing consisted of purchase of government bonds which were assigned a zero risk weight; i.e. considered riskless assets from the point of view of the need for own capital. Interbank lending, too, was treated as a low-risk activity.

EMU facilitated increased debt levels in some countries which were ultimately financed by other euro-area countries. Integrated financial markets were one of the aims of EMU, but the type of integration that occurred was not. Instead of giving rise to financial institutions operating in several countries and being able to diversify risks, banking consolidation was mostly nationally confined. Creation of larger national banks was encouraged, even though this led to national concentration of risks as well. Eurozone-wide integration was mainly limited to interbank markets and financial institutions of surplus countries purchasing deficit countries' government and other securities. Here integration progressed substantially, as is evidenced by the much faster growth of cross-border asset holdings in the Eurozone than elsewhere in the developed world.

Links between governments and banks, as well as between banks in different countries, made the risk of contagion of financial problems difficult to assess. This proved to be fatal for the no-bailout clause of Art. 125(1) TFEU. The principle of no-bailout was not only enshrined in the Treaty; it was also an important part of the economic basis of the macro-economic constitution. Yet, it failed at the first practical test. When Greece was excluded from market funding in early 2010, the European banking sector had already been severely hit by the financial crisis. Banks in big Eurozone countries, primarily Germany and France, had large exposures of Greek government debt in their balance sheet and at the wrong prices. They could argue that Greek default would entail extensive banking defaults and the exclusion of other euro-area countries from financial markets as well. Whether a timely Greek default would actually have reduced uncertainty and helped to sort out the crisis quickly or whether it would have led to a catastrophe, such as the crash of the euro, will probably remain an unresolved question, although a recent IMF report would tend to suggest that postponing debt restructuring led to a worsening of the situation and increased costs of the crisis for Greece in particular. Not unexpectedly, the EU Commission does not share these views.[33] What, however, is certain is that together with the principle of no-bailout, the principle of the primacy of national responsibility for financial stability had failed, too. Hence, central assumptions about financial markets and financial stability that underlie the Maastricht framework collapsed because of the extreme nature of events, because of deficient execution mainly at the national level, or simply because they had been unrealistic in the first place.

---

[33] IMF (2013b), 'Greece: Ex Post Evaluation of Exceptional Access under the 2010 Stand-By Arrangement', June 2013. For an EU reaction, see P. Spiegel (2013), 'EU's Olli Rehn Lashes out at IMF Criticism of Greek Bailout', *Financial Times*, 7 June 2013.

The exceptional force of the financial and economic shock in some euro-area countries can be explained by the rapidity with which the excesses of the real estate bubble and credit expansion were unwound. The virtuous cycle turned into a vicious one, as the financial-cycle theory has anticipated. Domestic private and public demand, which had been based on debt accumulation, was reversed. This caused unemployment and, consequently, further decline in consumption and investment.

A central assumption of Economist optimists had been that even if EMU did not constitute an optimal currency area at the start, it would converge towards one. Such a development would be prompted by, first of all, intensified internal trade and internal adjustment mechanisms. Reality has not matched the optimistic expectations. The share of internal trade has actually decreased during the euro era. Persistently high unemployment differences intimate that labour mobility does not play a significant role, and this lack is not compensated by wage flexibility. Fiscal transfers from EU structural funds have not had much impact on structural differences, and any steps towards a 'transfer union' are highly unpopular in netto-paying Member States. Yet, in support of a more positive assessment, the fact could be invoked that the crisis has enhanced labour mobility and wage flexibility in some of the worst troubled countries. In addition, the rescue measures taken to prevent state default could be seen as paving the way for more permanent and substantial fiscal transfers.

Finally, the mechanism which the Treaty and the Stability and Growth Pact had set up to advance fiscal prudence and, by the same token, to create the necessary room for manoeuvre for national fiscal policy, did not live up to expectations. As pre-crisis positive effects of secular trends were revealed to be only transitory, the fiscal position of many countries degenerated as regards both cyclically adjusted fiscal balances and medium-term fiscal sustainability. These countries include Spain, Portugal and Ireland, as well as Greece, whose starting position had already been weak but masked by falsification of up-cycle figures. In addition to worsening fiscal positions, the less optimistic economic environment made visible the lost competitiveness of many euro-area countries.

The fiscal-policy assumptions of the Maastricht macroeconomic constitution did not pass the test of the crisis, either. It appears that many Member States did not realise that the significance of fiscal policy would actually grow in EMU, because it was the primary instrument still available to national economic policy to confront asymmetric shocks. It may be that the obligations deriving from the Stability and Growth Pact were conceived of as external requirements rather than as an integral part of national preparations for downturns. Furthermore, in countries such as Spain and Ireland, the prolonged up-cycle made revenues appear sustainable and obscured the need for fiscal adjustments.

Particularities of the economies of five crisis countries

The euro-area countries hardest hit by the recent crisis display great variance with regard to both the path towards the crisis and the causes underlying their predicament.

The Greek economy has been vulnerable for a long time. At least since the mid 1990s, the main problems have been related to simultaneous current-account and public-sector deficits. Greek export development has been poor for two decades, while imports have kept growing. Domestically, external imbalance has manifested itself in constant investments and continuously declining savings, particularly by the public sector. Greece entered EMU in 2001, after which its external balance shifted from bad to catastrophic, reaching −14% of GDP in 2007. The development was fuelled by brisk domestic consumption and worsening competitiveness, as wage increases outpaced productivity gains. Assuming that Greece remains in the euro, the IMF has estimated that an internal devaluation of a magnitude of 20–30% would be required to restore competitiveness.[34] In the meanwhile, unemployment has kept increasing, attaining 28% in June 2013.

Initially, the Greek banking sector was relatively healthy, but increased holding of government debt and resulting losses as well as the steep recession have eroded its capital base.

Ireland was the success story of the EU after it overcame the economic predicament from which it still suffered in the 1980s. GDP growth was exceptionally high in the 1990s and continued at a healthy level until 2008. Unemployment declined despite growth in the workforce from more than 15% in the early 1990s to around 4% in 2000, and stayed at this level until 2008. It jumped quickly to 15% in 2012, but has since declined slightly. Irish problems stem from overheated real estate markets and the economy more generally. In addition, Irish banks have

---

[34] IMF (2013b), 'Greece: Ex Post Evaluation of Exceptional Access under the 2010 Stand-By Arrangement', June 2013.

been very active in cross-border operations, which all resulted in major losses during the crisis.

Public finances were in good shape in Ireland. The public sector showed a surplus until 2007, and public debt reached a low of 25% of GDP. The bursting of the real estate bubble and the banking crisis hit public finances on multiple fronts. Tax revenues related to real estate declined rapidly, and at the same time the state had to rescue banks. The public-sector deficit widened quickly and reached a colossal 31% of GDP in 2010, due mainly to bank recapitalisation. In turn, public-sector debt amounted to 118% of GDP in 2012. However, on most fronts Ireland has shown signs of improvement since 2010.

Portugal has faced structural difficulties similar to Greece. Its current account deficit has widened since the mid 1990s. The deficit has hovered around 10% of GDP since EMU entry. Portugal has been particularly hard hit by competitive pressures from emerging economies, but also by its inability to catch up with more advanced EU countries. The external deficit was financed by capital inflows stemming from declining domestic savings, both private and public. Public-sector finances deteriorated in the EMU era, with deficits varying mostly between 3% and 5% of GDP. Public debt increased gradually from 51% in 2000 to 124 % in 2012.

Spain shares many similarities with Ireland. In the 1990s, it witnessed a positive real estate development, which was then transformed into a boom in EMU and, finally, into a bubble. The boom fuelled employment, with unemployment declining from 20% in the mid 1990s to below 8% on the eve of the crisis. The real estate boom helped public finances by boosting revenues and reducing social security expenditure. A public deficit of 7% in 1995 was closed in 2000, and even turned into a surplus of 2% in 2006 and 2007. In turn, public sector debt declined to 36% of GDP in 2007. These positive developments were reversed when the real estate bubble burst. The unemployment rate exploded to 27% in 2013 and the public deficit to around 10% and public debt to 84% of GDP in 2012, part of which is related to recapitalisation of the banking sector. Moreover, the bursting of the bubble has most likely revealed structural weaknesses in Spain's competitive position which had been hidden by the domestic investment boom.

Finally, Italy is different from other crisis countries. Its main problems relate to the high level of public debt which was initially built up in the 1980s and early 1990s, but in the face of the current crisis Italy has not stood out as a relative underperformer. Being a large and economically heterogeneous country, Italy has demonstrated many of the structural weaknesses of Portugal, while also possessing structural strengths and wealth comparable to Germany. Italy's public deficit improved considerably in pre-EMU years and has subsequently remained at around 3% of GDP. Public debt declined almost continuously until 2007, when it equalled 103% of GDP. Even since the outbreak of the crisis, public deficit and debt have been relatively stable in comparison with other crisis countries. The reasons for Italy's debt problems are not obvious. A potential explanation lies in financial markets' lack of trust in the ability of the Italian political system to cope with a high debt level, if this is accompanied by rising interest rates.

Box 3.1: Timeline of the crisis

2007

The first clear signs of financial crisis appear, mostly related to real estate markets. Large global banks report major losses, particularly in the sub-prime market, and smaller specialised banks collapse not only in the US but also in Europe.

Central banks start operations to maintain sufficient liquidity in the increasingly nervous interbank markets.

2008

The largest global banks, including the US-based Citygroup and Merrill Lynch, Swiss UBS and British HSBC report record losses for 2007.

September 2008 marks the start of chaos in financial markets. First, federal mortgage companies Freddie Mac and Fannie May practically collapse in the arms of the US Government. The major shock is the fall of Lehman Brothers on 15 September, after which the US Federal Reserve decides to save AIG by practically taking it over.

The US Federal Reserve, in close cooperation with the US Treasury, launches various programmes to stabilise the financial system, including large-scale creation of liquidity and purchase of securities to compensate for malfunctioning of the financial markets. The ECB and other central banks follow suit.

The risk of a systemic banking crisis prompts European governments, too, to take extraordinary support commitments for their banking systems. This takes the form of a coordinated commitment on 12 October by Euro Summit to provide capital and guarantees for European banks. In Ireland, the government provides a blanket guarantee for all bank debts.

Financial-market distress continues with equity and corporate bond markets suffering various panic situations. The uncertainty begins to affect economic developments more generally.

In December, the Ecofin Council agrees on a recovery plan to support European growth. The total amount is reported to be 200 billion euro, financed mainly through national budgets.

2009

Financial markets remain under heightened stress but start recovering slowly in Spring 2009.

The economic situation in the euro area deteriorates. In April, the Ecofin Council decides on the existence of excessive deficits in France, Spain, Ireland and Greece. The fiscal crisis is about to erupt.

In October, the new Greek Government revises its 2009 deficit forecast to 12.5% up from 5%, blaming the bad economy and statistical errors. In December, Greece admits that its public debt will reach 300 billion euro (113% of GDP). Both announcements shock both Ecofin and creditors, given the Greek history of already being caught falsifying figures in 2004. Credit rating downgrades follow.

In December, Ecofin agrees to create three new European authorities to supervise the banking, insurance and securities markets: the European Banking Authority; the European Insurance and Occupation Pensions Authority; and the European Securities and Markets Authority.

Rapidly increasing deficits lead Ecofin to decide on an exit strategy from fiscal stimulus. Member States are supposed to start consolidating public finances in a gradual and differentiated manner as of 2010.

2010

In February, Greece unveils a fiscal package aimed at reducing the deficit. It fails to convince the markets. Nervousness spreads to other heavily indebted euro-area countries, particularly Portugal and Ireland.

In March, Prime Minister Papandreou insists that no bailout is needed.

In April, Greece finally asks for financial assistance.

In May, the euro-area states and the IMF agree on a 110 billion euro bailout package to rescue Greece, of which 80 billion is in bilateral loans from euro-area countries and 30 billion from IMF stand-by agreement.

The ECB starts its Securities Market Programme buying euro-area government bonds.

Ecofin decides on a package of measures, including a European Financial Stabilisation Mechanism (EFSM) and a European Financial Stability Facility (EFSF) – with a volume of up to 500 billion euro. The IMF agrees to an additional 250 billion euro.

The euro falls and interest rates on Irish and Portuguese bonds in particular continue to increase.

In October Chancellor Merkel and President Sarkozy call on Member States to set up a permanent crisis mechanism as of 2013. In particular they suggest that the private sector should be involved in all rescue measures.

In November, Ireland requests financial assistance.

In December, a package of 85 billion euro for Ireland is agreed on with contributions from the EU, euro-area Member States, bilateral contributions from the United Kingdom, Sweden and Denmark as well as funding from the IMF.

The European Systemic Risk Board (ESRB) is set up to prevent or mitigate systemic risks to financial stability in the EU.

2011

In February, Ecofin agrees on the European Stability Mechanism (ESM) with a capacity of 500 billion euro.

In May, the euro area and the IMF approve a 78 billion euro bailout for Portugal. 52 billion is provided by the EFSM and the EFSF, while the IMF stands for the remaining 26 billion.

In July, the Troika concedes that the Greek programme has failed to put public finances on a sustainable basis. The Greek parliament approves a new austerity package, and 12 billion euro of additional loans are granted.

Despite or because of the rescue measures, worries spread to Italy and Spain.

In August, the ECB states that it will buy Italian and Spanish bonds. The ECB Governor, together with his national counterparts, sends letters to the prime ministers of both countries calling for detailed reforms and austerity measures.

In September, Spain constitutionalises deficit constraint. In Italy, the Berlusconi Government reneges on its promises to consolidate public finances and to adopt structural reforms. The ECB stops buying Italian bonds.

In October, several crisis meetings are held among euro states and various proposals are put forth. Another instalment of the Greek bailout money is transferred (8 billion euro).

In November, the six-pack legislation is adopted to strengthen economic governance in the EU. In Italy, a new government led by Mario Monti takes office and announces significant fiscal consolidation measures.

In December, a compromise is reached on an intergovernmental treaty to introduce budgetary constraints in national legislation, after Treaty amendment has failed on the opposition of the UK and the Czech Republic.

2012

In January, France and the EFSF are downgraded by S&P.

The euro-area unemployment rate reaches a new record.

In February and March, long discussions on the second Greek package end up with a package of 130 billion euro, with the IMF joining in later. The package includes private sector involvement; i.e. in practice a restructuring of Greek debt but only to the extent that it is not owned by public authorities.

In March, the Treaty on Stability, Coordination and Governance (TSCG) is signed with the UK and the Czech Republic opting out.

In March and April, additional financial market worries emerge on Spain and Italy.

In May, election victory in Greece for parties opposing the bailout agreement. Formation of a new government is blocked, and new elections are announced.

In May, Bankia, Spain's fourth largest bank, announces a need for government support of 19 billion euro to survive. This initiates debates on Spain's ability to rescue its banking sector.

In June, new Greek elections result in more support for parties favouring the bailout agreements. Speculation on Greek exit from EMU calms down.

Spain and Cyprus request financial assistance.

The Ecofin Council agrees to set up a banking supervisory agent run by the ECB.

In July, the Eurogroup agrees to provide Spain with financial assistance for recapitalisation of the banking sector. The funds will be channelled to banks via Spanish government agent, the Fund for Orderly Bank Restructuring. Assistance of up to 100 billion euro will be provided by the EFSF until the ESM becomes available.

In August, the ECB announces the Outright Monetary Transactions programme: an unlimited bond-buying programme in secondary sovereign bond markets. The states involved must participate in an EFSF or ESM programme to ensure conditionality. Technical features are defined in September.

In December, Ecofin agrees on establishment of the Single Supervisory Mechanism (SSM).

2013

In March, a rescue package for Cyprus is agreed on, with up to 10 billion euro from ESM and with participation of the IMF. Owners and senior creditors of banks face considerable losses.

4   Responses to the crisis

European reactions to the Eurozone crisis fall into three categories. First, rescue packages have been assembled to pull the worst-hit countries out of the most acute difficulties, and financial stability mechanisms have been established. The objective has not merely been to provide emergency assistance but also to avert contagion and to enhance the confidence of financial markets in the euro area's ability to cope with the situation. Second, emergency measures and building financial and institutional capacity to meet future crises have been flanked by efforts to strengthen European economic governance. Here the aim has been to remedy the insufficiencies and inefficiencies of the Maastricht constraints on national fiscal economic policy which had proven unable to prevent turmoil erupting in Spring 2010. Third, interventions by the ECB have supported and complemented other emergency measures, at times even playing a decisive role. In the following, we shall outline the major developments on all three fronts and then turn to their constitutional analysis in Part II. As a prelude, we shall summarise European reactions to the financial turmoil which preceded the fiscal crisis.

Prelude: tackling the financial crisis

As late as June 2007, the ECB raised interest rates, which was a token that the upcoming financial crisis was not yet foreseen.[1] The first larger-scale indications of the upcoming financial crisis only became apparent

---

[1] In July 2008, after the crisis seemed to have soothed, the ECB again raised interest rates.

in the latter half of 2007.[2] The ECB responded with a series of measures that were mainly intended to ease liquidity shortage and ensure market funding for banks. General announcements on liquidity policy were accompanied by fine-tuning operations addressing short-term nervousness in the money market. As these were considered insufficient, the ECB engaged in a series of ad hoc or supplementary measures to guarantee longer-term financing to the banking sector and to normalise conditions in the money market.

With the collapse of Lehman Brothers on 15 October 2008, the financial crisis took a definitive turn for the worse. Confidence in financial markets in general and the interbank market in particular crashed. Along with other central banks, the ECB was forced to react quickly to compensate for the non-functioning of the interbank market and to prevent the liquidity crisis from turning into a solvency crisis. On 4 September 2008, that is, before the Lehman Brothers collapse, the ECB decided on first changes in its collateral policy. The main deviation from previous collateral policy was effected on 15 October,[3] when the ECB decided on a temporary expansion of the list of eligible collateral in Eurosystem credit operations. Eurosystem lending to banks is always protected by collateral offered by banks. When banks could no longer obtain financing from the markets, they had to substitute the market with central-bank financing. For that they needed a lot of new collateral. Otherwise they would have been forced to sell their assets or terminate loans to customers, both of these measures entailing adverse economic consequences.

In addition to renewed collateral policy, the ECB actively used other standard and ad hoc instruments in its operational framework. Ad hoc measures which had been started in the first phase of the financial crisis, such as provision of dollar liquidity, were continued and given a more permanent status. Special longer-term refinancing operations

---

[2] One of the key events was the disclosure by Bear Stearns, a major US investment bank, of severe losses of value of two hedge funds investing in so-called sub-prime loans. The surprise losses suffered by investment-bank-led hedge funds, related primarily to the US real estate markets, revealed that many risks had been heavily underestimated and hence undercapitalised. As a consequence, banks lost the mutual trust necessary for the proper functioning of the interbank market, which had become a major source of funding for the banking sector.

[3] The decision was quickly made in the form of Regulation (EC) No. 1053/2008 of the European Central Bank of 23 October 2008 on temporary changes to the rules relating to eligibility of collateral, [2008] OJ L282/17, because it amended, albeit temporarily, ECB Guideline 2000/7 and needed direct applicability throughout the Eurosystem. Soon afterwards, the ECB adopted a Guideline on temporary changes to the rules relating to eligibility of collateral (ECB/2008/18), [2008] OJ L314/14.

were made regular, and their maturity was prolonged.[4] Moreover, the ECB changed its normal tender procedure and the standing facilities corridor (lending and deposit rates for banks) on 8 October 2008, effectively replacing a major part of the by then largely defunct euro-area money market mechanism. Finally, a covered bond programme, carried out by means of direct purchases in both primary and secondary markets, was introduced on 7 May 2009.[5] The aim of the programme was to support a "specific financial market segment that is important for the funding of banks and that had been particularly affected by the financial crisis". The market situation appeared to calm down towards late 2009 and early 2010, and on 4 March 2010, the ECB decided to continue the gradual phasing-out of its non-standard operational measures. Yet the emerging Greek problems slowed down the process of phasing-out.

On 7 October 2008, the Ecofin Council agreed on common EU guiding principles on dealing with the banking crisis. These were complemented on 12 October by a Euro Summit declaration on a concerted action plan, involving a commitment to keep national banking sectors functional. The action plan included government guarantees for interbank lending and new debt issues by banks, enhanced retail deposit insurance and, if necessary, recapitalisation of banks.[6] The Irish Government took the most far-reaching step when on 1 October 2008 it gave a blank guarantee to its banking sector, which had a nominal value of 400 billion euro; i.e. ten times the then government debt.[7] Thereby, the ultimate risk of the banking sector was nationalised.

Complementing ECB measures, other EU institutions pursued financial stability and restoration of mutual trust in the banking sector through enhanced supervision. Following the US example, the Ecofin Council mandated the Committee of European Banking Supervisors[8]

---

[4] For example on 7 May 2009, the ECB announced for the first time a schedule of one-year auctions with fixed rate and full allotment.

[5] See, e.g., ECB (2009b), 'Press Release', 4 June 2009. See also the official decision, taken on 2 July 2009, on the implementation of the covered bond purchase programme (ECB/2009/16), [2009] OJ L175/18.

[6] A. van Riet (2010), p. 13.

[7] See Finfacts team (2008), 'Government's Emergency Legislation to Provide €400 Billion Guarantee for Irish Banking System to be Passed by Oireachtas Today', *Finfacts Ireland*, 1 October 2008.

[8] The Committee of European Banking Supervisors (CEBS) was an independent advisory group on EU banking supervision set up by Commission Decision of 5 November 2003 (2004/5/EC), [2004] OJ L3/28. It was composed of senior representatives of Member

"to coordinate, in cooperation with the European Commission and the ECB, an EU-wide forward-looking stress test of the banking system, building on common guidelines and scenarios, for a sample of 22 major European cross-border banking groups".[9] The report of the Committee estimated that in a negative scenario, banking losses could amount to 400 billion euro in 2009–10 but, optimistically enough, reckoned that all the banks examined possessed sufficient accumulated earnings and capital buffers.

The purpose of stress tests was to increase information and pacify markets. Unfortunately, the EU stress test probably made things worse by reducing trust in the honesty or capability of supervisors. If the banks knew that their own risks were grossly underestimated, they could hardly trust calculations concerning other banks. Renewal of the test in July 2010 did not dampen criticism. An OECD study showed that by ignoring the banking books, the test also overlooked the main exposures of European banks.[10] For example, the test took into account only slightly more than one-tenth of Greek and less than one-tenth of Spanish bonds. Hence the optimistic estimation that even in the worst scenario there would be no sovereign defaults and the implicit assumption that there would be no bank failures in the EU, either.

In October 2008, the European Commission tasked a specialist group chaired by Jacque de Larosière, a former Governor of the IMF and the Banque de France, to propose how European banking supervision could be strengthened. The group presented a lengthy report in February 2009, which concluded that supervisory arrangements should concentrate not only on supervision of individual financial institutions but also on the stability of the financial system as a whole.[11] This led to establishment of the European Systemic Risk Board (ESRB) in December 2010.[12] According to Regulation 1092/2010, the ESRB is responsible for

State bank supervisory authorities and central banks. In 2011, the committee was succeeded by the European Banking Authority.

[9] CEBS (2009), 'Press Release on the Results of the EU-wide Stress Testing Exercise', 1 October 2009.

[10] A. Blundell-Wignall and P. Slovik (2010).

[11] J. de Laroisière (2009).

[12] Regulation (EU) No. 1092/2010 of the European Parliament and of the Council of 24 November 2010 on European Union macro-prudential oversight of the financial system and establishing a European Systemic Risk Board (the 'ESRB Regulation'), [2010] OJ L331/1; and Council Regulation (EU) No. 1096/2010 of 17 November 2010 conferring specific tasks upon the European Central Bank concerning the functioning of the European Systemic Risk Board, [2010] OJ L331/162.

macro-prudential oversight of the financial system within the Union. It is supposed to contribute to preventing or mitigating systemic risks to financial stability which "arise from developments within the financial system and taking into account macro-economic developments, so as to avoid periods of widespread financial distress". It is further expected to promote the smooth functioning of the internal market and ensure a sustainable contribution by the financial sector to economic growth. The ESRB is part of the European System of Financial Supervision but operates under the ECB. The roadmap to a banking union, at present on the agenda of European institutions, includes as a first step creation of a Single Supervisory Mechanism for the Eurozone (see Chapter 8).

Rescue packages and stability mechanisms

Sticking to the no-bailout clause and letting Greece or other crisis states default was never a real option for euro-area decision-makers. A cynical observer would explain this by the interests of banks and other private investors, to whose lobbying the governments of large euro states have lent a sensitive ear. A less cynical explanation invokes the threat of contagion and the need to ensure the financial stability of the euro area as a whole: a viewpoint the Maastricht economic constitution had downplayed.

Yet, the possibility of bailout had never been seriously discussed in the run-up to Maastricht, and no resolution mechanism for fiscal turmoil was included in the macroeconomic constitution. Hence, the aggravation of the Greek debt crisis in early 2010 largely caught the EU and the euro states unprepared. The Maastricht economic constitution was based on the assumption that safeguards against fiscal imprudence in Arts. 123–126 TFEU, the convergence criteria of EMU and the Stability and Growth Pact would suffice to ensure fiscal stability and to impose the necessary restraint on euro-area Member States, although these still retained fiscal-policy sovereignty. The procedure for mutual assistance established by Art. 108 of the Treaty of Rome still existed, and, indeed had been activated after the financial crisis exploded. However, it only allows for financial assistance to non-euro states facing difficulties in their balance of payments (Art. 143 TFEU).[13] With regard to resolving a sovereign debt crisis in a euro state, the field was open for

---

[13] Financial assistance under Art. 143 TFEU has been provided to Latvia, Romania and Hungary.

legal improvisation. Indeed, legal experimentalism is a distinctive feature of European responses to the crisis.

The first Greek rescue package was anchored in instruments of varying legal nature: a *sui generis* decision on 2 May 2010 by the Ecofin Council meeting in its Euro Group composition;[14] a Loan Facility Agreement between Greece and the other euro-area states, settling the availability of credits in the form of pooled bilateral loans for Greece; an Intercreditor Agreement among the creditor states;[15] and a Memorandum of Understanding (MoU) signed by Greece and the Commission, on behalf of the Member States belonging to the Euro Group, and spelling out the adjustment programme to which Greece committed itself as a condition of the loans.[16] The package introduced some typical traits which have characterised subsequent financial stability mechanisms, too: reliance on intergovernmental agreements and institutional solutions outside the Treaty framework, as well as the centrality of an adjustment programme, set out in a MoU, as a condition for assistance. The Commission was assigned coordinating and monitoring tasks, but it was supposed to perform these outside its Treaty-based functions.

Shortly after the decision on Greek rescue measures, mechanisms for further assistance were set up in order to preserve financial stability within the EU; these made up what in German debates was called the rescue umbrella (*Rettungsschirm*). In addition to support from the IMF, the umbrella consisted of the European Financial Stabilisation Mechanism (EFSM) and the European Financial Stability Facility (EFSF).[17]

---

[14] Eurogroup (2010), 'Draft Statement', 2 May 2010. Euro-area Member States had already agreed upon the terms of financial support on 11 April 2010. This agreement was based on statements issued by the Heads of State or Government of the euro area on 11 February and 25 March, where the euro-area Member States affirmed "their willingness to take determined and coordinated action, if needed, to safeguard financial stability in the euro area as a whole". See European Council (2010c), 'Statement by Heads of State and Government of the Euro Area', 25–26 March 2010.

[15] Euro Area Loan Facility Bill (2010), Schedule 1.

[16] The MoU has since been reviewed five times. The present MoU is available as an annex to European Commission (2011b), *The Economic Adjustment Programme for Greece – Fifth Review*. As will be explained below, the main contents of the MoUs have been reiterated in Council Decisions taken in the excessive debt procedure under Art. 126(9). A further element complicating legal implementation of the rescue package consisted of an Agreement between Greece and the IMF in the form of Exchange of Letters, where the Greek Government undertook to fully implement the agreed measures, including the MoU.

[17] In its conclusions adopted on 9 May 2010, the Council also evoked the contribution of the ECB: "We also reiterate the support of the euro area Member States to the ECB

The EFSM was established on 11 May 2010 by Council Regulation 407/2010,[18] issued under the emergency provision of Art. 122(2) TFEU. This provision lays down that "where a Member State is in difficulties or is seriously threatened with severe difficulties caused by natural disasters or exceptional occurrences beyond its control, the Council, on a proposal from the Commission, may grant, under certain conditions, Union financial assistance to the Member State concerned". The EFSM constitutes an exception to the general policy of relying on legal and institutional frameworks outside the Treaty architecture. The Regulation defines its aim and scope in the following terms: "With a view to preserving the financial stability of the European Union, this Regulation establishes the conditions and procedures under which Union financial assistance may be granted to a Member State which is experiencing, or is seriously threatened with, a severe economic or financial disturbance caused by exceptional occurrences beyond its control …" (Art. 1). The EFSM is administered by the Council and the Commission, with the ECB in a consulting role. A Member State seeking Union financial assistance should discuss its needs with the Commission, in liaison with the ECB. It must also submit a draft economic and financial adjustment programme to the Commission and the Economic and Financial Committee. The Council decides on granting financial assistance or credit-line by a qualified majority and on a proposal from the Commission. The decision should contain, inter alia, "general economic policy conditions which are attached to the Union financial assistance with a view to re-establishing a sound economic or financial situation in the beneficiary Member State and to restoring its capacity to finance itself on the financial markets". These conditions are defined by the Commission, in consultation with the ECB. Moreover, the decision should contain approval of the adjustment programme prepared by the beneficiary Member State to meet the economic conditions attached to Union financial assistance. At regular intervals, the Commission verifies whether the economic policy of the beneficiary Member State accords with its adjustment programme and with the conditions laid down by the Council. Disbursement of the loan or release of funds depends on the results of Commission verification.

in its action to ensure the stability to the euro area." See Council of the European Union (2010), 'Economic and Financial Affairs – Extraordinary Council Meeting Press Release', 9–10 May 2010.

[18] Council Regulation (EU) No. 407/2010 of 11 May 2010 establishing a European financial stabilisation mechanism, [2010] OJ L118/1.

The capacity of the EFSM is relatively small, 60 billion euro. Consequently, it has played but a minor role in the whole of the 'rescue umbrella'. It is financed through bonds which the Commission is allowed to issue on behalf of the Union under an implicit EU budget guarantee. Hence, no direct Member State financial liability is involved. The EFSM has been activated to provide assistance to Ireland (Autumn 2010) and Portugal (Spring 2011).

Far more important has been the contribution of the European Financial Stability Facility (EFSF), which, despite the establishment of the EFSM, was designed to bear the main burden of future financial assistance. The legal anchorage of the EFSF is rather complicated. In connection with the Council meeting on 9–10 May 2010, representatives of euro-area state governments adopted a decision "to commit to provide assistance through a Special Purpose Vehicle", whereas the representatives of all Member State governments adopted another decision "allowing the Commission to be tasked by the euro area member states in this context".[19] The EFSF was registered as a limited liability company under Luxembourg law. Subsequently, the euro-area states and the EFSF concluded a Framework Agreement, laying down the institutional structure of the EFSF, as well as the forms and conditionality of available assistance and the grant procedure.[20]

The EFSF acquired its financial capacity from open markets, while the financial liability of the assisting states took the form of guarantees for loans issued by the EFSF. The total financial capacity of the EFSF was 440 billion euro, which was backed by Member State guarantee commitments of 780 billion euro, allotted in accordance with the states' shares in the paid-up capital of the ECB. The upper limit of guarantee liabilities for each euro state was defined by its guarantee commitment. Over-guarantees took into account the possibility that guarantors may become beneficiary states, which reduced the value of their guarantees. Ironically enough, the EFSF guarantees added to the financial liabilities of the vulnerable states and possibly hampered their credit position.

Assistance granted by the EFSF could take diverse forms: loan disbursements; precautionary facilities; facilities to finance recapitalisation of financial institutions in a euro-area Member State; facilities for the purchase of bonds in the secondary markets on the basis of an ECB

[19] See n. 17
[20] The consolidated version of the Framework Agreement is available on the EFSF website under legal documents.

analysis recognising the existence of exceptional financial market circumstances and risks to financial stability; or facilities for the purchase of bonds in the primary market.[21] A key element in the procedure consisted of a Memorandum of Understanding which the Commission was authorised to negotiate with the beneficiary state in liaison with the ECB and the IMF. The Commission was also authorised to sign the MoU on behalf of the euro-area Member States, after it had been approved by the Eurogroup Working Group.[22] The first financial assistance was released or utilised following the signing of the MoU. Each subsequent disbursement is, as a rule, preceded by a report where the Commission, again in liaison with the ECB, analyses compliance by the beneficiary state with the terms and conditions set out in the MoU. The Guarantor States evaluate compliance and unanimously decide on whether to permit disbursement of assistance.

The EFSF has been activated to provide assistance to Ireland, Portugal and Greece (the second Greek rescue package in early 2012). The total commitment under these programmes is 188 billion euro, of which the share of Greece is three-fourths. Recapitalisation of Spanish banks was also initially funded by the EFSF in July 2012. Of the total amount of 100 billion euro, nearly 40 billion was granted in December 2012, and a further 1.9 billion in February 2013. The programme was transferred to the European Stability Mechanism after the latter had become fully operational.

The EFSF decision-making body is the Board of Directors, whose composition is identical to the Eurogroup Working Group. Votes are weighed according to the shares the States hold in the issued share capital of the EFSF. Decisions of a principal nature and affecting the liabilities of the Guarantors require unanimity.[23]

Side by side with expansion of the EFSF, plans were drawn up for a permanent European Stability Mechanism (ESM), which would take over the functions not only of the EFSF but also of the EFSM, with regard to euro-area states. A decision to establish this mechanism was taken

---

[21] The instruments available to the EFSF were expanded through amendments to the Framework Agreement which entered into force in the autumn of 2011.

[22] The Working Group is a euro-area configuration of the Economic and Financial Committee. Only the euro-area Member States, the Commission and the ECB are represented. The Working Group prepares the work of the Euro Group, i.e. the euro-area composition of the Ecofin Council.

[23] The Commission and ECB are entitled to appoint an observer who may take part in meetings of the board of directors and present observations, without however having the power to vote. The board of directors may even permit other EU institutions to appoint observers.

by the European Council in December 2010, and the first draft Treaty on the ESM was presented to the Euro Summit in July 2011.[24] However, negotiations on the final shape of the Treaty dragged on to the following year, until it was finally signed by the euro-area states on 2 March 2012. After the German Constitutional Court on 12 September 2012 had – with certain qualifications – shown the green light to German ratification, the ESM was able to start functioning on 8 October 2012. Drafting and negotiating the TESM was accompanied by an amendment to the TFEU in the simplified procedure under Art. 48(6) TEU. The European Council decided on 25 March 2011 to amend Art. 136 TFEU by adding to it a new paragraph 3.[25] The new provision lays down that "the Member States whose currency is the euro may establish a stability mechanism to be activated if indispensable to safeguard the stability of the euro-area as a whole". Furthermore, "the granting of any required financial assistance under the mechanism will be made subject to strict conditionality". Yet, the amendment was only expected to enter into force on 1 January 2013, while the original date for the Treaty on the ESM was set for 1 July 2012. Consequently, the amendment was not even meant to constitute a legal basis for the TESM. The ratification process of the amendment was only completed in Spring 2013 so that it finally entered into force on 1 May 2013, while the TESM had been in force since 27 September 2012. In the Preamble to the TESM, the amendment is invoked but not as a competence basis. All in all, the purported legal significance of the amendment raises questions. We shall revert to this question below in Chapter 5.

The ESM has sometimes been characterised as the IMF of the EU.[26] It is an 'international organization under public international law', as it was characterised in the Conclusions of the European Council of 24–25 March 2011.[27] All euro-area states are members. In addition, it is also open to non-euro Member States, but so far none of these has joined. The ESM is governed by a Board of Governors, composed of ministers of finance of the euro-area states, with the Commissioner for economic and monetary affairs and the President of the ECB holding observer

---

[24] European Council (2010b), 'Conclusions', 16–17 December 2010; Treaty Establishing the ESM, 11 July 2011.

[25] European Council Decision of 25 March 2011 amending Art. 136 TFEU with regard to a stability mechanism for Member States whose currency is the euro (2011/199/EU), [2011] OJ L91/1.

[26] The Preamble explicitly evokes IMF practice (Recitals 12–13).

[27] European Council (2011), 'Conclusions', 24–25 March 2011.

status. The composition of the Board of Governors corresponds to that of the Eurogroup, that is, the Ecofin Council in its euro-area shape. Moreover, the Eurogroup President has been elected to act as President of the Board of Governors as well. Thus, in spite of institutional separateness, a personal union between the ESM and the Union (euro-area) framework has been created.

Major decisions on granting and financing assistance require mutual agreement, i.e. unanimity, in the Board of Governors. However, an emergency voting procedure allows decision-making by mutual agreement with a qualified majority of 85 per cent of the votes cast. This procedure can be used where the Commission and the ECB both conclude that failure to urgently adopt a decision to grant or implement financial assistance would threaten the economic and financial sustainability of the euro area. Reliance on the emergency voting procedure deprives all but the three largest euro states – Germany, France and Italy – of their veto power. In the negotiating process, the scope of procedure was restricted to decisions on granting or implementing financial assistance, so that decisions directly affecting Member States' financial liabilities were excluded. For reasons of parliamentary budgetary sovereignty, this had been a requirement of the EU Committee of the Finnish Parliament, which, in turn, relied on the opinion of the Constitutional Law Committee, the main constitutional review body in Finland (see Chapter 6).

In the ESM, the participating states' financial liability assumes the guise of share holding. Total authorised capital stock of the ESM amounts to 700 billion euro, of which the major part consists of callable instead of paid-in shares. Initial paid-in capital amounts to 80 billion euro and will be paid in five allotments by 2014. Hence, ratification of the Treaty directly obliged the respective states to redeem only 11.4 per cent of their total contribution, which has been calculated in accordance with the ECB Capital subscription key. As a rule, calls for callable shares require a unanimous decision of the Board of Governors; the emergency voting procedure with qualified-majority voting is not available. During a transitional period, which ended in June 2013, the ESM and the EFSF functioned in parallel, with a total lending capacity of 700 billion euro, while the lending capacity of the ESM amounts to 500 billion euro. After June 2013, the EFSF merely administers loans and bonds until they are repaid. In turn, the EFSM has not been wound up, but it will no longer be used in providing assistance to euro-area states.

The Board of Governors decides on stability support to an ESM Member on the basis of an assessment by the Commission and the ECB. Support may be provided if it proves to be indispensable to safeguard the financial stability of the euro area as a whole and of its Member States. Instruments available for stability support of the ESM are largely similar to those in the repertoire of the EFSF: financial assistance to an ESM Member for recapitalisation of financial institutions; a loan to an ESM Member; purchase of bonds of an ESM Member on the primary market; as well as operations on the secondary market in relation to the bonds of an ESM Member. The Board of Governors may also decide to grant precautionary financial assistance in the form of a precautionary conditioned credit line or in the form of an enhanced conditions credit line.

Furthermore, Art. 19 TESM empowers the Board of Governors to review the list of support instruments and make changes to it. An intricate legal issue is what the limits of the Board's reviewing power are. It could be argued that new forms of assistance must be in line with the assistance explicitly regulated in the ESM Treaty; otherwise, the decision of the Board would substantively amount to amending the Treaty. The options explicitly laid down in the Treaty only comprise support channelled through the recipient state. Direct recapitalisation of financial institutions, bypassing the state, could be economically justifiable by the objective of breaking the vicious circle of banking and sovereign debt crisis. However, legally speaking, doubts can be raised about its compatibility with the ESM Treaty. Yet, in June 2012, in the midst of the banking crisis in Spain, the Euro Summit took a principal decision on the admissibility of direct recapitalisation after creation of the Single Supervisory Mechanism.[28] In the meantime, stability support to Spain has taken the form of loans granted to Fondo de Restructuración Ordenado Bancaria, a bank recapitalisation fund of the Spanish Government, which channels the funds to the financial institutions concerned.[29] In March 2013, the Eurogroup decided that financial assistance to Cyprus is warranted to safeguard financial stability in Cyprus and the euro area as a whole.[30] Funds which were mainly

---

[28] Euro Area (2012), 'Summit Statement', 29 June 2012.
[29] See Master Financial Assistance Agreement between European Financial Stability Facility, Kingdom of Spain as Beneficiary Member State, Fondo de Reestructuración Ordenada Bancaria as Guarantor and the Bank of Spain.
[30] Eurogroup (2013a), 'Statement', 16 March 2013; Eurogroup (2013b), 'Statement', 25 March 2013.

intended for recapitalising Cypriot banks were again directed through the state.

Conditionality is an essential part of ESM assistance as well. Still here the provisions in the ESM Treaty are more flexible than in legal instruments regulating the EFSM or the EFSF. Art. 12 of the Treaty on the ESM presupposes that stability support must be subject to strict conditionality, but adds that conditionality must be appropriate to the chosen instrument. Conditionality may range from a macro-economic adjustment programme to continuous respect of pre-established eligibility conditions. Again, the Commission has been entrusted with the task – in liaison with the ECB and, wherever possible, together with the IMF – of negotiating and signing with the ESM Member the Memorandum of Understanding detailing the conditionality.

The stability mechanisms adopted since eruption of the sovereign debt crisis in Spring 2010 display both common and divergent traits. The shared features embrace reliance on intergovernmental legal and institutional structures – here the financially rather insignificant EFSM constitutes the only exception – as well as the conditionality of assistance. Common to diverse forms of financial assistance from loans to Greece in May 2010 to the ESM has also been involvement of the IMF. The IMF has not only made a significant financial contribution but has participated in drafting the conditions of assistance and in monitoring compliance with them. The Commission, the ECB and the IMF make up the renowned Troika, dominating much of the media coverage of the at times dramatic rescue operations. The involvement of the IMF is explicitly set out in the Treaty on the ESM. According to the Preamble, "the ESM will cooperate very closely with the International Monetary Fund … in providing stability support", and "the active participation of the IMF will be sought, both at technical and financial level". Furthermore, the involvement of the IMF is evoked in the provisions on negotiating the MoU and monitoring compliance with it. The crisis has de facto – partly even *de jure* – transformed the IMF into a European institution.

Where the mechanisms diverge is in their exact legal form; here the experimentalism labelling European reactions is highly conspicuous. Broadly speaking, management of the crisis has given rise to two types of intergovernmental agreement. First, there are agreements with primarily a private-law character. This category comprises the agreements for the first Greek rescue package – the Loan Facility Agreement and the Intercreditor Agreement – and the EFSF Framework Agreement.

Second, the Treaty on the ESM was concluded under public international law, as was also the case with the Treaty on Stability, Coordination and Governance (TSCG), which will be discussed below in the context of efforts to tighten European economic governance. A clear-cut division is complicated by the fact that agreements in the first category also possess features which point to the direction of public international law and which are of relevance from the perspective of EU law as well.

The above classification is based on the criterion of the applicable law. Agreements in the first category declare themselves to be governed by English law.[31] The ESM Treaty (or the TSCG) does not contain any reference to applicable law but is premised on the pertinence of public international law. As regards their substance, agreements of the first category involve provisions on, not merely typical private-law issues, but tasks of EU institutions as well; i.e. issues on which English law does not offer much guidance. Hence, substantively the agreements exceed the boundaries of private law. What is also noteworthy is that although the private-law company EFSF is a party to the Framework Agreement, the institutional provisions have been concluded only between the euro-area Member States. Indeed, the Framework Agreement can be argued to involve two agreements, one agreed on by and binding upon all the parties and another agreed on by and binding upon merely the state parties. Disputes arising from or in the context of the Greek agreements fall to the exclusive jurisdiction of the Court of Justice of the European Union. Thus, the ECJ is supposed to rule on private-law issues, applying English law. In turn, the EFSF Framework Agreement submits disputes between Member States to the jurisdiction of the ECJ, whereas disputes between one or more Member States and the EFSF belong to the jurisdiction of the Courts of the Grand Duchy of Luxembourg. All in all, institutional provisions and jurisdictional arrangements lend a hybrid character especially to the Greek Intercreditor Agreement and the EFSF Framework Agreement; an international-law flavour is added to the primary private-law character, and even EU law remains relevant. A further international-law element derives from the fact that both the Greek aid package and establishment of the EFSF were first agreed on by the representatives of the euro-area Member States through decisions which appear to fall under international law. According to

---

[31] See, e.g., Art. 14(1) of the Loan Facility Agreement, Art. 14(1) of the Intercreditor Agreement and Art. 18(1) of the EFSF Framework Agreement: "This Agreement and any non-contractual obligations arising out of or in connection with it shall be governed by and shall be construed in accordance with English law."

a Statement by the Euro Group issued on 2 May 2010, "following a request by the Greek authorities, euro area Ministers unanimously agreed today to activate stability support to Greece via bilateral loans centrally pooled by the European Commission under the conditions set out in their statement of 11 April".[32] In turn, establishment of the EFSF was agreed upon through a Decision taken by the Ministers of the euro-area Member States, "wearing their intergovernmental hats",[33] at the Council session on 9 May 2010.[34]

Differences between agreements under private law and agreements under public international law may be important for national constitutional law,[35] but less so for EU law. From the EU law perspective, the default position for both types of agreement is Member States' freedom of action: Member States may conclude agreements between themselves under both public international law and private law, if no ground to the contrary can be derived from EU law (see Chapter 5).

The legal status of the Member States providing assistance also varies from one mechanism to another. In the Greek aid package of May 2010 the assisting states appear as creditors, in the EFSF as guarantors (for loans issued by the EFSF) and in the ESM as shareholders, while in the EFSM the liability of Member States is restricted to their contributions to the EU budget. These differences may have constitutional implications at both European and Member State level, but from the perspective of beneficiary states they are largely irrelevant. Rather, what matters for the recipient states and their population is the foremost common feature of the mechanisms, which has also been spelled out in the amendment to Art. 136 TFEU: the 'strict conditionality' of financial assistance. The MoUs which the beneficiary states have been obliged to sign not only define in aggregate terms required cuts in public expenditure but also determine how those cuts should

---

[32] Eurogroup (2010), 'Draft Statement', 2 May 2010 (n. 14).
[33] B. de Witte (2011); see also C. Calliess (2011), p. 218.
[34] In the Greek aid case, decided by the German Constitutional Court, one of the claimants argued that a treaty under public international law had been concluded and that it should have been submitted to the *Bundestag* for approval, in accordance with Art. 59.2 of the Basic Law. However, the Constitutional Court denied the claimant's standing in this issue. BVerfG, 2 BvR 987/10, 7 September 2011.
[35] In Member States, a certain uncertainty is noticeable as to the legal character of the agreements and the necessity for their parliamentary approval. In Finland, the agreements for the first Greek rescue package were not submitted to Parliament for approval, but the EFSF Framework Agreement was. In Germany, none of these agreements was approved by the *Bundestag*.

be allocated. In addition, the MoUs indicate market-liberally oriented structural reforms. The Greek MoUs include commitments to, for instance, comprehensive healthcare and labour market reforms; in Ireland, the Government must, inter alia, reform legislation on the minimum wage and take other measures "to facilitate adjustment in the labour market"; and Portugal has vowed to reduce pension expenditure by detailed pension reductions, to control costs in the health sector on the basis of detailed measures listed in the MoU and even to reduce cash social transfers other than pensions by at least a fixed minimum amount by tightening eligibility criteria and decreasing average benefits in selected cases.[36] The MoU signed with Spain on 20 July 2012 has a more limited scope and is restricted to measures concerning the financial sector.[37] By contrast, the Cyprus MoU signed in April 2013 again has a wider scope and reaches out to taxation and public expenditure, as well as structural reforms.[38] The consequences of austerity programmes and reform packages for the functioning of democracy and the realisation of social rights in the respective states must be an important part of the constitutional analysis which we shall undertake in Part II.

In the wrangling around rescue packages and mechanisms, one of the most controversial issues has been the so-called bail-in; that is, private sector involvement in sharing the costs. In practice, bail-in can mean restructuring of debt by cutting the amount and changing the terms, including maturity and interest rate. The main argument against bail-in has been related to financial stability: bail-in has been feared to increase market nervousness and the likelihood of contagion. However, in dynamic terms the financial-stability argument favours bail-in: by eliminating moral hazard, bail-in prevents reckless lending by banks and other investors. Furthermore, as the Greek

[36] The MoUs have run through several updates. As a sample, see the third update of the Greek MoU, annexed to European Commission (2011a), *The Economic Adjustment Programme for Greece: Third Review – Winter 2011*; (2011c), Ireland's MoU annexed to *The Economic Adjustment Programme for Ireland: Spring 2011 Review*; and (2012b) the fifth update of Portugal's MoU, in *The Economic Adjustment Programme for Portugal: Fifth Review – Summer 2012*.
[37] Assistance to Spain was granted under the EFSF Guideline on Recapitalisation of Financial Institutions which does not presuppose a macroeconomic adjustment programme but only a more focused form of conditionality. Accordingly, only a Memorandum of Understanding on Financial-Sector Policy Conditionality was signed. See Master Financial Assistance Agreement (n. 29).
[38] See IMF (2013a), 'Cyprus: Letter of Intent, Memorandum of Economic and Financial Policies, and Technical Memorandum of Understanding', 29 April 2013.

case in particular makes plausible, bail-in could be the most feasible way to reach a sustainable debt level at the start of an adjustment programme.[39]

In the euro-area rescue operations, bail-in has been present to a varying degree. In the initial programmes for Greece, Ireland and Portugal, no bail-in was envisaged. Ireland was even obliged to take over the Anglo Irish Bank and effectively its liabilities, too, without losses to private investors. However, fierce criticism in many euro states and calls for investor responsibility retained bail-in on the agenda, and it was included in the first drafts of the Treaty on the ESM. In the final version, though, it only received a mention in the Preamble.[40] In the context of the second bailout package for Greece in March 2012, channelled through the EFSF, a formally voluntary private debt restructuring was adopted. This resulted in a massive bail-in on a debt of approximately 200 billion euro, still in the possession of private investors. Investors that had been repaid in the context of the first programme or had sold their bonds to the ECB were not affected. In the Cyprus programme, a bail-in of the largest debtors of the banks was included, but not in the Spanish banking rescue.

The ECB's contribution to combating the sovereign debt crisis

The ECB has played a vigorous, at times even crucial, role in fighting not only the financial but also the subsequent fiscal crisis in the Eurozone. In addition to its involvement in the rescue operations and stability mechanisms described above, the main activities of the ECB fall under three groups: first, verbal interventions addressed both to distressed Member States and financial markets; second, changed collateral policy and large-scale medium-term liquidity creation in order to encourage markets to invest in higher-yielding government bonds; and third, and most controversially, launching the Securities Market Programme, i.e. outright purchase of government bonds.

[39] This is a central point in the IMF (self-)criticism concerning the Greek assistance; see IMF (2013b), 'Greece: Ex Post Evaluation of Exceptional Access under the 2010 Stand-By Arrangement', June 2013.

[40] "In accordance with IMF practice, in exceptional cases an adequate and proportionate form of private sector involvement shall be considered in cases where stability support is provided accompanied by conditionality in the form of a macro-economic adjustment programme" (Recital 12).

In analysing the economic situation, central banks commonly comment on fiscal policy, too. Here the ECB has been no exception. Still, until the sovereign debt crisis it usually kept its comments at a general level and did not engage in discussing individual Member States' fiscal policy. Already on 4 February 2010, the ECB demanded that Greece and other countries should fully respect the Stability and Growth Pact.[41] A clear turn occurred the following month, when the ECB issued a special statement on the Greek Government's fiscal consolidation programme.[42] The statement was probably meant to convince financial markets of the adjustment measures, and perhaps the Greek people, too, of the necessity for consolidation. The ECB statement was followed by President Trichet's support for the statement of the European Council that "euro area Member States will take determined and coordinated action if needed to safeguard financial stability in the euro area as a whole".[43] At subsequent ECB press conferences, Trichet insisted that Greece would not default on its debt.

In addition to public statements, Trichet was reported to have communicated widely with finance ministers and heads of government. The most dramatic example of the ECB's direct pressure on governments is the letter which Trichet, together with the governors of the respective national central banks, sent to the prime ministers of Spain and Italy in August 2011,[44] calling for large-scale structural reforms.[45] On their face, the letters were not linked to the ECB's activities in the bond market, because these were labelled as merely monetary policy operations with no fiscal-support function.

The collateral policy changes of April 2010 may already have aimed to facilitate acceptance of Greek government bonds as collateral. Soon enough, a day after the Troika concluded negotiations with Greece, the ECB explicitly decided to suspend application of the minimum credit

[41] ECB (2010a, 2010b), 'Introductory statement with Q&A with J.-C. Trichet', 4 February and 4 March 2010.

[42] ECB (2010d), 'Statement by the ECB's Governing Council on the Additional Measures of the Greek Government', 3 March 2010.

[43] Trichet also caused some surprise by stating "I do not believe that it would be appropriate to introduce the IMF as a supplier of help through stand-by arrangements or through any such kind of help." He thus explicitly disregarded the only bailout mechanism that was deemed appropriate and available, and implicitly advocated Union bailout mechanisms. See *ibid.*

[44] *Corriere della Sera* (2010), 'Trichet e Draghi: Un'Azione Pressante per Ristabilire la Fiducia degli Investitori', *Corriere della Sera*, 6 August 2010.

[45] It has been claimed that the ECB even demanded the resignation of Berlusconi as a condition for its support.

rating threshold to debt issued or guaranteed by the Greek Government. The justification was that the ECB had assessed the Greek adjustment programme and considered it to be appropriate from the risk management perspective, too.[46] Similar decisions to relax collateral requirements for sovereign debt were subsequently adopted with regard to Ireland in March 2011[47] and Portugal in July 2011.[48]

The ECB had started to unwind its extraordinary liquidity-creating measures, when escalation of the Greek predicament caused it to retract its policy. A principal difference exists between creating liquidity to guarantee a functioning interbank market and producing incentives for investment in government bonds. Arguably, the latter purpose became increasingly important for ECB activities. Yet, the link between interbank market liquidity and investment in government bonds, which makes a strict separation between the two purposes impossible, must be kept in mind. Towards the end of 2011, the ECB announced two large-scale refinancing operations with a total of nearly 1015 billion euro and with an unprecedented maturity of three years. Undoubtedly, the operations procured strong incentives to banks to buy government debt instruments, particularly if these were eligible as collateral.

The most controversial of the ECB's actions, spawned initially by the Greek distress, has been outright purchase of government bonds. The ECB announced its Securities Market Programme on 10 May 2010 as part of a larger package to address severe tensions in financial markets.[49] The programme was declared to contain "interventions in the euro area public and private debt securities markets to ensure depth and liquidity in those market segments which are dysfunctional". The pronounced objective was to "address the malfunctioning of securities markets and restore an appropriate monetary policy transmission mechanism".[50] Yet, it soon became clear that the main purpose of the programme was

---

[46] Decision of the ECB of 6 May 2010 on temporary measures relating to the eligibility of marketable debt instruments issued or guaranteed by the Greek Government (ECB/2010/3), [2010] OJ L117/102. See also ECB (2010c), 'Introductory Statement with Q&A with J.-C. Trichet', 6 May 2010.

[47] ECB (2011a), 'Press Release', 31 March 2011: ECB announces the suspension of the rating threshold for debt instruments of the Irish Government.

[48] ECB (2011b), 'Press Release', 7 July: ECB announces change in eligibility of debt instruments issued or guaranteed by the Portuguese Government.

[49] Formally the programme was established by an ECB Decision on 14 May 2010 establishing a securities markets programme (ECB/2010/5), [2010] OJ L124/8.

[50] Decision of the ECB of 14 May 2010 establishing a securities market programme (ECB/2010/5), [2010] OJ L124/8.

to buy government bonds of the troubled Member States; first Greece, Ireland and Portugal, and later Spain and Italy, too. The programme was to be sterilised to ensure that the monetary policy stance was not affected; i.e. the same amount of liquidity that was provided by the programme was reduced from the market by other means.

The programme started off immediately after the decision, but was practically suspended in July 2010, to be again reactivated with large-scale purchases from August 2011 onwards. In March 2012, the total amount spent was nearly 218 billion euro, while the largest holdings were in Italian (101 billion), Spanish (44 billion) and Greek (34 billion) government bonds.[51]

On 6 September 2012, the ECB announced the termination of the Securities Markets Programme and its replacement with Outright Monetary Transactions. These involve "outright transactions in secondary sovereign bond markets that aim at safeguarding an appropriate monetary policy transmission and the singleness of the monetary policy". In spite of the pronounced emphasis on monetary policy transmission, it is clear that the central objective of the new programme was to calm down sovereign debt markets and to restore financial stability in the euro area. Secondary market operations would only be launched on condition that the state concerned had accepted the conditionality attached to an EFSF or ESM programme. On the other hand, no *ex ante* quantitative limits have been set on the size of transactions.[52] Although the programme has not been activated, its adoption is often claimed to have been a turning point which initiated the at least temporary alleviation of the Eurozone sovereign debt crisis.

The ECB's role as a member of the Troika is not very well documented. Most likely, the role has been rather active. Based on mainly unofficial sources, a report by a European think tank specialising in economics states that the ECB has vigorously opposed any debt restructuring, particularly in the case of Greece. The report also repeats the claim according to which the ECB insisted that private unguaranteed bondholders of Irish banks had to be paid in full, although such a requirement was not included in the rescue programme. This would have substantially increased the bill that Irish taxpayers had to pay.[53]

---

[51] ECB (2013b), 'Press Release', 21 February 2013: Details on securities holdings acquired under the Securities Markets Programme.

[52] ECB (2012), 'Press Release', 6 September 2012: Technical features of outright monetary transactions.

[53] J. Pisani-Ferry *et al.* (2013).

Tightening fiscal discipline

Financial assistance to individual euro-area states and building up a firewall credible enough to prevent the crisis from spreading, complemented with unconventional monetary-policy measures by the ECB, constitute one of the major prongs of responses to the Eurozone crisis. Simultaneously, European economic governance has step-by-step been reinforced with a view to tightening fiscal policy discipline in Member States and intensifying coordination of their macroeconomic policies. Another characteristic of the incrementalist reinforcement of European economic governance has been increased intrusion into the procedural and substantive budgetary autonomy of the Member States. In addition, the crisis has brought about a further differentiation of the legal framework applicable to the euro area.

The explosion of the fiscal crisis brought to light the inherent weaknesses of the Stability and Growth Pact.[54] Art. 126 TFEU and the related Protocol employ two criteria for assessing and disciplining Member State fiscal policy: government deficit and government debt. The Stability and Growth Pact put clear emphasis on the former, with the implicit expectation that shrinking the budget deficit would also reduce indebtedness. Regulation 1466/97 on the preventive arm of the multilateral surveillance procedure concentrated on budgetary targets, and the corrective arm under Regulation 1467/97 could only be triggered off in the case of a Member State exceeding the budget-deficit reference value.[55] Furthermore, in 2005 the Stability and Growth Pact was watered down by amendments to the two Regulations, which increased the discretion of the Commission and the Council in the multilateral surveillance and excessive deficit procedure.[56] This occurred as a reaction to application of the excessive deficit procedure to Germany and France; that is, the two biggest Member States.

The procedure was launched against Germany in November 2002 and against France in April 2003. In both cases, the Council had, in accordance with Art. 104 TEC (present 126 TFEU) and Regulation 1467/97,

---

[54] Tellingly enough, the excessive deficit procedure has been launched for most Member States – in May 2013 the procedure was pending for 21 of them – but never has it led to the imposition of sanctions.

[55] Council Regulation (EC) No. 1466- and 1467/97 of 7 July 1997 on the strengthening of the surveillance of budgetary positions and the surveillance and coordination of economic policies, and, on speeding up and clarifying the implementation of the excessive deficit procedure, [1997] OJ L209/1.

[56] Council Regulations (EC) 1055- and 1056/2005, [2005] OJ L174/1.

established that an excessive deficit existed and recommended the German and French governments to bring the deficit to an end. The Council had also set a deadline for taking the necessary measures and ending the deficit. As the next step, the Commission had recommended to the Council that it establish that France and Germany had not taken adequate action to correct the excessive deficit and give them notice to put an end to their excessive deficit situation by 2005 at the latest. In the vote in the Council, the required qualified majority was not reached for approving the Commission's recommendations. In its conclusions, the Council decided not to act on the basis of the Commission recommendation, but agreed to hold the excessive deficit procedure in abeyance. Neither France nor Germany was allowed to vote in its own case, but they could reciprocally influence the result of the vote in each other's case. The Commission took the cases to the ECJ. The Court found the action inadmissible in so far as it sought annulment of the Council's failure to adopt the formal instruments contained in the Commission's recommendations. By contrast, the Court found that neither Art. 104 TEC (present Art. 126 TFEU) nor Regulation 1467/1997 provided for the possibility of deciding to hold the procedure in abeyance in the situation covered by the Council's conclusions.[57]

The Court's ruling manifested a partial victory for the Commission, which favoured strict observance of the excessive deficit procedure. But events clearly showed the ineffectiveness of a procedure where states monitor each other – and not only each other but even themselves – at least when launched against large Member States. The conclusion the Council drew from the incident was not tightening but loosening the provisions of the Regulations on the preventive and corrective arm of the Stability and Growth Pact. The sovereign debt crisis produced an abrupt reversal of policy. Now the direction has been to intensify European economic governance, particularly, but not solely, in supervising national fiscal policy.

The first crisis-induced move to reinforce economic governance was the legislative package which the Commission introduced in Autumn 2010 and which entered into force in December 2011. The package, composed of five Regulations and one Directive, was nicknamed the 'six-pack'.[58]

---

[57] Case C-27/04 *Commission v. Council* [2004] ECR I-6649.
[58] European Parliament and Council Regulation (EU) No. 1173/2011 of 16 November 2011 on the effective enforcement of budgetary surveillance in the euro area, [2011] OJ L306/1; European Parliament and Council Regulation (EU) No. 1174/2011 of 16

The primary objective was to increase the efficacy of the preventive and corrective arm of the Stability and Growth Pact: that is, the multilateral surveillance procedure under Art. 121 and the excessive deficit procedure under Art. 126 TFEU.

After the amendments to the Stability and Growth Pact Regulations in 2005, the excessive deficit procedure had lost much of its significance and credibility. Furthermore, the procedure only kept an eye on one of the two reference values alluded to in Art. 126 TFEU, namely the budgetary deficit. After the six-pack amendments, not only excessive government deficit but even excessive public debt can activate the procedure under Art. 126 TFEU. Leeway for Member State justifications for exceeding reference values has been narrowed. Moreover, procedural time limits have been shortened and sanctions made more substantial. In the euro area, the probability of sanctions has been increased through introduction of reverse majority voting: the Council may only reject or amend a Commission recommendation by qualified majority. Such a semi-automatic decision-making procedure in the Council enhances the position of the Commission and makes it more difficult than before for Member States to form blocking majorities.

A central objective of the Directive on requirements for Member State budgetary frameworks (2011/85) is to ensure consistency of national fiscal planning with the Stability and Growth Pact, which is seen to require a multiannual perspective and pursuit of medium-term budgetary objectives. Each Member State should have in place numerical fiscal rules which promote compliance over a multiannual horizon with obligations deriving from the TFEU in the area of budgetary policy. Member States are obliged to establish a credible and effective medium-term budgetary framework, which ensures that national fiscal planning follows a multiannual perspective.[59]

In November 2011, that is, shortly before entry into force of the six-pack, the Commission introduced further proposals for legislation reinforcing European control of national economic, especially fiscal,

November 2011 on enforcement measures to correct excessive macroeconomic imbalances in the euro area, [2011] OJ L306/8; Council Regulations (EU) No. 1175- and 1177/2011 of 8 November 2011 amending Council Regulations 1466- and 1467/97; European Parliament and Council Regulation (EU) No. 1176/2011 of 16 November 2011 on the prevention and correction of macroeconomic imbalances, [2011] OJ L306/25; Council Directive 2011/85/EU of 8 November 2011 on requirements for budgetary frameworks of the Member States, [2011] OJ L306/41.

[59] A further objective of the Directive is to increase the transparency of government finances in the budget process (see Chapter 6).

policy and making further incursions into national budgetary autonomy. These proposals were promptly nicknamed the 'two-pack'. The
legislative procedure was exceptionally difficult and complicated, and it
took the European Parliament more than a year to reach the necessary
agreement on the two, in many points amended, Regulations. The two-
pack Regulations finally entered into force on 1 June 2013.[60] They were
issued under Art. 136 TFEU and, hence, apply only to the euro area.

Regulation 473/2013, applicable to all euro-area states, widens the
inroad into Member States' budgetary sovereignty which was opened
by the six-pack Directive 2011/85. While the Directive addressed multiannual budgetary planning, the new Regulation focuses on the annual
budgetary process, and, therefore, is much more sensitive from the point
of view of national budgetary autonomy. Euro-area states are required to
introduce a common budgetary timeline, ensuring temporal harmony
of the national budgetary process with the European semester. New
monitoring mechanisms are introduced at both national and European
levels. Member States are required to set up independent fiscal bodies
monitoring compliance with fiscal rules. For the purposes of European
monitoring, euro-area states are obliged to submit their draft budgetary plans for the following year to the Commission and the Eurogroup.
The Commission adopts an opinion on each draft budgetary plan. If
the Commission identifies "particularly serious non-compliance" with
the budgetary policy obligations laid down in the Stability and Growth
Pact, it will request a revised plan, on which it issues a new opinion.
Commission opinions do not have binding legal effect, but are, of course,
meant to influence national decision-making. The requirement that opinions addressing a "particularly serious non-compliance" with the budgetary policy obligations be made public is intended to give them additional
thrust. Moreover, defiance may lead to sanctions under the excessive deficit procedure. Accordingly, the Regulation includes explicit provisions
on the relationship of the annual monitoring of draft budgetary plans
to the excessive deficit procedure. It also provides for specific reporting
requirements for Member States in the excessive deficit procedure.

---

[60] European Parliament and Council Regulation (EU) No. 472/2013 of 21 May 2013 on
the strengthening of economic and budgetary surveillance of Member States in the
euro area experiencing or threatened with serious difficulties with respect to their
financial stability, [2013] OJ L140/1; European Parliament and Council Regulation (EU)
No. 473/2013 of 21 May 2013 on common provisions for monitoring and assessing
draft budgetary plans and ensuring the correction of excessive deficit of the Member
States in the euro area, [2013] OJ L140/11.

Diverging from country-specific rescue measures and establishment of stability funds, European economic governance has been reinforced and expanded within the EU's legislative and institutional framework. The necessary competence basis has been found, primarily, in the – rather broadly interpreted – competences established by Art. 121 (multilateral surveillance), Art. 126 (excessive deficit procedure) and Art. 136 TFEU (specific regime for the euro area). Still, a major exception to this legislative and institutional policy exists: namely, the Treaty on Stability, Coordination and Governance in the Economic and Monetary Union (TSCG). The Treaty is an agreement under public international law and, thus, extends the intergovernmental option from financial assistance into European economic governance. The Treaty has been signed by 25 out of 27 Member States, with the UK and the Czech Republic opting out.

The Fiscal Compact is the most important Title of the TSCG, on which political, economic and legal debates have largely concentrated.[61] The TSGC is a vital element in the strategy to constrain national fiscal policy with a view to ensuring financial stability in the euro area as well as the European Union as a whole. From the very beginning, the central objective of the Treaty, forcefully promoted especially by the German Government, has been to create in Member States legally binding guarantees for compliance with EU rules on a balanced government budget. This objective had already inspired the Commission proposal for two-pack legislation issued in November 2011. The Commission proposed the following provision on Member State rules on budgetary balance: "Member States shall have in place numerical fiscal rules on the budget balance that implement in the national budgetary processes their medium-term budgetary objective as defined in Article 2a of Regulation (EC) No. 1466/97. Such rules shall cover the general government as a whole and be of binding, preferably constitutional, nature."[62] Serious constitutional doubts can be raised on imposing through EU secondary regulation such an obligation to undertake legislative, preferably constitutional, measures. This, probably, is the backdrop to the change of

---

[61] The Treaty as a whole is sometimes called the Fiscal Compact. Actually, the Fiscal Compact constitutes only one, albeit the most important one, of the eight Titles of the TSCG.

[62] Proposal for a regulation of the European Parliament and of the Council on common provisions for monitoring and assessing draft budgetary plans and ensuring the correction of the excessive deficit of the Member States in the euro area (COM(2011) 821 final), Art. 4(1).

strategy: to attain the objective through an amendment to the TFEU. This road, however, was blocked by the veto of the UK and Czech governments, which in turn led to recourse to the intergovernmental option. Thus, the intergovernmental way was entered into only after discussions on a Treaty amendment had fallen through. We shall resume discussing the constitutional aspects of the TSCG saga in Chapter 5.

The TSCG underwent several transformations in inter-state negotiations, and the most controversial of the original provisions were dropped from the final version signed in the margins of the European Council meeting on 1–2 March 2012.[63] The first draft version, advocated by the German Government, would have directly encroached on the constitutional autonomy of the Contracting Parties: these would have been obliged to make the requirement of a balanced or surplus budget and the country-specific medium-term objective as defined in the revised Stability and Growth Pact constitutionally binding.[64] Furthermore, Member States would have been required to entrust national courts with the power to monitor compliance with these constitutionally anchored criteria. In most Member States, both of these obligations would have presupposed constitutional amendments. The requirement of national guarantees of budgetary discipline was gradually loosened. In its final version, Art. 3(2) stipulates that "the rules mentioned under paragraph 1 shall take effect in the national law of the Contracting Parties at the latest one year after the entry into force of this Treaty through provisions of binding force and permanent character, preferably constitutional, *or otherwise guaranteed to be fully respected and adhered to throughout the national budgetary processes*" (emphasis added).

Contrary to the first drafts, in its final shape the Fiscal Compact does not involve national courts in the monitoring process. However, a national correction mechanism must be put in place and triggered automatically if significant deviations from the medium-term objective or the adjustment path towards it are observed. National constitutional concerns have been heeded in a provision which lays down that the correction mechanism "shall fully respect the prerogatives of national Parliaments". While national courts are excluded from the monitoring process, a Contracting Party may bring the matter to the Court of Justice of the European Union if it considers that another Contracting

---

[63] See European Council (2012a), 'Conclusions', 1–2 March 2012.
[64] Germany had already amended its Basic Law in 2009 and anchored the so-called debt brake (*Schuldenbremse*) constitutionally (Arts. 109 and 115 of the Basic Law).

Party has failed to comply with its obligation under Art. 3(2). The case can be raised either on the basis of a report by the Commission or independently of such a report.

Expanding economic coordination

As was the case before the crisis, fiscal policy still lies at the centre of European economic governance. Still, a characteristic of recent developments has been not only tightening fiscal-policy surveillance but also extending the scope of European instruments to general macroeconomic policy. The six-pack includes a Regulation on the prevention and correction of macroeconomic imbalances (1176/2011), introducing a new – and controversial – excessive imbalances procedure, which considerably widens the reach of European monitoring. In the Preamble, the new procedure is justified by reference to the need to broaden "surveillance of the economic policies of the Member States … beyond budgetary surveillance to include a more detailed and formal framework to prevent excessive macroeconomic imbalances and to help the Member States affected to establish corrective plans before divergences become entrenched". Thus, the Preamble argues, it is appropriate to supplement the multilateral surveillance procedure with specific rules for the prevention, detection and correction of macroeconomic imbalances.

The procedure includes an alert or early-warning system based on ten indicators (the scoreboard), supposedly covering the major sources of macroeconomic imbalances. The system is managed by the Commission. The Commission and the Council may adopt preventive recommendations under Art. 121(2) TFEU at an early stage before imbalances become large. For more serious cases, a corrective arm exists where an excessive imbalance procedure can be opened. The Member State concerned will have to submit a corrective action plan with a roadmap and deadlines for implementing corrective action. The Commission will step up surveillance on the basis of regular progress reports submitted by the Member State. For euro-area states, a two-step enforcement regime has been established. First, an interest-bearing deposit can be imposed after one failure to comply with recommended corrective action. After a second compliance failure, this interest-bearing deposit can be converted into a fine of up to 0.1 per cent of GDP. Sanctions can also be imposed for twice failing to submit a sufficient corrective action plan. In accordance with the new euro-area rules on the excessive deficit procedure, decision-making in the excessive imbalance procedure is streamlined by prescribing use of reverse qualified majority voting to take all the relevant decisions leading up to sanctions.

For its part, the two-pack introduced two new instruments which exceed the confines of fiscal policy. The first of these is enhanced surveillance set out in Regulation 472/2013. This procedure has been designed with a view to financial stability; i.e. the new overriding economic policy objective (see Chapter 6). The decision to subject a Member State to enhanced surveillance falls to the Commission. The substantive prerequisite is that the Member State is "experiencing or threatened with serious difficulties with respect to its financial stability which are likely to have adverse spill-over effects on other Member States in the euro area". The procedure includes, inter alia, review missions by the Commission. The Council, acting by a qualified majority on a proposal by the Commission, recommends to the Member State adoption of precautionary corrective measures or preparation of a draft macroeconomic adjustment programme. It can also decide to make the recommendation public.

The other two-pack Regulation (473/2013) complements the excessive deficit procedure with an economic partnership programme, which Member States against whom the procedure has been opened must present to the Commission and the Council. The programme must describe the policy measures and structural reforms needed to ensure an "effective and lasting correction" of the deficit. In particular it must "identify and select a number of specific priorities aiming to enhance competitiveness and long-term sustainable growth and addressing structural weaknesses in the Member State concerned".

In addition to the requirements on national budgetary legislation and procedure, the TSCG contains general and rather vaguely formulated provisions on economic policy coordination and convergence. These provisions do not seem to add anything new to existing obligations and procedures under EU primary and secondary legislation, complemented by such soft-law instruments as the EuroPlus Pact. Art. 9 lays down that "building upon the economic policy coordination as defined in the Treaty on the Functioning of the European Union, the Contracting Parties undertake to work jointly towards an economic policy fostering the smooth functioning of the Economic and Monetary Union and economic growth through enhanced convergence and competitiveness". To further this end, "the Contracting Parties shall take the necessary actions and measures in all the domains which are essential to the good functioning of the euro-area in pursuit of the objectives of fostering competitiveness, promoting employment, contributing further to the sustainability of public finances and reinforcing financial stability". Benchmarking and peer review practices evoked by Art. 11 are not a novelty in European economic policy coordination, either: "With a view to benchmarking best practices and working towards a more closely coordinated economic policy, the Contracting Parties ensure that all major economic policy reforms that they plan to undertake will be discussed ex-ante and, where appropriate, coordinated among themselves." Reliance on existing EU law is confirmed by the provision according to which "this coordination shall involve the institutions of the European Union as required by European Union law".

The TSCG was preceded by the EuroPlus Pact, which is a political commitment by the Signatory States to reforms in the fields of competitiveness, employment, sustainability of public finances, reinforcement of financial stability and tax policy. The EuroPlus Pact lacks direct legal relevance: it is a typical soft-law document which even in its implementation relies on soft-law methods, such as peer review. The Pact was agreed on in March 2011 by Heads of State or Government of 23 Member States.[65] Subsequent developments and more stringent measures for strengthening policy coordination have largely surpassed the EuroPlus Pact and reduced its significance in the arsenal of European economic governance.

Coordinating coordination

European responses to the fiscal crisis have led to a plethora of procedures for monitoring and coordinating national fiscal and macroeconomic policies. This, in turn, has created a need for their mutual integration. Introduction of the European semester is an effort to achieve meta-level coordination. The European semester is an annual cycle of economic and fiscal policy coordination, which was first followed in 2011 and subsequently formalised through the six-pack Regulation 1175/2011. The semester starts with publication by the Commission of an Annual Growth Survey which is supposed to provide a basis for integrating macroeconomic, thematic and fiscal surveillance. At its spring meeting,

[65] Conclusions of the Heads of State or Government of the Euro Area, 11 March 2011, Annex I.

the European Council issues policy orientations covering fiscal, as well as macroeconomic structural-reform and growth-enhancing areas, and advises on linkages between them. This takes the form of broad economic and employment-policy guidelines, invoked in Arts. 121(2) and 148(2) TFEU. In April, Member States send to the Commission their Stability and Convergence Programmes for assessment, as presupposed by the multilateral surveillance procedure under Art. 121 TFEU. The states also submit their national reform programmes, introduced by the new economic imbalances procedure. In June or July, on the basis of the Commission's assessment, the Council issues country-specific guidance which is supposed to influence Member States when these finalise their draft budgets for the following year.[66] Under the two-pack legislation, the annual cycle continues for euro states with submission of their draft budgets by 15 October, as well as the subsequent opinion(s) of the Commission.

Attention has also been paid to obtaining the formal blessing of the Council for conditionality of assistance, thus involving it in operations which have mainly been realised outside the Union institutional and legal framework. For Greek, Spanish and Cypriot assistance, Art. 126 TFEU, together with Art. 136(1), has functioned as a bridge between the excessive deficit procedure and the economic adjustment programme set out in the MoUs. The Preamble to the Greek Loan Facility Agreement and the Intercreditor Agreement explicitly invoked Arts. 126(9) and 136.[67] Indeed, the main contents of the adjustment programme have been included in Council decisions taken in the excessive deficit procedure under Art. 126(9) and even referring to Art. 136.[68] Art.

---

[66] See European Commission, 'Making it Happen – the European Semester' (announcement on the Commission website).

[67] "Measures concerning the coordination and surveillance of the budgetary discipline of Greece and setting out economic policy guidelines for Greece will be defined in a Council Decision on the basis of Arts. 126(9) and 136 of the Treaty on the Functioning of the European Union (the 'Council Decision'), and the support granted to Greece is made dependent on compliance by Greece amongst others with measures consistent with that act and laid down in a Memorandum of Economic and Financial Policies, Memorandum of Understanding on Specific Economic Policy Conditionality and Technical Memorandum of Understanding (hereinafter referred together as the 'MoU') each signed on 3 May 2010 by the Borrower and the Bank of Greece."
See Intercreditor Agreement, Recital 6 of the Preamble; see also Loan Facility Agreement, Recital 6 of the Preamble.

[68] See Council Decision (EU) of 12 July 2011 addressed to Greece with a view of reinforcing and deepening fiscal surveillance and giving notice to Greece to take measures for the deficit reduction judged necessary to remedy the situation of excessive deficit, [2011] OJ L296/38; and subsequent amendments: Council Decision of 8 November 2011, [2011] OJ L320/28, and Council Decision of 13 March 2012, [2012] OJ L113/8.

126(9) addresses the situation where a Member State persists in failing to put into practice recommendations the Council has issued under the excessive deficit procedure. It authorises the Council to give notice to a Member State to take, within a specified time limit, such measures for deficit reduction which the Council judges necessary. The Council may also request the Member State to submit reports following a specific timetable in order to examine the adjustment. In turn, the announced competence basis for the Council decisions on Spain and Cyprus was Art. 136(1), in conjunction with Art. 126(6).[69] The latter provision addresses an earlier stage of the excessive deficit procedure and provides the Council merely with the power to decide, on a proposal from the Commission and after an overall assessment, whether an excessive deficit exists. In the cases of Ireland and Portugal, involvement of the Council was facilitated by the participation of the European Financial Stabilisation Mechanism (EFSM), which was established in the Union institutional and legislative mechanism. The MoUs were summarised in Council decisions taken under Art. 3(3) of Regulation 407/2010, establishing the EFSM.[70]

The two-pack Regulation 472/2013 signifies a further effort to anchor the conditionality of intergovernmental financial assistance in Union legislation. It contains provisions on a macroeconomic adjustment programme which Member States requesting financial assistance from other Member States or the EFSM, the EFSF, the ESM or the IMF have to prepare by agreement with the Commission. The Commission, in turn, is supposed to act in liaison with its Troika partners, the ECB and the IMF. Approval of the macroeconomic adjustment programme falls to the Council, which acts by qualified majority and on a proposal by the Commission. The Commission is obliged to ensure that the MoUs it signs on behalf of the ESM or the EFSF are fully consistent with the macroeconomic adjustment programme. Furthermore, the Regulation aims to coordinate monitoring under the macroeconomic adjustment programme – and, indirectly, the MoUs related to financial assistance – with the multilateral surveillance and excessive deficit procedure

---

[69] Council decision of 23 July 2012 addressed to Spain on specific measures to reinforce financial stability (2012/443/EU), [2012] OJ L202/17; Council decision of 25 April 2013 addressed to Cyprus on specific measures to restore financial stability and sustainable growth (2013/236/EU), [2013] OJ L141/32.

[70] See Council implementing decision of 7 December 2010 on granting Union financial assistance to Ireland (2011/77/EU), [2011] OJ L30/34; and Council implementing decision of 30 May 2011 on granting Union financial assistance to Portugal (2011/344/EU), [2011] OJ L159/88.

under Arts. 121 and 126 TFEU (i.e. the preventive and corrective arm of the Stability and Growth Pact), as well as the new excessive imbalances procedure, introduced by the six-pack.

A link has also been created between the Treaty on the European Stability Mechanism and the Treaty on Stability, Coordination and Governance. These treaties are located on different sides of the division between emergency measures and general economic governance. Yet, their negotiating and ratification processes largely overlapped, and the respective Preambles include mutual references. Moreover, according to the Preamble to the Treaty on the ESM, financial assistance within the framework of new programmes under the ESM may not be granted to a Member State which has not ratified the TSCG or complied with the obligation to introduce national legal guarantees for balanced budgets.[71] A further coordinating issue concerns the relations of the TSCG to primary and secondary EU legislation, especially Arts. 121, 126 and 136 TFEU, as well as the Regulations falling under the Stability and Growth Pact. We shall discuss the constitutional aspects of these issues in Chapter 5. Here it suffices to refer to Art. 16 TSCG which expresses the Contracting States' intention to incorporate the treaty into the EU framework.[72]

---

[71] "On 9 December 2011 the Heads of State or Government of the Member States whose currency is the euro agreed to move towards a stronger economic union including a new fiscal compact and strengthened economic policy coordination to be implemented through an international agreement, the Treaty on Stability, Coordination and Governance in the Economic and Monetary Union ('TSCG'). The TSCG will help develop a closer coordination within the euro area with a view to ensuring a lasting, sound and robust management of public finances and thus addresses one of the main sources of financial instability. This Treaty and the TSCG are complementary in fostering fiscal responsibility and solidarity within the economic and monetary union. It is acknowledged and agreed that the granting of financial assistance in the framework of new programmes under the ESM will be conditional, as of 1 March 2013, on the ratification of the TSCG by the ESM Member concerned and, upon expiration of the transposition period referred to in Art. 3(2) TSCG on compliance with the requirements of that article" (Recital 5).

[72] "Within five years, at most, of the date of entry into force of this Treaty, on the basis of an assessment of the experience with its implementation, the necessary steps shall be taken, in accordance with the Treaty on the European Union and the Treaty on the Functioning of the European Union, with the aim of incorporating the substance of this Treaty into the legal framework of the European Union."

PART II

Constitutional mutation

5   Constitutionality of European measures

European responses to the Eurozone crisis raise constitutional issues in both the European Union and its Member States. Furthermore, constitutional implications can be discussed at two levels, remembering the multi-layered nature of constitutions in general and the economic constitution in particular: in addition to explicit constitutional provisions and precedents, constitutions include a 'sub-surface' level of underlying principles, concepts and theories. In this chapter, we focus on doctrinal questions, related to 'surface-level' constitutional law[1] and postpone 'matters of principle' to Chapter 6. Of course, these two levels neither can nor should be hermeneutically isolated from each other. The tougher doctrinal issues are, the more frequently legal argumentation must take recourse to the principles underlying individual provisions. Principles, in turn, can only be identified through the traces they have left in such 'surface-level' constitutional material as the Treaties or the case law of the ECJ, i.e. the constitutional court of the EU. It is perhaps more appropriate to speak of different emphases than two separate levels of discussion.

   We shall argue that the *Pringle* judgment of the ECJ, together with the amendment to Art. 136 TFEU, which explicitly acknowledged Member States' competence to establish a stability mechanism, have confirmed that significant changes in the macroeconomic constitution have occurred. We take these for granted, deferring to the weight the speech acts of the constitutional legislator and the constitutional court (ECJ) have in EU constitutional discourse. Yet, we feel free to criticise

---

[1] The role of the IMF raises specific questions of compatibility with the IMF Statute. These questions fall under public international law and will be left unexplored here. See C. Gaitanides (2011); D. Thym (2011); M. Ruffert (2011).

the argumentation in the *Pringle* ruling and the preceding view of AG Kokott,[2] as well as in European Council Decision 2011/99 on the amendment to Art. 136 TFEU. Furthermore, we shall comment on the constitutionality of ECB action and thus enter a territory largely uncharted by constitutional scholarship. We shall also discuss the constitutional basis of reinforced economic governance, in particular the reach of Art. 136(1) TFEU in justifying specific Eurozone measures and the use of intergovernmental agreements to circumvent political obstacles blocking recourse to primary or secondary EU legislation.

During the three hectic years from Spring 2010 to Spring 2013, Europe seemed to proceed, not only from one crisis to another, but also from one measure to another, reacting to often abrupt economic developments and without a coherent and comprehensive roadmap. Legal services of the European institutions – the Commission, the Council, the Presidency of the European Council and the ECB – and Member State Governments were entrusted with the intricate and usually extremely urgent task of garbing political decisions in legal form. Legal improvisation and innovative constitutional interpretations – if we are allowed a euphemism – were felt a necessity. However, when the dust starts to settle it is important to tackle the constitutional aspects of all major prongs of European responses – rescue packages and mechanisms, ECB action as well as measures aimed to tighten European economic governance.

The two-order telos of the no-bailout clause

Constitutional assessment of rescue packages and mechanisms must start with their relationship to the no-bailout clause in Art. 125(1) TFEU. *Pringle* has taken a position on the major interpretative questions, and it must be accorded due significance as a major intervention in the ongoing constitutional discourse. Still, *Pringle* does not discuss all the relevant problems, nor is its argumentation always persuasive. Art. 125(1) TFEU raises three main interpretive questions, one methodological and two substantive. The major methodological options are a literal interpretation, emphasising the wording of the provision, and a teleological reading, emphasising its purpose – *Sinn und Zweck*. As we shall demonstrate, the teleological method, in turn, includes alternative

---

[2] Case C-370/12 *Thomas Pringle* v. *Government of Ireland*, not yet reported, view of Advocate General Kokott, delivered on 26 October 2012.

ways to conceive of the relevant telos, implying different interpretive conclusions.[3] On our reading, *Pringle* combines literal interpretation with two-level teleology. This corresponds to our own methodological premises. Individual provisions must be construed in the light of the purposes of constitutional regulation. However, the criterion of what Ronald Dworkin called institutional support[4] must be heeded as well. In EU law, this criterion can be related to the principle of legal certainty which can be argued to require that interpretation must always be sustained by discursively formulated surface-level constitutional material, such as explicit Treaty provisions.[5] In order to prepare the ground for discussing the implications of the no-bailout clause, allow us to quote Art. 125(1) *in extenso*:

The Union shall not be liable for or assume the commitments of central governments, regional, local or other public authorities, other bodies governed by public law, or public undertakings of any Member State, without prejudice to mutual financial guarantees for the joint execution of a specific project. A Member State shall not be liable for or assume the commitments of central governments, regional, local or other public authorities, other bodies governed by public law, or public undertakings of another Member State, without prejudice to mutual financial guarantees for the joint execution of a specific project.

The two main substantive interpretive questions concern the personal (institutional) and the substantive scope of the no-bailout clause, i.e. its *ratione personae* and *ratione materiae*.[6] The questions are the following: (1) who is obliged by the clause, and (2) what forms of financial support does the clause prohibit? Note that we do not consider the obligatory/voluntary nature of the support to be a problem really worth discussing. No persuasive arguments following either literal or teleological interpretation have been presented to defend a narrow view which would restrict the bailout prohibition merely to obligatory financial assistance to a Member State in fiscal distress. The wording of Art. 125(1) TFEU (*shall not be liable for or assume commitments*) clearly indicates that both obligatory and voluntary liability commitments are addressed, and it is hard to imagine any teleological viewpoints favouring a restrictive

---

[3] Cf. the way V. Borger (2013), pp. 129–31, classifies the methodological options.
[4] R. Dworkin (1978), p. 40.
[5] See on legal certainty as a general principle of EU law Tridimas (2006), Ch. 5.
[6] A. de Gregorio Merino (2012) employs a similar grouping of the legal issues.

interpretation. The Court, too, evidently held the issue to be so clear that no explicit stand on it was needed.[7]

As we showed in our presentation of emergency measures and mechanisms in Chapter 4, financial assistance has assumed a variety of forms. Ignoring for the moment the role of the ECB, a distinction should be made between

(1) assistance directly by Member States (bilateral loans making up the first Greek rescue package);

(2) assistance from funds established by Member States through private- or international-law agreements and constituting distinct legal subjects, such as the European Financial Stability Facility (EFSF) and the European Stability Mechanism (ESM); and

(3) financial assistance by the EU through a mechanism under its legislative and institutional framework, such as the European Financial Stability Mechanism (EFSM).

Pursuant to the wording of Art. 125(1) TFEU, the bailout prohibition is addressed to both the Union and Member States. Consequently, it should be evident that it covers *ratione personae* alternatives (1) and (3). Yet, in a detailed examination of the bailout prohibition assistance by the Union and by Member States must be scrutinised separately. This is due to the provision on emergency assistance in Art. 122(2) TFEU, which, unlike the no-bailout clause, deals merely with assistance by the Union and not by Member States. Consequently, we shall postpone our discussion of the no-bailout clause's significance for Union assistance to the next section, where we relate it to the emergency provision in Art. 122(2). We shall also deal separately with the possible relevance of the no-bailout clause for the ECB.

The only case on our list which merits brief discussion with regard to the *ratione personae* dimension is the second and in practical terms most important one: namely, assistance from funds established by Member States through private- or international-law agreements and constituting distinct legal subjects. In *Pringle*, the claimant argued that the approach of a financial institution under international law had been chosen in order to circumvent the prohibition on bailouts. Jonathan Tomkin, a member of Mr Pringle's legal team, has found

---

[7] In the academic debate, the issue has been commented on by, e.g., K. Fassbender (2010), p. 800; L. Knopp (2010), p. 1779; C. Calliess (2011), p. 260.

corroboration for this view in the observations some Member States lodged before the ECJ in the *Pringle* proceedings. Some state interveners claimed that as an international financial institution with a legal personality distinct from Member States, ESM is not subject to the bailout provision.[8] This consideration may have played a role especially in the context of the EFSF.[9] Yet, most likely the main reason for opting for the intergovernmental way has simply been the fact that only Member States but not the Union possessed the necessary fiscal means for rescue operations. In *Pringle*, the Court avoided any direct discussion on the *ratione personae* issue. The Court's silence can be interpreted in two ways: either it considered the issue self-evident or it held an explicit position to be unnecessary after it had concluded that financial assistance under the ESM Treaty did not fall under the bailout prohibition *ratione substantiae*. Either way, side-stepping the issue is somewhat surprising, given that it had been raised in state observations and that AG Kokott had devoted considerable attention to it.

In our mind, the premise should be clear enough: if EU law prohibits Member States a certain action, the prohibition extends to Member States acting both individually and in concert, through intergovernmental agreements, whether under private or international law. The prohibition also covers intergovernmental facilities, established by Member States, regardless of whether these possess a distinct legal subjectivity or not. As AG Kokott has demonstrated with regard to the ESM, in spite of its distinct legal subjectivity, in its decision-making bodies and procedure it is indistinguishable from its Member States (para. 110). Its Board of Governors is composed of Member States' Ministers of Finance, and as a rule decisions are made by mutual agreement. Correspondingly, the composition of the EFSF decision-making body, the Board of Directors, is identical to the Eurogroup Working Group.[10]

---

[8] J. Tomkin (2013), pp. 174–5.

[9] In the context of the EFSF, some discussants have also accorded relevance to the fact that Member States did not appear as guarantors for loans the EFSF granted to beneficiary states but to loans issued by the EFSF in the financial markets. See, e.g., C. Calliess (2011), p. 263. In a literal interpretation this certainly is relevant, but not so much in a teleological reading.

[10] In her view, AG Kokott argued that whether granting financial assistance through the ESM is contrary to the no-bailout clause does not actually depend on whether the clause obliges the ESM. What is at issue is whether the Member States act in breach of Art. 125(1) TFEU when bringing about the grant of financial assistance by the ESM.

The second and actually more important and complicated interpretive issue concerns the *ratione materiae*, i.e. the substantive reach, of the prohibition on bailouts; that is, the forms of assistance it embraces. The first Greek rescue package was made up of bilateral loans by the assisting Member States. The only instruments the EFSM has at its disposal are loans or credit lines. By contrast, the EFSF and the ESM possess a broader range of instruments. Arts. 14–18 of the ESM Treaty provide for the following options:

- precautionary financial assistance in the form of a precautionary conditioned credit line or in the form of an enhanced conditions credit line;
- loans to an ESM Member for the specific purpose of recapitalising the financial institutions of that ESM Member;
- a loan to an ESM Member;
- purchase of bonds of an ESM Member on the primary market;
- operations on the secondary market in relation to the bonds of an ESM Member.

In addition, Art. 19 TESM grants the Board of Governors the power to complement the list of instruments.

Art. 125(1) TFEU explicitly forbids "liability for" and "assumption of commitments" of a Member State. Following AG Kokott's view in *Pringle*, a literal interpretation would entail that the prohibition comprises merely discharging a Member State's commitment through payment; directly replacing the Member State as a debtor of sovereign debt; or providing legally for such a replacement through a guarantee commitment.[11] Both AG Kokott and the Court apply literal interpretation as a vital means of reasoning. AG Kokott argues that "neither loans nor the purchase of bonds guarantee to the creditors of a Member State repayment of the sums owed to them" (para. 116). As regards loans, they are not equivalent to becoming liable for commitments of a Member State (para. 117), nor is an existing commitment of another Member State

Both in assuming commitments under international agreements and in giving effect to such commitments, Member States must comply with the requirements EU law imposes on them, including the no-bailout clause (paras. 109–12).

[11] AG Kokott examines separately 'becoming liable' and 'assumption of commitments'. As regards the latter part of the no-bailout clause, she argues that it "prevents a Member State … from taking upon itself the commitments of another Member State, either by discharging the commitment by making payment or by itself becoming the obligated party subject to the commitment, which it then has to discharge at a later date" (para. 121).

assumed or discharged by granting a loan; "instead a new commitment is imposed on that Member State" (para. 122). AG Kokott treats acquisition of a bond on the primary market from the issuing State merely as a particular form of loan. With regard to purchases on the secondary market, she claims that they do not "in principle" signify assumption of the commitments of the state, because no commitment of that state is discharged: "the Member State issuing the bonds continues to be the party subject to the commitment", and "the Member State's commitment therefore remains substantively unaltered, only the creditor changes" (para. 156).

The Court, in turn, first states that Arts. 14–18 TESM "demonstrate that the ESM will not act as guarantor of the debts of the recipient Member State" and that "the latter will remain responsible to its creditors for its financial commitments". After this opening statement, the Court separately discusses loans and purchases of bonds on the primary or secondary market. Pursuing a literal interpretation, the Court contends that granting credit lines or loans "in no way implies that the ESM will assume the debts of the recipient Member State" but "on the contrary, such assistance amounts to the creation of a new debt, owed to the ESM by that recipient Member State, which remains responsible for its commitments to its creditors in respect of its existing debts". Purchase of bonds on the primary market, in turn, is comparable to a loan and does not, either, entail that the ESM would assume debts of the recipient state. Finally, as regards purchases of bonds on the secondary market, the Court points out that "the issuing Member State remains solely answerable to repay the debts in question". The Court further indicates that "the fact that the ESM as the purchaser on that market of bonds issued by an ESM Member pays a price to the holder of those bonds, who is the creditor of the issuing ESM Member, does not mean that the ESM becomes responsible for the debt of that ESM Member to that creditor" (paras. 138–41). Indeed, nobody can be responsible for a debt to a creditor that is no longer a creditor![12]

---

[12] *Pringle* did not address assistance by the EFSF but merely by the ESM. If it had, it would probably have had to consider the second Greek package adopted in March 2012 legally problematic. In the restructuration, loans by the Greek Government were partly directly replaced by debt certificates of the EFSF. Here, the EFSF directly replaced Greece as debtors, which falls under AG Kokott's definition of the literal sense of the no-bailout clause. See the Greek Financial Assistance Facility Agreement.

Even adhering to a literal interpretation, AG Kokott's and the Court's reasoning is vulnerable to criticism. Purchases on the secondary market certainly amount to discharging the issuing state's commitment to the former creditor and thus imply, at least when following AG Kokott's explication of the literal sense, violation of the explicit prohibition on bailouts. It is true, though, that the ESM member remains indebted to the ESM. This would, however, also be the case if the ESM discharged the original debt as a guarantor. No relevant difference from the perspective of either the original creditor or the debtor state exists between a guarantor's discharging the debt and a secondary-market purchase.

The literal interpretation, as employed by AG Kokott and the Court, focuses merely on the relationship between the ESM and the debtor state, and wholly misses the perspective of the (original) creditor. This is the essential perspective for moral-hazard and market-discipline considerations. In order to encourage creditors to monitor and assess the risks of bonds issued by a Member State, creditors' financial compensation of the risks should be based on the expectation of that Member State's paying or not paying their debt. If other Member States or the Union step in, market discipline is lost, regardless of what the ultimate relationship between the bailing-out Member States (or the Union) and the bailed-out state is.

These considerations serve as a bridge from a literal to a teleological reading of the no-bailout clause. AG Kokott vacillates between a "pure" literal interpretation and complements literal interpretation with teleological considerations, but leans ultimately to the former option. She concedes that the objectives of Art. 125(1) TFEU, its *Sinn und Zweck*, might favour an interpretation to the effect that not only direct but even indirect assumption of liabilities would be included. However, in her mind such "basic fundamental principles of the Treaties" as sovereignty and solidarity of Member States militate against a broad interpretation. She does, though, concede some relevance to the *Misbrauchsverbot* argument, familiar from German academic debates. Many German discussants have stressed that circumventing the bailout prohibition through assistance which in effect equals the explicitly banned forms of bailout should not be allowed.[13] AG Kokott argues that "Article 125 TFEU cannot be interpreted in such a way that the prohibitions laid down therein become entirely devoid of meaning". Yet for her, this only entails that loans are included in the scope of the no-bailout clause

---

[13] See, e.g., C. Calliess (2011), pp. 261 ff.

merely if they directly benefit the creditors of the recipient Member State. This would be the case if this state had no control over disposal of the loaned funds. In sum, the no-bailout clause "prohibits only the *direct* assumption of the commitments of another Member State in the sense of taking responsibility for or discharging those commitments, whereby the creditors are directly benefited" (paras. 145–9, emphasis added).

The Court grants teleological viewpoints a more prominent role than AG Kokott. The Court's message can be summarised as follows: the prohibition on bailouts addresses, first, all assistance covered by the wording of Art. 125(1) TFEU, irrespective of the objectives it serves; and, second, even other financial assistance, such as the facilities the ESM is entitled to provide, if it contradicts the objective of the prohibition. This brings us to a discussion of the teleology of the no-bailout clause.

A broad consensus exists among academic commentators of the primary objective: the bailout prohibition aims to prevent moral hazard on the side of both Member States and their creditors, to prevent excessive public debt, and thus to contribute to budgetary discipline and sound public finances. The Court adopts the prevailing view and argues that "the prohibition laid down in Article 125 TFEU ensures that the Member States remain subject to the logic of the market when they enter into debt, since that ought to prompt them to maintain budgetary discipline" (para. 135). The Court also emphasises that the main function of the provisions on economic policy in the TFEU, especially Arts. 123–5, is preventive, "to reduce so far as possible the risk of public debt crises". The objective of establishing a stability mechanism such as the ESM is different: it is "the management of financial crises which, notwithstanding such preventive action as might have been taken, might nonetheless arise" (para. 59).

This reading corresponds to our reconstruction of the Maastricht principles. The no-bailout provision in Art. 125(1) expresses the principle of Member States' fiscal liability. It was expected to encourage Member States to a solid fiscal policy and avoidance of excessive indebtedness. It was supposed to ward off the moral hazard which could arise if states and their creditors were allowed to rely on other Member States or the Union coming to the rescue in case of a threatening insolvency. The provision expressed confidence in the disciplinary effect of the credit market. States would have to pay for reckless fiscal policy in the form of higher interest rates, which would induce them to adhere to a policy of sound public finances. Yet, as we explained in Chapter 2, the drafters of the Maastricht economic constitution were also aware of the limited effect of market discipline, based as it was on default risk premia which possess a conspicuous on-off nature. That is why it was so important to have in place the monitoring mechanism set out in Art. 126 TFEU and further specified in the Protocol on the excessive deficit procedure and the Stability and Growth Pact.

The crisis which erupted in early 2010 has proved the point of those who had cautioned against too much confidence in the disciplining effects of credit markets. As the Delors Committee had warned, neither creditors nor Member States as debtors had stuck to the rationality of market logic. But nor was the excessive deficit procedure able to prevent the sovereign debt crisis. Yet, the Maastricht macroeconomic constitution did not include any crisis resolution mechanism, beyond the provision on emergency assistance in Art. 122(2) TFEU. Two alternative explanations exist for this lack. Either the drafters of the Maastricht constitution considered an insolvency crisis so improbable that there was no need to prepare for that eventuality.[14] Or the implicit normative message was that a no-bailout clause should be taken seriously at a time of crisis, too, and a Member State threatened by insolvency should be left to default and to negotiate a resettlement of its debts. Either way, since early 2010 the Eurozone leaders have grappled with a most intricate economic and political problem which *Pringle* then put before the Court in its constitutional shape. They had to decide how to deal with a situation which the macroeconomic constitution introduced in Maastricht did not, at least not explicitly, address. This was a situation where Art. 125(1), together with other 'basic safeguards against fiscal profligacy', had manifestly failed to realise its primary objective. Furthermore, in Spring 2010, when Greece had drifted close to the brink of insolvency, exit through default and resettlement of debts was considered to be closed. According to the prevailing, but by no means uncontroversial judgment, imminent danger existed of contagion and spread of the debt crisis to other euro states. In addition, through losses inflicted on creditor financial institutions default of a Member State was assessed to have serious repercussions on the financial system of the whole Eurozone.[15]

---

[14] G. Majone (2013) has referred to the "political culture of total optimism", often characterising EU politics.
[15] These arguments were not uncontested even among central-bank economists, which reflects the all but certain nature of macroeconomic causalities. See also IMF

One possibility to find a way out, which was intimated by the legal service of the German Government, was to postulate the silence of the Treaties as a regulatory lacuna which responsible Eurozone leaders were called on to remedy.[16] But the political and legal dilemma arose from the fact that crisis resolution was seen to require measures which at least in economic terms amounted to a bailout. Because of the tension with the principle of Member States' fiscal liability and the economic price the assisting states and their taxpayers had to pay, such measures were hard to defend before national constituencies, too. The justification was sought in a higher-order objective which was expressly invoked in both political resolutions and legal instruments: the financial stability of the euro area as a whole. On this view, at stake was not only the solvency of the crisis states and the continuation of their EMU membership, but the very future of EMU as a whole and the common currency in general; indeed, ultimately, the very idea(l) of European integration.[17]

Pringle explicitly consecrated in constitutional terms the idea of two-level teleology and the definition of a higher objective as the financial stability of the euro area as a whole. This objective seems to harmonise crisis prevention, which includes the prohibition on bailouts, with crisis resolution, which may require measures deviating from this prohibition. The Court postulates that compliance with budgetary discipline, which is the primary objective of the no-bailout clause, contributes at Union level to a higher objective; namely, maintaining the financial stability of the euro area. And it is this very same objective which stability mechanisms, such as the ESM, also serve (para. 136).

(2013b), 'Greece: Ex Post Evaluation of Exceptional Access under the 2010 Stand-By Arrangement', June 2013.

[16] See the reference in C. Calliess (2011), p. 263, fn. 235.

[17] This alarmist tone was conspicuous in Chancellor Angela Merkel's speech before the *Bundestag* on 19 May 2010: "Es geht um viel mehr als um eine Währung. Die Währungsunion ist eine Schicksalsgemeinschaft. Es geht deshalb um nicht mehr und nicht weniger als um die Bewahrung und Bewährung der europäischen Idee. Das ist unsere historische Aufgabe; denn scheitert der Euro, dann scheitert Europa. Wenden wir diese Gefahr aber ab, dann werden der Euro und Europa stärker als zuvor sein." [It is about much more than a currency. The Monetary Union is a community of destiny. It therefore involves no more and no less than the preservation and probation of the European idea. This is our historic task; if the euro fails then Europe fails. We avert this danger but then the euro, and Europe too, will be stronger than before.] A. Merkel (2010), 'Regierungserklärung von Bundeskanzlerin Merkel zu den Euro-Stabilisierungsmaßnahmen', 19 May 2010.

The conclusion is that the interpretation and application of the no-bailout clause should not prevent attaining the higher-level objective it shares with crisis management. Yet, harmonisation of crisis prevention and resolution through a common higher objective does not solve all the tensions between them.

Should the higher-order telos be used broadly to derogate from the bailout prohibition, it could even increase the risk of financial instability it aims to prevent. The dilemma arises from the fact that crisis resolution must be related not only to past (and failed) but also to future crisis prevention. Crisis management is considered necessary when the no-bailout clause, together with other safeguards against fiscal profligacy, has failed in its preventive function, such as elimination of moral hazard. But measures amounting to – at least in economic terms – a bailout may spawn a future risk of moral hazard; sovereigns and creditors learn that, ultimately, other Member States or the Union come to the rescue to prevent insolvency. So focusing on the second-order objective may endanger realisation of the primary objective and ultimately, paradoxically enough, the second-order objective itself. This dilemma has not, of course, remained unobserved either by European decision-makers or the ECJ. The intended solution to the potential contradiction between second- and first-order teleology lies in the 'strict conditionality' of assistance, although the role of conditionality in preventing future moral hazard is not usually explicitly spelled out.[18]

Invoking the opinion of the ECB on the draft amendment to Art. 136 TFEU,[19] the Court sets out two criteria which financial assistance by a stability mechanism such as the ESM must meet in order to be compatible with Art. 125(1). First, it must be indispensable for safeguarding the financial stability of the euro area as a whole, i.e. the higher objective of economic-policy provisions; and, second, it must be subject to strict conditions (para. 136). As may be recalled, the Court defined through literal interpretation the assistance which is in any case prohibited and which even the second-order telos cannot justify. The summarising paragraph of *Pringle* combines this definition and the teleological determination of other, justifiable assistance: "Article 125 TFEU

---

[18] Another means to thwart moral hazard consists of involving the private sector in sharing the burden in rescue operations through so-called bail-in.

[19] Opinion of the European Central Bank of 17 March 2011 on a draft European Council Decision amending Article 136 of the Treaty on the Functioning of the European Union with regard to a stability mechanism for Member States whose currency is the euro (CON/2011/24), [2011] OJ C140/8.

does not prohibit the granting of financial assistance by one or more Member States to a Member State which remains responsible for its commitments to its creditors provided that the conditions attached to such assistance are such as to prompt that Member State to implement a sound budgetary policy" (para. 137).

The Court does not explicitly tie strict conditionality to general moral hazard but to inducing the beneficiary state to prudent fiscal policy. The argument seems to be that, first, moral hazard retains its relevance even when retreat from stringent bailout prohibition is constitutionally permitted. But, second, strict conditionality is needed in order to restrict the ensuing moral hazard. The conditions laid down in the Memoranda of Understanding imposed on beneficiary states have required spending cuts and other measures considered necessary for reducing budgetary deficits and government indebtedness, as well as lowering the price of credit. Hence, through its conditionality, financial assistance arguably pursues the very same objectives which the no-bailout clause – and, it may be added, the excessive deficit procedure under Art. 126 TFEU – is expected, but has not managed, to achieve. According to this line of reasoning, financial assistance can only be a temporary measure, aiming at (re-)establishing in the beneficiary state the circumstances where Arts. 125 and 126 can reassume their role in guaranteeing the fiscal discipline which financial stability in the euro area requires. The Court's reasoning, such as we have reconstructed it, is open to the criticism that the potential contradiction between the second-order telos and the primary objective of the no-bailout clause is addressed merely in relation to the recipient state, but not with regard to a more general moral hazard.

In our view, a cogent constitutional justification of the measures undertaken to resolve the Eurozone crisis in the face of the no-bailout clause of Art. 125(1) TFEU presupposes resort to a two-level teleology and the dialectic between the first- and second-order objectives. We also agree with the ECJ, AG Kokott and the academic discussants on the primary objective of the no-bailout clause: inducement of Member States to budgetary discipline and prudent fiscal policy through elimination of the moral hazard connected with mutualisation of debt. Still, we see problems in the Court's arguments; problems which relate to definition of the higher objective and the way the potential contradiction between the first- and second-order telos is supposed to be resolved.

The objective of preserving the financial stability of the euro area as a whole has been the main justification for emergency measures and mechanisms ever since the first Greek rescue package.[20] Yet, when the crisis broke out and the hectic experimentation with rescue packages and stability mechanisms started, the objective had no textual support in the Treaties. The Treaty provisions on EMU do enshrine a stability objective but that is not the financial stability of the euro area as a whole but price stability as the primary objective of common monetary policy, falling under the responsibility of the ECB. In the Stability and Growth Pact, too, 'stability' was understood as price stability and sound public finances as a means to achieve it. The Resolution of the European Council of 17 June 1997 (97/C 236/01) was quite explicit in the subordination of fiscal supervision to price stability as the primary objective of monetary policy. The European Council underlined "the importance of safeguarding sound government finances as a means to strengthening the conditions for price stability and for strong sustainable growth conducive to employment creation", and declared it "necessary to ensure that national budgetary policies support stability oriented monetary policies".

Introducing the objective of the financial stability of the euro area as a whole in order to justify rescue packages and mechanisms must be regarded as a legal innovation. It was only provided with explicit institutional support by *Pringle*, as well as by the amendment to Art. 136, which inserted the concept in a slightly different form in the text of the Treaty.[21] At issue is an important modification of the European macroeconomic constitution, although the Court does not spell this out. Financial stability of the euro area as a whole has taken the place

---

[20] In their statement Euro Group Ministers concurred "with the Commission and the ECB that market access for Greece is not sufficient and that providing a loan is warranted to safeguard financial stability in the euro area as a whole". See Eurogroup (2010), 'Draft Statement', 2 May 2010. Correspondingly, the EFSF was established "in order to financially support euro-area Member States in difficulties caused by exceptional circumstances beyond such euro-area Member States' control with the aim of safeguarding the financial stability of the euro area as a whole and of its Member States" (Recital 1 of the Preamble to the EFSF Framework Treaty). In turn, the Treaty on the ESM defines the purpose of the ESM in the following terms: "The purpose of the ESM shall be to mobilise funding and provide stability support under strict conditionality, appropriate to the financial assistance instrument chosen, to the benefit of ESM Members which are experiencing, or are threatened by, severe financing problems, if indispensable to safeguard the financial stability of the euro area as a whole and of its Member States" (Art. 3).

[21] Interestingly enough, in the Preamble to Regulation (EU) No. 1175/2011 of the European Parliament and of the Council of 16 November 2011 amending Council Regulation (EC) No. 1466/97 on the strengthening of the surveillance of budgetary positions and the surveillance and coordination of economic policies, [2011] OJ

of price stability as the second-order telos of the provisions on EMU aiming at ensuring prudent fiscal policy in Member States.

Another problem afflicting the Court's reasoning in *Pringle* concerns conceptual clarity: what 'financial stability of the euro area as a whole' exactly means is far from evident. None of the legal or political instruments employing it, *Pringle* included, have made any attempt at a definition. The wide variety of European measures taken to re-establish financial stability also testifies to the vagueness of the concept. Yet one can surmise that the concept reacts to two fundamental failures in the economic assumptions underlying the Maastricht principles of the European macroeconomic constitution: underestimation of, on the one hand, the intertwinement of public finances and private financial institutions and, on the other hand, the importance of cross-border financial relationships, due inter alia to the liberation of capital markets and the common monetary-policy framework. Obviously, the financial stability of the euro area as a whole is intended to be a broad concept comprising both sovereigns and private financial institutions, and heeding cross-border financial integration. It presumably disregards financial-stability considerations related to individual institutions or even Member States when these do not have broader financial stability consequences. It may be that particularly in the context of rescue operations and stability mechanisms, the precise meaning of 'financial stability' was intentionally kept open. In order to avoid moral hazard, financial institutions and Member States were left in ambiguity with regard to possible financial rescue measures.

The solution *Pringle* offers to the potential tension between rescue operations aiming at the higher-level objective of financial stability of the euro area as a whole and the future realisation of the primary objective of eliminating moral hazard merits a critical comment, too. *Pringle*, again flanked by the amendment to Art. 136 TFEU, has constitutionalised the requirement of strict conditionality. Should this be interpreted in terms of austerity programmes, such as those Greece, Portugal, Ireland and Cyprus had to accept? An affirmative answer

---

L306/12, the objective of the Stability and Growth Pact was rendered in a revised form, by adding a reference to financial stability which the Resolution of the European Council of 17 June 1997 did not contain. According to Recital 3, "the SGP is based on the objective of sound government finances as a means of strengthening the conditions for price stability and for strong sustainable growth underpinned by financial stability, thereby supporting the achievement of the Union's objectives for sustainable growth and employment".

seems to be suggested both by the epithet 'strict' and the Court's explicit reference to the opinion of the ECB, one of the members of the Troika, devising and monitoring the MoUs of the beneficiary states. A further consideration points in the same direction: in order for the conditionality to fulfil its future preventive role, it should evidently not only attempt to reinstate fiscal prudence and to tackle the macroeconomic root causes of fiscal problems, but also include a punitive element, making assistance unattractive for sovereigns and national constituencies. Yet, such an interpretation would have wide-reaching implications. It would constitutionalise a highly controversial economic policy aiming for economic flexibility. This policy is mostly based on supply-side measures, such as reducing labour costs. Imposing such measures from the outside have far-reaching consequences for national democratic procedures and cooperation between social partners.

In sum, *Pringle*, taken together with the amendment to Art. 136 TFEU, not only constitutionally sanctioned the rescue packages and mechanisms produced by the experimentalism of the preceding two and a half years. It also confirmed that the macroeconomic constitution has been complemented and modified with three new elements: first, with regard to Member State fiscal policy, the macroeconomic constitution provides not only for crisis prevention but for crisis management as well; second, preventive fiscal policy constraints and crisis resolution share the same higher objective of the financial stability of the euro area as a whole; third, crisis resolution by means of financial assistance for the purpose of such financial stability is only permitted if it is accompanied by strict conditionality.

Finally, to conclude our examination of the no-bailout clause in light of *Pringle*, we want to draw attention to some arguments which the Court did not employ but which have been embraced in previous contributions to constitutional discourse; as is well known to lawyers, what a court does not say may tell as much as what it does say. First, some academic debaters have derived from the scattered references in the Treaties a master-principle of solidarity for which they claim relevance even in the constitutional assessment of financial assistance to Member States hit by fiscal crisis.[22] AG Kokott, too, invoked solidarity

---

[22] The solidarity argument is discussed by, inter alia, C. Calliess (2011).

as a general constitutional principle which militates against an extensive interpretation of the no-bailout clause (paras. 142–3).

Indeed, solidarity is one of the foundational EU-law principles addressing the relationships among Member States and underpinning the whole European project. It is evoked in the Preamble to the TEU, where the Contracting parties proclaim their desire to deepen the solidarity between their peoples, and Art. 3(3) TEU includes promoting solidarity among Member States in the objectives of the Union. In turn, pursuant to Art. 120(1) TFEU, Member States are supposed to conduct their economic policies with a view to contributing to the achievement of the objectives of the Union, as defined in Art. 3 TEU. In addition, Member State solidarity is expressly referred to in Art. 122(1) TFEU, located in the chapter on economic policy.[23] Yet, from the quite vague principle of solidarity we find it difficult to derive exact legal consequences in individual legal doctrinal issues.[24] We also find it rather artificial to conceive of recent rescue operations in the euro area as a token of assisting states' solidarity towards beneficiary states. Arguably, the motives of the former have been rather egotistic: to avoid contagion and repercussions inflicting their own economies. Nor should one close one's eyes to the impact in big euro states of lobbying by national financial institutions with investments in the bonds of crisis states. There is not much solidarity in such background factors. It would also be a tough task to convince the peoples of the beneficiary states that the socially very harsh austerity programmes are a token of European solidarity.

Second, in *Pringle* the Court avoided any reference to unwritten emergency powers – a *Unionnotstand* and consequent *Notrecht* – as a justification for rescue measures. Such a reference would have implied that the Court admits that these measures contravened the constitutional prohibition on bailouts but argues that they were warranted by the unwritten constitutional principle of emergency powers. This argument has been put forth in German academic debates, sometimes expressly

---

[23] Without prejudice to any other procedures provided for in the Treaties, the Council, on a proposal from the Commission, may decide, in a spirit of solidarity between Member States, upon the measures appropriate to the economic situation, in particular if severe difficulties arise in the supply of certain products, notably in the area of energy.

[24] AG Kokott did not, either, infer from the solidarity principle any obligation to financial assistance. Her point was that an extensive reading of the no-bailout clause would prevent voluntary assistance in the spirit of solidarity.

alluding to Carl Schmitt's theorising on the state of exception.[25] The most alarmist tones of European political leaders, too, bear resemblance to emergency-law thinking: *Not kennt kein Gebot* or – to use the Latin expression – *necessitas not habet legem*.[26] The Court's particular combination of literal interpretation and two-level teleology exhausts the need to resort to unwritten emergency law. We agree with this strategy: opening the door for emergency-law reasoning is as risky in a transnational as in a national setting, due to the threat of relativising the legal effect of Treaty law. Yet as we have shown – and shall continue to show – keeping the door closed may presuppose argumentation which entails other kinds of risk, such as introducing constitutional norms with little or non-existent institutional support in the text of the Treaties.

Financial assistance under Art. 122(2) TFEU

The emphasis in rescue packages and mechanisms has lain on intergovernmental arrangements: bilateral loans (the first Greek rescue package) and assistance from intergovernmental funds, such as the EFSF and the ESM. Financial assistance by the Union has played but a minor role. The framework of Union assistance has been provided by the European Financial Stability Mechanism (EFSM), which has been activated in rescue operations involving Ireland and Portugal but not, interestingly enough, Greece. EFSM was established on 11 May 2010 through Regulation 407/2010 as part of the 'rescue umbrella', which also comprised the EFSF as an inter-governmental financial institution – a 'Special Purpose Vehicle' – under private law and a commitment on assistance from the IMF. As a legal basis, Regulation 407/2010 invoked Art. 122(2) TFEU.

The no-bailout clause of Art. 125 TFEU is explicitly addressed to both the Union and the Member States. Neither the Union nor a Member State is to be "liable for or assume the commitments" of a(nother) Member State. In contrast, Art. 122(2) regulates merely financial assistance by the EU: "Where a Member State is in difficulties or is seriously threatened with severe difficulties caused by natural disasters or exceptional occurrences beyond its control, the Council, on a proposal from

---

[25] In his analysis, Ulrich Hufeld detects three instances of *Verfassungsdurchbrechung* (breaking the Constitution). The Union level *Verfassungsdurchbrechung* consists of violation of the no-bailout clause. U. Hufeld (2011). On *Unionnotstand* see the discussion in F. Schorkopf (2011), pp. 341–3; C. Calliess (2011), pp. 271–3.

[26] Supra note 17.

the Commission, may grant, under certain conditions, Union financial assistance to the Member State concerned."

Art. 122(2) TFEU is a competence provision, which, in accordance with the principle of conferral enshrined in Art. 5(2) TEU,[27] empowers the Union (the Council) with a competence it would not otherwise possess. Accordingly, in *Pringle* the Court emphasises that Art. 122 TFEU deals solely with financial assistance by the Union and not that by the Member States (para. 118). It is no accident that Member States are not mentioned in Art. 122(2). Member States, acting individually or in concert, do not need an explicit competence basis in the Treaties. They are free to act, provided that no legal obstacles deriving from EU law exist.[28] Their competence is assessed not on the principle of conferral but on the principle of comprehensive powers.[29] Union and Member State competences are appraised from opposite premises. This also entails that no direct legal conclusions with regard to Member State financial assistance can be drawn from Art. 122(2). Member State measures fall outside the scope of this article, and for instance an *e contrario* argument deriving a prohibition of Member State assistance from Art. 122(2) would be wholly groundless. If the legality of Member State assistance is rejected, this has to be supported with arguments drawn from elsewhere. Two possible grounds exist: the no-bailout clause of Art. 125(1) TFEU and the principle of pre-emption. The former potential obstacle we have already discussed, and the latter we shall examine below in this chapter.

[27] According to Art. 5(1), "the limits of Union competences are governed by the principle of conferral". In turn, Art. 5(2) lays down that "under the principle of conferral, the Union shall act only within the limits of the competences conferred upon it by the Member States in the Treaties to attain the objectives set out therein".

[28] This point has been made by many in academic debate, see, e.g., C. Calliess (2011), pp. 213 and 222. It was also spelled out by AG Kokott in para. 125:

> In particular however, measures taken by the Union and measures taken by the Member States are in different contexts. For Union measures, in accordance with Article 4(1) and the first sentence of Article 5(1) TEU, the principle of conferred powers applies, while for the actions of Member States the principle of comprehensive power applies. In that light, Articles 122(2) and 143(2) TFEU empower the Union to grant credit facilities; a power which the Member States on the other hand do not need. To infer, from the fact that powers are conferred on the Union to grant credit facilities and that those powers are subject to restrictive conditions, that there is a comprehensive prohibition preventing the Member States from granting loans would be at variance with the principles relating to the division of powers between Member States and the Union.

[29] This is a principle not explicitly mentioned in the Treaties but evoked by, for instance, AG Kokott in para. 125.

Thus, when discussing the interpretation and implications of Art. 122(2) TFEU, attention should be restricted to Union measures. Is this article an adequate competence basis for Regulation 407/2010, establishing the EFSM, and assistance channelled through this mechanism? At first glance, with its explicit reference to natural disasters, the article seems to address other types of 'exceptional occurrence' than economic or fiscal crises. Yet, legislative history ties emergency assistance under present Art. 122(2) TFEU to the balance-of-payments assistance which the Treaty of Rome had already facilitated. Art. 108 of the Rome Treaty had provided for the possibility of the Council granting mutual assistance, including credits by other Member States, to a Member State facing difficulties in its balance of payments. The provision was retained by the Maastricht Treaty and found its way into the TFEU as Art. 143. Yet its scope has been narrowed down so that it only applies to non-euro states ('Member States with a derogation'). In pre-Maastricht negotiations, the Delors Commission and economically weaker Member States pushed for allowing for financial assistance even to Member States which had already joined EMU. In turn, Germany advocated a no-bailout clause and abolition of even the existing possibility of financial assistance to Member States suffering from difficulties in their balance of payments. The end-result was a compromise, which included the no-bailout clause (Art. 125(1) TFEU) but also facilitated financial assistance, not only to non-euro states (Art. 143 TFEU), but to euro states as well (Art. 122(2) TFEU)).[30] Indeed, in drafting and negotiating what became the Maastricht Treaty, the general presumption seems to have been that the emergency provision would also cover financial assistance to a Member State struck by an economic crisis.

In light of this legislative history, excluding economic crises in general or fiscal crises in particular *a priori* from the scope of application of Art. 122(2) TFEU appears to be ungrounded. This history also highlights the connection between assistance under Art. 122(2) and under Art. 143 TFEU. The connection was made explicit in Regulation 407/2010, which includes two references to Regulation 332/2002, establishing a facility providing medium-term financial assistance for Member States' balances of payments under the present Art. 143 TFEU. The Preamble to Regulation 407/2010 declares that the existing facility providing medium-term financial assistance for non-euro-area Member States, as established by

---

[30] U. Häde (2009), pp. 402–3; J.-V. Louis (2010), pp. 981–3; A. de Gregorio Merino (2012), p. 1633.

Regulation 332/2002, should remain in place. In turn, Art. 1 of Regulation 407/2010 requires that in granting assistance, the possible application of the already existing facility providing assistance for non-euro-area Member States' balances of payments be taken into account.

Yet, including fiscal or economic crises in the 'exceptional circumstances' where financial assistance under Art. 122(2) TFEU may be granted does not solve all the constitutional issues involved with the establishment or activation of the EFSM. Again the main question is the relationship of financial assistance to the prohibition on bailouts. In academic debates, different views have been propounded. Some discussants have contended that financial assistance must be regarded as an exception to the no-bailout clause in Art. 125(1) TFEU and that, consequently, Art. 122(2) should be given a narrow interpretation.[31] By contrast, others have argued that Arts. 122(2) and 125(1) stand at the same level, and that the former constitutes a counter-weight rather than an exception to the latter.[32] In *Pringle*, the Court seems to lean towards the latter reading: "If Article 125 TFEU prohibited any financial assistance whatever by the Union or the Member States to another Member State, Article 122 TFEU would have had to state that it derogated from Article 125 TFEU" (para. 131). We do not find this argument very persuasive: a provision may be legally construable as an exception to another provision even if it does not expressly declare itself to be a derogation.

Member States' fiscal liability as one of the main Maastricht principles of the European economic constitution underlies Art. 125(1) TFEU. Financial assistance by the Union under Art. 122(2) for the purpose of resolving a sovereign debt crisis diverges from this principle, and in this sense it constitutes an exception. Although this does not warrant the conclusion that such financial assistance would inevitably contradict the no-bailout clause, in interpreting Art. 122(2) the no-bailout clause of Art. 125(1) must be taken into account, and a reading which harmonises the two provisions should be sought. If the two-order teleology of the no-bailout clause, embraced by *Pringle* with regard to Member State assistance, is accepted, it is relevant in assessing Union assistance under Art. 122(2) TFEU as well.

Indeed, in line with the justifications and criteria for rescue measures and mechanisms in general, Regulation 407/2010 invokes the principle of financial stability. However, this is expressed in even wider

---

[31] See, e.g., K. Fassbender (2010), pp. 800–1; L. Knopp (2010), pp. 1780–1.
[32] See, e.g., U. Häde (2009), p. 403; J.-V. Louis (2010), p. 983.

terms than the second-order telos whose constitutional status was later confirmed by *Pringle* and the amendment to Art. 136 TFEU. At issue is the financial stability of not only the euro area but the Union as a whole. This accords with the definition of potential recipients, which includes all the Member States and not only those belonging to the euro area. The Preamble to the Regulation evokes "a serious threat to the financial stability of the European Union as a whole", which necessitates "a Union stabilisation mechanism to preserve financial stability in the European Union". Art. 1, which defines the aim and scope of the Regulation, also gives expression to the comprehensive, supra-state objective of assistance.[33] The Regulation establishes the conditions and procedures under which Union financial assistance is granted "with a view to preserving the financial stability of the European Union". Such a comprehensive second-order telos is afflicted by problems of lacking support either in the text of Treaties or in underlying principles; problems which we have already addressed when discussing assistance by Member States. Moreover, the wording of Art. 122(2) focuses exclusively on circumstances in the respective state. However, this is not a problem in so far as the more comprehensive criterion of the financial stability of the European Union as a whole does not replace but complements country-specific preconditions.[34]

[33] Interestingly enough, Art. 1 also establishes a link between financial assistance under Art. 122(2), available to all Member States, and assistance under Art. 143, available only to non-Euro states:

> With a view to preserving the financial stability of the European Union, this Regulation establishes the conditions and procedures under which Union financial assistance may be granted to a Member State which is experiencing, or is seriously threatened with, a severe economic or financial disturbance caused by exceptional occurrences beyond its control, taking into account the possible application of the existing facility providing medium-term financial assistance for non-euro-area Member States' balances of payments, as established by Regulation (EC) No. 332/2002.

[34] This is in line with the presuppositions of financial assistance under Art. 143 TFEU, which also sets out both country-specific and more general criteria, although these are not related to financial stability:

> where a Member State with a derogation is in difficulties or is seriously threatened with difficulties as regards its balance of payments either as a result of an overall disequilibrium in its balance of payments, or as a result of the type of currency at its disposal, and where such difficulties are liable in particular to jeopardise the functioning of the internal market or the implementation of the common commercial policy ...

However, even if financial assistance under Art. 122(2) TFEU could be brought into harmony with the no-bailout clause through a common (higher) objective, the moral hazard issue still retains its significance, both with regard to the recipient state and its creditors and with regard to other Member States and their creditors. Here the criteria for assistance expressly set out in the article appear to offer a solution. Granting assistance presupposes that the exceptional occurrences causing already realised or seriously threatening difficulties are 'beyond the control' of the Member State at issue. Art. 1 of Regulation 407/2010 specifies the difficulties at issue as a severe economic or financial disturbance and repeats the requirement of exceptional occurrences beyond the control of the afflicted Member State: "financial assistance may be granted to a Member State which is experiencing, or is seriously threatened with, a severe economic or financial disturbance caused by exceptional occurrences beyond its control ..." In academic legal debates, much ink has been spilled over the question whether financial assistance may be granted to a Member State whose fiscal crisis is not a mere consequence of external factors but at least partly self-induced through reckless fiscal policy and maybe even conscious statistical falsifications. Two readings of Art. 122(2) seem plausible. Some commentators have claimed that assistance is excluded where the crisis is self-induced, because then the background developments have not been beyond the control of the Member State.[35] According to the alternative reading, the requirement of 'beyond the control' relates to the situation 'as is' and not to preceding developments. Following this interpretation, what is essential for the Council's competence to grant assistance is a Member State's inability to cope with the crisis, which the market discipline pursued by the no-bailout clause or the excessive deficit procedure have not been able to prevent.[36] For moral hazard, what is decisive is the path towards the crisis. Yet the discussion also reflects the uncertainty of macroeconomic analysis, which should call for caution in deriving legal consequences from such an analysis. In all economic situations, a large number of factors lie beyond the control of the state. Correspondingly, one can always point to potential measures that the state could have taken, all with uncertain economic impacts.

---

[35] See, e.g., K. Fassbender (2010), p. 800; L. Knopp (2010), p. 1780.
[36] See the discussion in C. Calliess (2011), pp. 242–3, where he ultimately rejects this interpretation.

In the Preamble to Regulation 407/2010 establishing the EFSM, any reference to self-causation is avoided. The crisis is exclusively attributed to external factors: "a serious deterioration in the international economic and financial environment" and "the unprecedented global financial crisis and economic downturn that have hit the world over the last two years have seriously damaged economic growth and financial stability and provoked a strong deterioration in the deficit and debt positions of the Member States". Such an account of the causality might be understood to hint at the relevance of the afflicted state's contribution to the crisis, when considering financial assistance.[37] On the other hand, the Preamble focuses on the general situation in the Union, and relates the 'beyond control' criterion, too, to Member States in general, and not to a particular state in distress, as does Art. 122(2) TFEU. The deepening of the financial crisis is claimed to have led to a severe deterioration in the borrowing conditions of several Member States so that if the situation is not addressed as a matter of urgency, it seriously threatens the financial stability of the European Union as a whole.

Yet, it should be recalled that Regulation 407/2010 contains general provisions and does not replace case-by-case assessment of the preconditions for assistance. These are set out in Art. 1 of the Regulation, and here the 'beyond control' criterion is expressly linked to the recipient state: the exceptional occurrences causing the severe economic or financial disturbance must lie beyond the control of this state. The EFSM has been activated for assistance to Ireland and Portugal but not to Greece, which is the usual culprit in the debate on self-causation of the crisis. This is perhaps not accidental and may be seen as testifying to the significance of a *culpa* assessment. And if an interpretation is sought which reconciles financial assistance under Art. 122(2), not only with the (postulated) second-order telos, but also with the primary objective of the no-bailout clause, the behaviour of the state at issue can hardly be ignored. The moral hazard viewpoint clearly favours a reading which excludes assistance in the case of a self-induced crisis. Furthermore, such a reading is supported by the wording of both Art. 122(2) TFEU and Art. 1 of Regulation 407/2010: 'beyond control' is attached to the causes of present difficulties and not to these difficulties as such – defined in the latter provision as a severe economic or financial disturbance. Note, however, that even if financial assistance by the Union under

---

[37] This account is questionable at least with regard to Greece, which, however, has not received assistance from the EFSM.

Art. 122(2) TFEU is excluded, the constitutional innovations adopted during the crisis may still allow for assistance by Member States. As we showed in the preceding section, *Pringle* has expressly blessed these innovations – the availability of a crisis resolution mechanism, financial stability of the euro area as a whole as a second-order objective and strict conditionality as a prerequisite for assistance.

In line with assistance through intergovernmental facilities, Regulation 407/2010 ties EFSM assistance to conditionality, which, as we have argued, is also a means to cope with the moral-hazard issue. Even Art. 122(2) TFEU lays down that the Council may only grant assistance 'under certain conditions'. It is, though, doubtful that the intention was to require similar conditionality as has now been attached to the rescue packages meant to pull crisis states out of their fiscal predicament. If our interpretation is correct, the 'beyond control' criterion was supposed to prevent the moral-hazard issue from arising in the first place.[38]

So, a strong case can be made that Art. 122(2) TFEU authorises such financial support as has been channelled to Ireland and Portugal. Yet, this conclusion does not efface all constitutional concerns raised by Regulation 407/2010. The Preamble to the Regulation mentions merely Art. 122(2) as its competence basis. However, as the Court points out in *Pringle*, Art. 122(2) confers on the Union the power to grant ad hoc assistance. The Court continues its argument by stating that this provision does not constitute an 'appropriate legal basis' for establishing a permanent stability mechanism of the ESM kind, envisaged in Decision 2011/199 of the European Council (para. 65). This leaves the reader a little perplexed. What should one make of the constitutionality of Regulation 407/2010 and the EFSM in the light of this statement? Does the Regulation, issued under Art. 122(2), not establish a permanent stability mechanism?

A possible interpretation exists which might help to dissolve the perplexity. The EFSM actually does not constitute a distinct stability fund with its own institutional structure as does the ESM. It can be characterised as a procedure to be followed in granting and financing ad hoc assistance; such a 'mechanism' cannot be equated with a stability fund in the likeness of the ESM or its predecessor the EFSF. In addition, the Regulation specifies the substantive conditions of ad hoc assistance. Here

---

[38] See, however, A. de Gregorio Merino (2012), p. 1634, where the phrase "under certain conditions" is explicitly linked to the strict conditionality aimed to prevent moral hazard.

a parallel can be drawn to Regulation 332/2002 which regulates the facility providing balance of payments assistance to non-euro Member States and which is expressly evoked in Regulation 407/2010. But this does not seem to be the Court's argument. The Court claims that the EFSM has been established to attend *temporarily* to the tasks which the ESM will take over. Yet, nowhere in Regulation 407/2010 or the Conclusions of the Ecofin Council meeting of 9–10 May 2010 can support be found for the merely temporary character of the EFSM.[39] Evidently, the Court needed to claim the temporary nature of the EFSM in order to be able to dispel any doubt that by establishing the ESM, Member States would have entered a field pre-empted by EU legislation (see below).

The constitutional situation is further complicated by the fact that Art. 122(2) is confined to creating a competence which the Council may use directly under the Treaty. It does not refer to complementary secondary legislation, nor does any other delegation in the TFEU cover Art. 122(2).[40] Arguably, to justify the Regulation in the light of the principle of conferral, recourse should have also been made to the auxiliary competence established by the flexibility clause of Art. 352(1) TFEU, which the Preamble does not allude to.[41] Such recourse would seem to have been necessary even for the competence the Regulation creates for the Commission to finance loans issued by the EFSM by borrowing on the capital markets or from financial institutions. Again, a parallel can be made with Regulation 332/2002 on financial assistance to non-euro states with a balance of payments problem. Art. 143(2) TFEU empowers the Council to adopt directives or decisions laying down the conditions and details of assistance. This delegation does not cover Regulations. Indeed, according to its Preamble, Regulation 332/2002 has been issued under Art. 308 TEC (present Art. 352 TFEU).

---

[39] Pursuant to the conclusions of the Ecofin Council, "the mechanism will stay in place as long as needed to safeguard financial stability".

[40] Art. 125(2) sets out that "the Council, on a proposal from the Commission and after consulting the European Parliament, may, as required, specify definitions for the application of the prohibitions referred to in Articles 123 and 124 and in this Article".

[41] Art. 352(1) TFEU provides that

> if action by the Union should prove necessary, within the framework of the policies defined in the Treaties, to attain one of the objectives set out in the Treaties, and the Treaties have not provided the necessary powers, the Council, acting unanimously on a proposal from the Commission and after obtaining the consent of the European Parliament, shall adopt the appropriate measures.

In German debates, U. Häde (2009), p. 403, and C. Calliess (2011), pp. 246–7, have pointed to the necessity of invoking Art. 352(1) (former Art. 308(1)).

In *Pringle*, the Court does discuss even recourse to Art. 352 TFEU as a competence basis for establishing a Union stability mechanism. The Court states that "as to whether the Union could establish a stability mechanism comparable to that envisaged by Decision 2011/199 on the basis of Article 352 TFEU, suffice it to say that the Union has not used its powers under that article and that, in any event, that provision does not impose on the Union any obligation to act" (para. 67).[42] Read together with the Court's rejection of Art. 122(2) TFEU as a competence basis for establishing a permanent stability mechanism, this again raises some perplexity. It can only be dissolved by assuming that the Court does not treat the EFSM as "a stability mechanism comparable to that envisaged by Decision 2011/199".

The significance of the amendment to Art. 136 TFEU

The amendment to Art. 136 TFEU is closely intertwined with establishment of the ESM. The decision of the European Council to initiate the amendment procedure was taken at the same meeting of 28–29 October 2010 where the need to create a permanent stability mechanism was recognised. The exact motive for the Treaty amendment remains unclear. As we shall show below, not very much help is offered by the text of either the amendment itself or the European Council Decision 2011/199, through which the amendment was formally adopted following the simplified procedure under Art. 48(6) TEU. Most probably debates in Member States, especially in Germany, on the legality of the Greek rescue package and the EFSF played a role. In Germany, applications claiming unconstitutionality with regard to the Basic Law but having at least indirect implications for the European economic constitution, too, had been submitted to the Constitutional Court. Yet the German Government also wanted to retain the no-bailout provision as it was. Accordingly, in October 2010 the European Council invited its president, Van Rompuy, to consult the Member States "on a limited treaty change required to that effect (creating a permanent stability mechanism), not modifying Article 125 TFEU".[43]

---

[42] See even para. 105 where the Court states that "neither Article 122(2) TFEU nor any other provision of the EU and FEU Treaties confers a specific power on the Union to establish a permanent stability mechanism such as the ESM".

[43] European Council (2010a), 'Conclusions', 28–29 October 2010, para. 2.

The unlawfulness of the amendment was one of Mr Pringle's central claims before the Irish High Court, and the validity of Decision 2011/199 was the first of the two questions the High Court referred to the ECJ for a preliminary ruling. The question had two aspects, the first of them being whether the Amendment met the criteria for the simplified procedure under Art. 48(6) TEU and, in particular, whether it involved an increase in the competences conferred on the Union in the Treaties. This was a procedural issue but required substantive discussion. So did the other aspect, too, which concerned the harmony of the amendment with the Treaties and general principles of EU law.

The simplified procedure allows the European Council to adopt a Treaty amendment under two substantive conditions.[44] First, only the provisions of Part III of the TFEU may be amended. And, second, the amendment may not increase the competences of the Union. As regards the first requirement, the Court did not content itself with noting that the amended Art. 136 was located in Part III TFEU. It also assessed whether the amendment affected Treaty regulations falling outside this Part, even if not formally changing them. In particular the Court examined Union competences in monetary and economic policy. The Court's conclusion was that the exclusive competence in monetary policy in the euro area, which the Union possessed under Art. 3(1) TEU, was not affected. Establishing a stability mechanism as envisaged in the amendment did not fall within monetary but economic policy and served to complement the new regulatory framework for strengthened economic governance of the Union (paras. 58–63). Consequently, the Court appraised whether the amendment affected Union competence in the area of coordination of Member State economic policies, as this competence is defined in Arts. 2(3) and 5(1) TFEU. The Court noted that the Treaties do not confer any specific power on the Union to establish a stability mechanism of the kind envisaged by Decision 2011/199. The Court also invoked its position that the emergency provision in Art. 122(2) is not applicable for creating a permanent mechanism for safeguarding the financial stability of the euro area as a whole. The Court did not engage in detailed discussion of the residual powers established by the flexibility clause Art. 352 but only emphasised that in any case this provision does not entail any obligation for the Union to act. The

---

[44] In the procedural respect, the European Council must act by unanimity, and consult the European Parliament and the Commission, as well as the ECB in the case of institutional changes in the monetary area.

Court invoked the principle of conferral applicable to the Union's powers, and concluded that the amendment does not interfere with Union competences in economic policy. In turn, under their comprehensive powers, Member States are entitled to conclude an agreement to establish a stability mechanism of the kind envisaged by Art. 1 of Decision 2011/199. Although the Court does not spell it out, its reasoning seems to be premised on the possibility of a pre-emptive effect of Union measures and competences on Member State freedom to act under national or international law. Interestingly enough, the Court evokes a second possible source of restrictions, too: namely, Member States general obligation to comply with EU law. This obligation can be related to the duty of loyalty or sincere cooperation, at present enshrined in Art. 4(3) TEU. We shall return to these issues.

The Court still had to establish that the amendment does not increase the competences of the Union. Here, too, the Court first invokes the principle of comprehensive powers, applicable to Member States. Member States were entitled to create a stability mechanism even regardless of the amendment; the amendment merely confirms this power (para. 73). What, however, is crucial for the conditions set out in Art. 48(6) TFEU is that the amendment "does not confer any new competence on the Union" and that it "creates no legal basis for the Union to be able to undertake any action which was not possible before". This is the general position taken in academic discussion, too: the amendment does not create any new competence either for the Union or the Member States, but merely confirms the power the latter possess as part of their general competence under international law. This view was also adhered to in establishing the European Stability Mechanism. The Treaty on the ESM not only was concluded and ratified but even entered into force before entry into force of the amendment; consequently, the amendment cannot have served as its legal basis. In its Preamble, the TESM does allude to the amendment but not as a competence basis.[45]

We have only one difficulty with the dominant view and especially the reasoning of the Court in *Pringle*. The Court does not examine the possible *indirect* effects the amendment may have on Union competences.[46] These indirect effects may especially derive from the objective

---

[45] As AG Kokott reported in para. 65 of her view, both the European Council and the intervening Member States submit that the amendment was solely designed to provide clarification.

[46] In this respect, AG Kokott is much more comprehensive in her argumentation.

of the 'stability of the euro area as a whole', which the amendment enshrined in the text of the TFEU. The Court would probably have claimed that at issue is not a new objective but one that has underlain the macroeconomic constitution from the very beginning. By contrast, as regards confirmation of Member State competences, we see no reason to disagree with the prevailing view, consecrated in *Pringle*. But this view raises a corollary question: why was an explicit acknowledgement of Member State competence deemed necessary? Why was the treaty amendment procedure, which even under Art. 48(6) TEU is complicated enough, launched in the first place?

Decision 2011/99 is not very helpful in our search for an explanation. Rather, it seems to add to the confusion. In the Preamble to the Decision, the European Council explicitly states that the amendment does not increase the competences conferred on the Union in the Treaties. This corresponds to *Pringle* and the majority academic opinion.[47] What causes puzzlement is the reference to Art. 122(2) TFEU in the Preamble. The European Council first states that the permanent stability mechanism "will provide the necessary tool for dealing with such cases of risk to the financial stability of the euro-area as a whole as have been experienced in 2010, and hence help preserve the economic and financial stability of the Union itself". Then it declares to have "agreed that, as this mechanism is designed to safeguard the financial stability of the euro-area as a whole, Art. 122(2) of the TFEU will no longer be needed for such purposes". Therefore, the European Council has also agreed that this provision "should not be used for such purposes". Yet, the amendment does not regulate Union financial assistance, which Art. 122(2) TFEU addresses, but Member State assistance, which, in turn, is not covered by this Treaty provision. As the Preamble to Decision 2011/99 makes clear, Union assistance cannot be based on the new Art. 136(3) TFEU. Here recourse to Art. 122(2) – and possibly also to Art. 352 TFEU – is still needed. By contrast, Member State assistance does not require explicit authorisation by the Treaty, nor did Art. 122(2) ever function as a legal basis for such assistance.

Perhaps reference to Art. 122(2) TFEU in the Preamble and the very instigation of the amendment procedure must simply be explained by the confusion which in late 2010 and early 2011 still prevailed as to the constitutionality of both Union and Member State assistance. Perhaps the amendment sought, for its part, merely to dissipate this confusion.

---

[47] See, e.g., A. de Gregorio Merino (2012), p. 1629.

The then uncertainty extended to justifiability of assistance in light of the prohibition on bailouts in Art. 125(1) TFEU. Yet the Preamble is silent on the no-bailout clause. By contrast, in *Pringle* the Court postulates another purpose for the amendment. In the Court's view, the amendment not only confirms Member State competence to create a permanent stability mechanism. It "is further intended to ensure, by providing that the granting of any financial assistance under that mechanism will be made subject to strict conditionality, that the mechanism will operate in a way that will comply with European Union law" (para. 73). As we showed above, in the Court's reasoning, strict conditionality is essential in securing that crisis management, serving the second-order objective of the financial stability of the euro area as a whole, complies with the primary purpose of the no-bailout clause to avert moral hazard and to induce Member States to budgetary discipline. Despite the silence on the delicate issue of the no-bailout clause, it may well be that the amendment was intended to confirm that EU law allows for financial assistance by Member States as an *ultima ratio* in emergency situations, notwithstanding the no-bailout clause in Art. 125(1) TFEU.[48]

Decision 2011/99 preceded *Pringle*, although it only entered in force on 1 May 2013, that is, after the issuance of *Pringle*. Still it is tempting to read the amendment and *Pringle* together and see both these constitutional speech acts as serving the same purpose: sanctifying constitutionally the innovations which legal and institutional experimentation in management of the Eurozone crisis had brought about. The three constitutional innovations we distilled from *Pringle*'s treatment of the no-bailout clause are present in the amendment as well: constitutionalisation of crisis management; postulation of a second-order telos of the (financial) stability of the euro area as a whole; and constitutionalisation of the requirement of strict conditionality, which helps to harmonise financial assistance with the primacy objective of the ban on bailouts. With regard to the postulated second-order telos of the Treaty provisions on EMU, *Pringle*, in harmony with the majority of legal and political documents produced during the crisis, evokes *financial* stability. The amendment, by contrast, has dropped the epithet 'financial' and refers merely to the 'stability of the euro area as a whole'. Perhaps

---

[48] A. de Gregorio Merino (2012), p. 1629 argues that "article 136(3) TFEU provides legal certainty as to the fact that mechanisms of assistance referred to therein (the ESM) are compatible with Article 125 TFEU, as all provisions of the Treaties must be consistent with each other".

too much should not be made of this divergence, which could be purely accidental; this assumption finds corroboration in the fact that when discussing the amendment in *Pringle*, the Court alternates the two terms. But, of course, the wording of the amendment leaves room for a wide reading which includes not only financial but general economic stability too.[49] The future will show whether this leeway will have any legal repercussions.

The pre-emptive effect of EU legislation?

The *Pringle* doctrine of two-order teleology and the dialectic between the higher objective of financial stability and the primary objective of budgetary discipline, levels the hurdle which the no-bailout clause of Art. 125(1) TFEU Art erected to Member State financial assistance. Yet this is not the only possible obstacle which EU law may pose to Member States' acting in their capacity of international- and private-law subjects and under the principle of comprehensive powers. A central argument in Mr Pringle's pleading was related to what can be called the pre-emptive effect of EU legislation.

   The doctrine of pre-emption is an import from federal states, primarily the US.[50] In the context of EU law, it has mainly been elaborated in the literature. By contrast, the ECJ has not explicitly employed it or clarified its normative contents in general terms.[51] The doctrine prohibits action by federated entities if the federation has through its own action pre-empted the issue. The doctrine only finds use where both the federation and the federated entities are competent to act; exclusive competence of either level is omitted from the scope of the doctrine. The general provisions of the TEU and TFEU on the division of competences between the Union and the Member States, complemented by the Protocol on shared competences attached to the Lisbon Treaty, set out the terms for discussing the relevance of the pre-emption doctrine for EU law.

---

[49] See V. Borger (2013), pp. 137–8.
[50] R. Schütze (2006), p. 1034: "The doctrine of pre-emption is a federal theory of normative conflict."
[51] In specific fields, relevant ECJ case law exists, even if the term 'pre-emption' is not employed. This goes especially for foreign relations, where the *ERTA* ruling is the early landmark case. Case 22/70 *Commission v. Council* (ERTA) [1971] ECR 263. On the relevance of ERTA for the pre-emption discussion see J. Weiler (1999), pp. 169–74, and R. Schütze (2012), pp. 329–40.

In the area of exclusive competence of the Union, the starting-point is Member States' non-competence, and no recourse to the doctrine of pre-emption is needed. Art. 2(1) TFEU lays down that "when the Treaties confer on the Union exclusive competence in a specific area, only the Union may legislate and adopt legally binding acts, the Member States being able to do so themselves only if so empowered by the Union or for the implementation of Union acts". If in a particular area no competence at all has been conferred upon the EU, the law is equally clear. As is expressly stated in Arts. 4(1) and 5(2) TEU, competences remain with the Member States, and no pre-emptive EU legislation can exist. In EU law, too, problems can only arise in areas of shared competences. Here the Lisbon Treaty introduced an explicit provision (Art. 2(2) TFEU):

> When the Treaties confer on the Union a competence shared with the Member States in a specific area, the Union and the Member States may legislate and adopt legally binding acts in that area. The Member States shall exercise their competence to the extent that the Union has not exercised its competence. The Member States shall again exercise their competence to the extent that the Union has decided to cease exercising its competence.

In US doctrine, a distinction is made between field, rule and obstacle pre-emption.[52] In field pre-emption, the federation has, simply by taking action, occupied the policy field as a whole; in rule pre-emption, federated entities are precluded from adopting rules which contradict existing federal legislation; whereas in obstacle pre-emption federated entities may not adopt legislation which would hamper realising the objectives of federal legislation.[53] On its face, the provision in Art. 2(2) TFEU does not take any clear position on alternative understandings of pre-emption. Yet the general tone of the provisions on the division of legislative competences between the Union and the Member States points to rejection of the widest reading, i.e. field pre-emption. The subsidiarity principle, as defined in Art. 5(3) TEU, establishes a presumption of Member State action in areas of shared competence; "the Union shall act only if and in so far as the objectives of the proposed action cannot be sufficiently achieved by the Member States, either at central level or at regional and local level, but can rather, by reason of the scale or effects of the proposed action, be better achieved at Union level". Field pre-emption would clearly militate against the presumption of Member State action.

[52] On different accounts of pre-emption, see R. Schütze (2006).
[53] As a succinct discussion see *ibid.*, p. 1038.

Excluding the widest sense of pre-emption finds confirmation in the Protocol on shared competences. The Protocol lays down, with reference to the Treaty provision on shared competence, that "when the Union has taken action in a certain area, the scope of this exercise of competence only covers those elements governed by the Union act in question and therefore does not cover the whole area".[54] 'Area' obviously refers to the areas of shared competence enumerated in Art. 4 TFEU. Yet, it would also be erroneous to restrict pre-emption merely to rule pre-emption which would only restrain Member States from adopting legislation which stands in conflict with EU law. Actually, such an effect would coincide with the principle of the supremacy of EU law, now understood as a principle addressed not only to Member State courts but to Member State legislatures as well. Arguably, the Protocol is intended to exclude Member State action within the scope of the Union act, even in the absence of an outright contradiction. Moreover, Member States' duty of sincere cooperation extends the prohibition on Member State action to what the US doctrine calls obstacle pre-emption: even outside the scope of a Union act, Member States are prohibited to take action which jeopardises achievement of the acts' objectives.[55]

Indeed, legal effects largely analogous to the doctrine of pre-emption can be derived from EU principles of supremacy and sincere cooperation. Hence one might doubt the wisdom of importing the former doctrine to EU law in the first place. As the preceding discussion has made clear, the Treaty bases for assessing use of shared competence are dispersed. Though the pre-emption doctrine by itself does not justify any normative conclusions in EU law, it may be helpful for systematising purposes. Yet, the general relevance of the doctrine does not yet warrant employing it in the area of economic policy.

In *Pringle*, the claimant contended that economic policy is a shared competence, and that Arts. 2(3), 119 to 121 and 129 TFEU confer on

[54] ECJ case law preceding the Lisbon Treaty also seems to have rejected field pre-emption. In its *Bangladesh* ruling on development aid, the Court confirmed that since Community competence in the field of development aid was not exclusive, the Member States remained free to act collectively, individually or jointly with the Community. (Joined Cases C-181/91 and C-248/91 *Parliament v. Council and Commission* [1993] ECR I-3685.) The same argument was employed in *Lomé* (Case C-316/91 *Parliament v. Council* [1994] ECR I-625).

[55] Art. 4(3) TEU lays down, inter alia, that "the Member States shall facilitate the achievement of the Union's tasks and refrain from any measure which could jeopardise the attainment of the Union's objectives".

the Union's institutions the power to coordinate economic policy. Mr Pringle further claimed that the conditionality of stability support by the ESM serves the same function as the recommendations under Arts. 121 (multilateral surveillance) and 126 TFEU (excessive deficit procedure). Therefore, he concluded, the ESM is in breach of Art. 2(2) TFEU, which stipulates that Member States are entitled to act in an area of shared competence only to the extent that the Union has not exercised its competence.

How should we locate EU competences in (non-monetary) economic policy with regard to the distinction between exclusive and shared competences? Both before and after entry into force of the Lisbon Treaty, some authors have characterised economic policy as disguised shared competence, with the clear implication of applicability of the pre-emption doctrine.[56] This position does not seem to stand critical examination.

In the US doctrine of pre-emption, the focus is on legislative acts. At least according to their wording, the Treaty provisions on exclusive and shared competences, too, primarily concern legislation and adoption of other legally binding acts. Reference is to acts which are legally effective within Member States and where pre-emption encroaches on Member State legislative sovereignty. The Treaty provisions at issue focus on legislative competences, which have been in the spotlight of scholarly discussion as well. However, the relevance of these provisions must be extended to Member States' treaty-making power, too. For discussing the division of competences between the Union and the Member States, it does not matter whether the latter adopt legally binding acts acting separately or jointly through agreements *inter se*.[57] The fact that in establishing and administering stability mechanisms, such as the EFSF and the ESM, Member States do not act individually but in concert does not affect the possible applicability of the pre-emption doctrine.

Yet, this doctrine's focus on legally binding acts and legislative sovereignty raises doubts as to its relevance for economic policy. Here the Union's main task is to facilitate coordination among Member States. Both Treaty provisions and secondary legislation, which includes the original Regulations of the Stability and Growth Pact as well as the six- and two-pack, lack direct effect within Member States

---

[56] R. Smits (2005); A. Antoniadis (2011).
[57] For the purposes of the present discussion, treaties involving non-Member States – treaties *cum tertiis* – can be ignored.

and are largely irrelevant for their internal legislative sovereignty. Hence, we are inclined to argue that economic policy should not be assessed in light of the dichotomy of exclusive and shared competences. Significantly enough, in the general provisions of the TFEU the Union's economic policy competencies are regulated outside this division. Art. 2(3) contains the principal provision on coordination of economic policy: "The Member States shall coordinate their economic and employment policies within arrangements as determined by this Treaty, which the Union shall have competence to provide." This provision follows those on exclusive (Art. 2(1)) and shared (Art. 2(2)) competences. The areas of the Union's exclusive competences are enumerated in Art. 3 and shared competences in Art. 4 TFEU. Again economic policy coordination, together with coordination of employment and social policy, is left outside this distinction and subsumed under a specific provision in Art. 5.[58] An additional consideration, related to the specificity of macroeconomics, favours our conclusion: macroeconomic concepts and competences are difficult to define as precisely as applying the dichotomy exclusive and shared competencies would require.

In *Pringle*, the Court considered it unnecessary to examine whether the EU-law concept of shared competence is applicable to economic policy. By contrast, AG Kokott briefly discussed the issue. She clearly leans towards a negative answer, although in the end, she, too, declared that her argument did not necessitate taking a definite position. She draws attention to the wording of the provisions of Arts. 2(3) and 5 TFEU on coordination of economic policy: no competence is established for the Union but instead the Member States are supposed to coordinate their economic policies within the Union. Furthermore, she points to the fact that in Art. 4(2) TFEU, economic policy is not included in the areas of shared competence.

Evidently, EU legislation and other EU measures restrict Member State freedom of action in resolving fiscal and financial crises. Yet, instead of a pre-emption doctrine built on Treaty provisions and the Protocol on shared competence, the restrictions should, more appropriately, be related to the particular EU-law principles of supremacy and sincere cooperation. Supremacy is usually discussed in the context

[58] Art. 5(1) repeats the Member States' obligation to coordinate their economic policies within the Union and adds that "to this end, the Council shall adopt measures, in particular broad guidelines for these policies". It also lays down that "specific provisions shall apply to those Member States whose currency is the euro".

of national courts' duty, in cases before them, to accord precedence to EU law over conflicting national law.[59] Yet, taken together with Member States' duty of sincere cooperation, the principle can be extended to national legislatures as well: these should refrain from enacting legislation contradicting EU law. The duty of sincere cooperation expands the restrictive effects even further: to all measures jeopardising the objectives of EU legislation or other EU measures.[60] In economic policy, the principles of supremacy and sincere cooperation entail normative consequences which come close to what in the pre-emption doctrine has been called rule and obstacle pre-emption. By contrast, they do not give rise to such a prohibition for Member States to take action within the scope of Union measures as seems to derive from the Treaty provisions and the Protocol on shared (legislative) competence, not to speak of anything resembling field pre-emption. But if restrictions exist, they concern both individual and joint Member State action, as does pre-emption in areas of shared competence, too.

In sum, Union financial assistance under Art. 122(2) TFEU, including the conditions attached to it, or secondary legislation or other measures of economic governance under Arts. 121 and 126 TFEU do not prevent Member States from pursuing crisis resolution through intergovernmental agreements under private or international law. For instance, establishing the EFSM through Regulation 407/2010 is not an obstacle to Member States' creating stability mechanisms, such as the EFSF or the ESM, which aim at similar objectives of crisis resolution as the Regulation and Union assistance. Nor do Arts. 121 and 126 TFEU, complemented by secondary legislation, bar provisions in intergovernmental agreements on the conditionality of financial assistance, contrary to what Mr Pringle argued.

Yet, the principles of supremacy and sincere cooperation entail that the intergovernmental agreements or measures taken under them may not contradict EU primary or secondary legislation or other EU measures. This also means that 'strict conditionality' of financial assistance must be in congruence with the country-specific guidance in the multilateral surveillance procedure under Art. 121 and the excessive deficit procedure under Art. 126. Moreover, harmony is required with the conditionality under Regulation 407/2010, establishing the Union's financial stability

---

[59] Here the proper term is actually 'primacy'.
[60] Art. 4(3) TEU lays down, inter alia, that "the Member States shall facilitate the achievement of the Union's tasks and refrain from any measure which could jeopardise the attainment of the Union's objectives".

mechanism EFSM. This conclusion concurs with the ECJ's position in *Pringle*.[61] The Court's reasoning, though, differs from ours. The Court emphasises that "the ESM is not concerned with the coordination of the economic policies of the Member States, but rather constitutes a financing mechanism", and that "the conditionality prescribed ... does not constitute an instrument for the coordination of the economic policies of the Member States" (paras. 110–11). This is not persuasive: certainly, financial assistance falls under economic policy and certainly the Member States coordinate their economic policies when establishing a joint mechanism for providing such assistance through an international agreement.

The Court also postulates for conditionality under the ESM an objective of securing compliance with Union measures. Conditionality would be intended to bring crisis resolution in harmony not only with the primary telos of the no-bailout clause but also with measures of economic policy coordination under Arts. 121 and 126 TFEU (para. 113). The Court's view may appear surprising. No reference to such a general harmonising aim can be found either in European Council Decision 2011/99 on amending Art. 136 TFEU or in the Preamble to the Treaty on the ESM. It is true, though, that the TESM does include a consistency clause, which is generally typical for intergovernmental agreements among Member States, such as the Schengen and Prüm Conventions.[62] Art. 13(3) TESM provides that the Memorandum of Understanding, laying down conditionality, "shall be fully consistent with the measures of economic policy coordination provided for in the TFEU, in particular with any act of European Union law, including any opinion, warning, recommendation or decision addressed to the ESM Member concerned". In turn, Art. 13(4) obliges the Commission to check for consistency before signing the MoU on behalf of the ESM.[63]

---

[61] The Court states in para. 121 that "the Member States remain free to establish a stability mechanism such as the ESM, provided however that, in its operation, that mechanism complies with European Union law and, in particular, with measures adopted by the Union in the area of coordination of the Member States' economic policies".

[62] Convention implementing the Schengen Agreement of 14 June 1985 between the Governments of the States of the Benelux Economic Union, the Federal Republic of Germany and the French Republic on the gradual abolition of checks at their common borders; and the Convention between the Kingdom of Belgium, the Federal Republic of Germany, the Kingdom of Spain, the French Republic, the Grand Duchy of Luxembourg, the Kingdom of the Netherlands and the Republic of Austria on the stepping up of cross-border cooperation, particularly in combating terrorism, cross-border crime and illegal migration.

[63] "The European Commission shall sign the MoU on behalf of the ESM, subject to prior compliance with the conditions set out in paragraph 3." Art. 2(1)(a) of the EFSF

In practice, congruence of conditionality with Union measures has been ensured by including the essential contents of MoUs in Council Decisions under Arts. 126 and 136 (Greece, Spain and Cyprus) or the EFSM Regulation (Ireland and Portugal). Yet, this practice implies that actually the MoUs determine and constrain the contents of Council decisions and not vice versa! In future financial assistance, however, the two-pack provisions on macroeconomic adjustment programmes will be applied. These require that Member States requesting assistance prepare such programmes, which are submitted to the Council for approval. The Commission, in turn, is obliged to ensure that the consequent MoU is in compliance with the programme (see above Chapter 4).

Conferral of new tasks on EU institutions

If Member States are free to establish financial stability mechanisms for the purpose of crisis resolution through intergovernmental agreements, may they also involve EU institutions in these mechanisms? Does not the regulation of Treaty-based EU institutions and their tasks fall under the exclusive competence of EU legislation? This question receives additional weight from the provision in Art. 13(2) TEU which sets out that each EU institution "shall act within the limits of the powers conferred on it in the Treaties, and in conformity with the procedures, conditions and objectives set out in them".[64] This provision extends the principle of conferral, applicable to the Union as a whole under Art. 5(2),

Framework Agreement lays down that the MoU shall be consistent with a decision the Council may adopt under Art. 136(1) TFEU. In addition the Preamble (Recital 2) to the Agreement sets out a more general requirement of consistency: "The conditions attached to the provision of Financial Assistance by EFSF as well as the rules which apply to monitoring compliance must be fully consistent with the Treaty on the Functioning of the European Union and the acts of EU law." The Greek Loan Facility Agreement also involves a provision which implies the primacy of EU law. Art. 6(6) of the Agreement lays down that if "the Court of Justice of the European Union in a final decision decides that this Agreement or the making of the Loans violates European Union law and such violation cannot be remedied then the Facility as a whole (i.e. the Commitments of all of the Lenders hereunder) shall immediately and irrevocably be cancelled".

[64] See P. Craig (2012), p. 2012 where Art. 13(2) TEU is also invoked. AG Kokott, too, in para. 169 defines the issue in the context of the principle of conferral:

It is therefore now necessary to examine whether the tasks laid down in the ESM Treaty for the Commission (Section (a) below), the European Central Bank (Section (b) below) and the Court of Justice (Section (c) below) are in breach of the first

to individual EU institutions as well. All the intergovernmental agreements concluded for coordinating Member State financial assistance confer tasks on EU institutions, mainly the Court and the Commission, but even the ECB. Have the Member States here encroached on an area reserved for the exclusive competence of EU legislation, primarily the Founding Treaties?

In *Pringle*, the applicant contended that Member States may confer new tasks on EU institutions merely through the procedure of enhanced cooperation, regulated in Art. 20 TEU and Arts. 326–34 TFEU. The ECJ rejected the claim. The Court argued, first, that enhanced cooperation may only be established in areas where the Union itself is competent to act and, second, that the Treaties do not grant the Union specific competence to establish a permanent stability mechanism such as the ESM (paras. 167–8). We shall discuss the alleged primacy of enhanced cooperation in the context of the Treaty on Stability, Coordination and Governance (TSCG), where it appears to be even more relevant than in examining intergovernmental stability mechanisms. Suffice it to say now that even if enhanced cooperation were possible, an *e contrario* conclusion that this would be the only way available to Member States to entrust new tasks to Union institutions needs additional justification.

Yet reference to enhanced cooperation may serve as a reminder of the backdrop to the legal issue now under discussion. In the decision-making on launching enhanced cooperation, all the Union institutions which constitute the Union legislator and, through them, all the Member States have a say. If Union institutions are entrusted new tasks through intergovernmental agreements, Union legislative institutions are bypassed, as are non-participating Member States.

We start by examining the constitutionality of involving EU institutions in intergovernmental stability mechanisms from the competence of the Court. Disputes arising from or in the context of the Greek agreements fall under the jurisdiction of the ECJ, which is thus supposed to rule on private-law issues, applying English law. In turn, the EFSF Framework Agreement submits disputes between Member States to the jurisdiction of the ECJ, whereas disputes between one or more Member States and the EFSF belong to the jurisdiction of the Courts of

sentence of Article 13(2) TEU, which provides that each institution is to act within the limits of the powers conferred on it in the Treaties.

Even the Court refers to Art. 13(2) TEU; see para. 153. Yet in accordance with AG Kokott, the Court merely invokes the principle of conferral in the definition of the issue but does not let it affect normative argumentation.

the Grand Duchy of Luxembourg. Finally, in the first phase of dispute settlement in the ESM the Board of Governors decides on the question of interpretation or application which has arisen between an ESM Member and the ESM or between ESM Members. If an ESM Member contests the Board's decision, the dispute will be submitted to the ECJ.

Due to an explicit authorisation by the TFEU, involving the Court does not seem to raise constitutional concerns. Art. 273 TFEU lays down that "the Court of Justice shall have jurisdiction in any dispute between Member States which relates to the subject matter of the Treaties if the dispute is submitted to it under a special agreement between the parties". As the Court stated in *Pringle*, the provisions on the jurisdiction of the ECJ in intergovernmental agreements amount to such 'special agreements'.[65] Furthermore, according to the *Pringle* doctrine, confirmed by the amendment to Art. 136 TFEU, EU constitutional law implies a mechanism not only for preventing fiscal crises but for resolving them, too. Hence, the intergovernmental agreements on stability mechanisms relate to 'a subject matter of the Treaties'. In *Pringle*, the Court also addresses the potential objection that Art. 37(3) of the ESM Treaty also covers disputes between Member States and the ESM, while Art. 273 TFEU merely allows for granting the ECJ jurisdiction in disputes between Member States. Again, it is easy to agree with the Court's reasoning: "… since the membership of the ESM consists solely of Member States, a dispute to which the ESM is party may be considered to be a dispute between Member States within the meaning of Article 273 TFEU" (para. 175).

Let us now turn to the Commission and the ECB. These Union institutions are involved in assessing the need for assistance, as well as negotiating and monitoring compliance with MoUs specifying the conditionality for assistance. As regards the Commission, the Preambles to the Greek Intercreditor Agreement, the EFSF Framework Agreement and the ESM Treaty refer to authorisation by the representatives of all the Member States to entrust the Commission with tasks of implementation.[66] Yet, it is difficult to see what legal significance such authorisations possess. Member

---

[65] The Court argues that "there is no reason, given the objective pursued by that provision (Art. 273 TFEU), why such agreement should not be given in advance, with reference to a whole class of pre-defined disputes, by means of a provision such as Article 37(3) of the ESM Treaty" (para. 172).

[66] Recital 3 of the Preamble to the Intercreditor Agreement: "Representatives of the Member States of the European Union have decided on 5 May 2010 to entrust the Commission with the tasks in relation to coordination and management of the

State representatives have acted under international law. Consequently, the authorisations, too, raise the constitutional problem of sidestepping EU legislation through intergovernmental agreements in assigning new tasks to EU institutions. Inclusion of all Member States – that is, even, non-euro-area states – does not suffice to remove the problem.

In relation to the Commission, a point of reference is provided by two rulings of the ECJ from the early 1990s, *Bangladesh* and *Lomé*. In *Bangladesh*, the Court held that the TEC did not prevent Member States from entrusting the Commission with the task of coordinating their collective action, which was based on an act approved by their representatives meeting in the Council.[67] Correspondingly, in *Lomé* the Court stated that no provision of the Treaty prevented Member States from using, outside its framework, procedural steps drawing on the rules applicable to Community expenditure and from associating Community institutions with the procedure thus set up.[68] In *Pringle*, the Court invoked *Bangladesh* and *Lomé* to support its statement that "it is apparent from the case-law of the Court that the Member States are entitled, in areas which do not fall under the exclusive competence of the Union, to entrust tasks to the institutions, outside the framework of the Union, such as the task of coordinating a collective action undertaken by the Member States or managing financial assistance" (para. 158).[69] We see problems in matching the tasks the Commission accomplishes in stability mechanisms with those examined in *Bangladesh* and *Lomé*. The tasks now assigned to the Commission are much wider and possess much more economic policy significance.[70]

In *Pringle*, the Court, now with reference to some of its Opinions, sets only one condition on tasks that Member States may allocate to EU institutions outside the Union framework: they may not alter the essential character

---

Pooled Bilateral Loans as set out in this Agreement." Recital 3 of the Preamble to the EFSF Framework: "By a decision of the representatives of the governments of the 16 euro-area Member States dated 7 June 2010, acting on the basis of the conclusions of the 27 European Union Member States of 9 May 2010, the Commission was tasked with carrying out certain duties and functions as contemplated by the terms of this Agreement." Recital 10 of the Preamble to the ESM Treaty: "On 20 June 2011, the representatives of the Governments of the Member States of the European Union authorised the Contracting Parties of this Treaty to request the European Commission and the ECB to perform the tasks provided for in this Treaty."

[67] Joined Cases C-181/91 and C-248/91 *Parliament* v. *Council and Commission* [1993] ECR I-3685.

[68] Case C-316/91 *Parliament* v. *Council* [1994] ECR I-625.

[69] See even AG Kokott's opinion, para. 171.

[70] See also P. Craig (2012), p. 240.

of the powers conferred on the institutions by the TEU and TFEU (para. 158).[71] If no other limitation exists, the derogation from the principle of conferral enshrined in Art. 13(2) TFEU is extensive enough. We would also argue that the relevance the Opinions the Court invokes possess for agreements on financial facilities for managing Member State fiscal crises is questionable: the Opinions the Court invokes concern international agreements where the Community/Union itself is one of the parties.

After formulating the general doctrine, it was easy for the Court to prove that no constitutional obstacle exists to entrust new tasks to the Commission in intergovernmental financial assistance. No objections can be made to the Court's observation that the tasks conferred on the Commission do not alter the essential character of its powers, such as they are under the TEU and TFEU. Indeed, the new tasks are largely analogous to those the Commission already exercises under EU legislation. For instance, the Commission's monitoring tasks are similar to those under Arts. 121 and 126 TFEU, and the Stability and Growth Pact. By contrast, the Court's argument invoking the Commission's overall task to "promote the general interest of the Union" and "to oversee the application of Union law" (Art. 17(2) TFEU) seems rather far-fetched in light of the requirement for an explicit competence basis, established by Art. 13(2) TEU. The Court argues that by its involvement in the ESM, the Commission promotes the general interest of the Union and is able to ensure that MoUs are consistent with EU law (paras. 163–4).

The case of the ECB might be seen as constitutionally even more problematic than that of the Commission. First, the ECB is an EU institution within the meaning of Art. 13(2) TEU. But, second, as Art. 130 TFEU makes clear, the ECB is supposed to function under an enhanced principle of independence. This warrants special caution in allowing Member States to assign new tasks to it. Hence, it is not self-evident that a doctrine developed with a view to the Commission can be transposed to tasks the Member States entrust to the ECB, as both the Court (para. 158) and AG Kokott (para. 180) claim. Unlike the Court, AG Kokott does comment on the independence of the ECB. Yet, she dispenses with it simply by stating that the ECB is under no obligation to perform the tasks allocated to it in the ESM Treaty (para. 181). For us, this does not settle the issue. External influences which the enhanced independence aims to fence off are not exhausted by legal obligations.

---

[71] Reference is to Opinion 1/92 [1992] ECR I-2821, paras. 32 and 41; Opinion 1/00 [2002] ECR I-3493, para. 20; and Opinion 1/09 [2011], not yet reported, para. 75.

Our discussion leads us to conclude that *Pringle* develops constitutional law even with regard to Member States' right to engage EU institutions in implementing intergovernmental agreements *inter se*. The enlarged doctrine articulated in *Pringle* may have far-reaching consequences for the unity of the EU's legal and institutional framework. It seems to open up possibilities for a group of Member States to establish through inter-governmental agreements institutional structures which lie outside the Union framework but which still involve Union institutions. At issue is a vital element in the ongoing constitutional mutation.

ECB action in financial and fiscal crises

A doctrinal constitutional scrutiny of the activities of the ECB is an intri-cate, yet important task. In a way exceptional for central banks, the whole legal framework for the ECB is enshrined in constitutional law, and needs to be assessed from that perspective. On the other hand, the ECB's missing democratic accountability and its enhanced independence emphasise the need for and significance of constitutional constraints. The ECB has played a key role in efforts to re-establish economic, financial and fiscal stability, in a manner not foreseen in the Maastricht Treaty.

The legal position of the ECB is given a general basis in the TEU, where EMU is defined as the Union's task and price stability as its aim (Arts. 3(3)–(4)), and where the ECB is included in the list of EU institu-tions (Art. 13(1)). The more detailed provisions are in Title VIII *Economic and monetary policy* of the TFEU and in the Statute of the ECB, which possesses a hierarchical status equivalent to the Treaties. The main doc-trinal issues raised by ECB action relate to the ECB venturing beyond traditional conduct of monetary policy. First, the measures taken to combat the financial crisis must be assessed in the light of Art. 127 TFEU, which defines the objectives and basic tasks of the ECB. Second, more specific questions derive from the relationship of the ECB's col-lateral policy to Art. 18(1) ECB Statute, which lays down the criteria for collateral. Third, purchase of government bonds and other meas-ures to relieve Member States' fiscal predicament should be looked at from the perspective of the prohibition of central-bank financing in Art. 123(1) TFEU and the no-bailout clause of Art. 125(1) TFEU. Finally, a separate discussion is needed of the implications of the deep involve-ment of the ECB in management of the crisis for its position as an independent expert body, with its primary focus on monetary policy oriented towards price stability; i.e. one of the pillars of the Maastricht macroeconomic constitution. This, however, we postpone to Chapter 7, where we analyse the mutation of constitutional principles.

As the first signs of financial crisis appeared in 2007, the ECB operated broadly in line with its preannounced operational framework, corresponding to the provisions of the TFEU and the Statute. The exceptional liquidity provision was conducted by standard weekly main refinancing operations. The usual operational mode and structure were maintained. The slightly more uncommon structural longer-term measures, too, were closely linked to the operational framework. In this regard, the only truly ad hoc measure was acting as agent for the US Fed in using Eurosystem collateral. A serious attempt was made to maintain the market conformity of operations, which reflected the ECB's own view about its constitutional obligations. The ECB's influence on financial-market price mechanisms increased but remained under control. Although the ECB's risks grew substantially, it could not be doubted that the purpose was to provide liquidity in order to keep the interbank market functioning. Liquidity provision was not mixed with indirect solvency support for the banking sector, nor could it be regarded as indirect public financing. The ECB aimed to guarantee sufficient liquidity while distancing itself from specific banking problems which fell under the competence of national authorities. The ECB explicitly stayed aloof from discussions on solvency support, which also helped to maintain its institutional independence.[72] Actions which complied with the preannounced monetary policy strategy and operational framework were in line with the ECB's basic task "to define and implement the monetary policy of the Union" (Art. 127(1) TFEU), and adhered to general principles pronounced in advance, as is required by Art. 18(2) ECB Statute.[73] Liquidity provision could be seen "to promote the smooth operation of payment systems", too, which also belongs to

[72] When a German bank failed over US subprime liabilities, Trichet stated at an ECB Press briefing on 2 August 2007 that "I will not add anything to what has been said by the German entities concerned themselves, by the authorities and by Axel Weber", making it very clear that the ECB had nothing to do with bank failures in the euro area. He was even more explicit on rejecting any responsibility for Fortis Bank at an ECB Introductory Statement with Q&A on 2 October 2008: "And in a period when it appears that the situation calls for government responsibility, I confirm that we judge it appropriate that governments take up their responsibilities. I think they did well in the case you mentioned, they did well in other cases, including in this country: I confirm that I think the government did well in Germany."

[73] "The ECB shall establish general principles for open market and credit operations carried out by itself or the national central banks, including for the announcement of conditions under which they stand ready to enter into such transactions."

the basic tasks of the ECB under Art. 127(2) TFEU. Against this background, it is not surprising that in public debates the ECB's focus on its primary objective of price stability was not seriously questioned.

The ECB's initial reactions, preceding Autumn 2008, can be used as benchmarks for subsequent measures during the full-blown financial crisis. These form a pattern and need to be seen as elements of the ECB's comprehensive effort to cope with an unforeseen and rapidly evolving situation. Their main aim was to maintain a functioning European interbank market in the face of the losses incurred and likely to be incurred after the Lehman Brothers collapse, as well as the blow inflicted on trust among banks and in financial supervision. In order to continue providing the banking sector with liquidity in the circumstances of a non-functioning interbank market, the ECB increasingly replaced the money market with its operational framework. The ECB guaranteed unlimited funding to banks as long as they had eligible collateral, the list of which it considerably expanded. When this was deemed not to suffice, the ECB started direct purchase of covered bonds. Such an involvement of the ECB in the functioning of financial markets is difficult to judge in the light of its basic tasks under Art. 127(2) TFEU. Even after escalation of the financial crisis, liquidity support could be justified by reference to implementing monetary policy and promoting the functioning of the payment system. It can, though, be asked whether the ECB acted "in accordance with the principle of an open market economy with free competition" (Art. 127(1)) when it practically replaced interbank markets.

With regard to collateral, the main issue is whether the ECB's policy relaxation entailed retreat from the requirement of 'adequate collateral', set out in Art. 18(1) of the ECB Statute. No clear-cut definition exists of the adequacy of collateral. Yet, it should be kept in mind that the ECB's lending and collateral policy does not allow for risk to be flexibly and adequately priced in interest rate margin; hence, the safety requirement should be more extensive than in private banks. In more dynamic terms, the question is whether collateral policy led to a reduction of market discipline and to a potential rise of systemic risk. The U–turn in collateral policy after the collapse of Lehmann Brothers responded to an unprecedented situation and, for the first time for the ECB, elevated financial stability to a primary consideration. Consequently, one can argue that increased use of bank-created assets as collateral has questioned the primacy of the ECB's monetary-policy tasks in a constitutionally problematic manner. Furthermore, one could claim that the new collateral policy has created the very moral hazard which especially German designers of EMU had wanted to prevent by excluding responsibility for financial stability from the ECB's narrowly defined objectives and tasks under Art. 127 TFEU and by stipulating strict collateral requirements in Art. 18(1) of the ECB Statute. As may be recalled, moral hazard was feared to derive from banks' assessment that the ECB would have incentives to come to their rescue, which could induce banks facing probable insolvency to reckless risk-taking and even lead to systemic risks in the banking sector. But, of course, one should also keep in mind that Member States had failed to supervise and control banks' risks, and were becoming less and less willing or able to use national resources to cover losses. In this sense, the justification for ECB policy lies in national policy failure.

The constitutional doubts which seem to be the most difficult to dispel relate to the Securities Markets Programme,[74] subsequently replaced by the programme of Outright Monetary Transactions. At first glance, Art. 123(1) TFEU, which seeks to curb Member State profligacy by prohibiting central-bank financing of public expenditures, appears to facilitate such purchases while explicitly banning merely primary-market operations.[75] Indeed, this has been a central argument for the constitutionality of the Securities Markets Programme and the programme of Outright Monetary Transactions. Furthermore, the officially announced aim of the latter programme is "safeguarding an appropriate monetary policy transmission and the singleness of the monetary policy".[76] The difference Art. 123(1) TFEU makes between primary- and secondary-market purchase of government bonds needs to be read in its proper context. A central bank may have a legitimate need to use government bonds in its monetary-policy operations, as they are the largest and most liquid financial-market instruments in most countries. Yet, the Treaty is very clear in not allowing the ECB to finance governments

[74] Decision of the ECB of 14 May 2010 establishing a securities markets programme (ECB/2010/5), [2010] OJ L124/8.
[75] "Overdraft facilities or any other type of credit facility with the European Central Bank or with the central banks of the Member States … in favour of Union institutions, bodies, offices or agencies, central governments, regional, local or other public authorities, other bodies governed by public law, or public undertakings of Member States shall be prohibited, as shall the purchase directly from them by the European Central Bank or national central banks of debt instruments."
[76] ECB (2012), 'Press Release', 6 September 2012.

and be in a position of an actual creditor vis-à-vis governments. Hence, mere reference to the permissibility of secondary-market operations under Art. 123(1) TFEU does not disperse all constitutional misgivings surrounding ECB policy. The ECB's argument that the two programmes are part of its monetary policy and designed to correct malfunctions in the transmission mechanism deserves a fair assessment, which must be informed by economic theory and monetary-policy practices. Still, as we have already contended, it should be evident that regardless of their role in monetary policy, both programmes have primarily aimed to solve the sovereign debt crisis. It does not come as a surprise that many economists, in particular in Germany, have not been convinced by the monetary-policy justification.[77]

Purchases of government bonds must also be examined in the context of the no-bailout clause in Art. 125(1) TFEU. Pursuing a textual interpretation, it may be discussed whether the ECB is directly affected by the clause. The clause is addressed to the Union, and at the time of its introduction the Treaties did not yet include the ECB among Union institutions; this only happened through Art. 13(1) TEU-Lisbon.[78] Yet, regardless of the direct applicability of Art. 125(1) TFEU to the ECB, this provision belongs to the same regulative whole as Art. 123(1) TFEU and, consequently, should be taken into account in interpreting the latter. Hence, one can argue that even though secondary-market operations are permitted by Art. 123(1), they should not be used for bailout purposes. The telos of the exception made in Art. 123(1) in favour of secondary-market purchases is to facilitate 'normal' liquidity operations and not emergency measures amounting to the bailout of a Member State threatened by insolvency.[79]

Significant differences exist between holding government bonds as collateral and holding them directly. Collateral is problematic in the sense that exposure is not controlled by the ECB, even though it can

---

[77] T. Mayer (2012), p. 111.

[78] Before Lisbon, the status of the ECB was a controversial issue in legal doctrine. See the discussion in C. Zilioli and M. Selmayr (2007).

[79] The constitutionality of the ECB operations has been questioned by, e.g., M. Ruffert (2011), pp. 1787–8. The Preamble to the 1993 Council Regulation specifying definitions for the application of the prohibitions on central-bank financing and bailouts also emphasised that purchases on the secondary market must not be used to circumvent the objective of Art. 104 TEC (present Art. 123 TFEU). Council Regulation (EC) No. 3603/93 of 13 December 1993 specifying definitions for the application of the prohibitions referred to in Articles 104 and 104b (1) of the Treaty, [1993] OJ L332/1.

influence the collateral it receives by haircut requirements[80] and eligibility criteria. Yet, with collateral the ECB incurs losses only when both collateral and debtor fail. In the case of purchases of bonds, the ECB faces losses as soon as the bond declines in value. In addition, purchases put the ECB in the position of a direct creditor to a Member State, which may cause problems for its constitutional independence. The ECB steps outside its central-bank role and becomes a stakeholder in Member States' interwoven financial and fiscal troubles.

Exposure to the European financial market may have reached the limit beyond which the ECB can no longer ignore solvency problems of individual institutions. If this is the case, the ECB faces the very moral hazard which Bundesbank representatives cautioned against in drafting the Maastricht macroeconomic constitution. Furthermore, financial-market and sovereign debt issues have become interwoven for the ECB, too. As the ECB has become a large lender to Member States' financial sector, and as it accepts government bonds as collateral, one can argue that the ECB cannot afford a state default. The role the Eurosystem plays in financing some Member States' banking sectors and the proportion of local banking or government-bond collateral threatens the ECB's operational independence and even its ability to focus on its primary objective. The large-scale and medium-term auctions of money to banks conducted by the ECB can also be appraised from this perspective. Through auctions in late 2011 and March 2012, the ECB lent a total of more than 1000 billion euro to banks for three years. This created incentives for banks to invest in government bonds particularly in the troubled countries. By the same token, it increased the ECB's direct exposure to banks and indirect exposure via collateral in government bonds.

The Securities Markets Programme and its successor, the programme of Outright Monetary Transactions, are only one element in the ECB's recent involvement in the fiscal problems of individual Member States. Other elements include participating as a member of the Troika in the austerity programmes imposed on countries receiving financial assistance; relaxing collateral requirements with regard to government bonds; and verbal interventions addressed not only to financial markets and the general public but to individual Member States, too. Taken together, activities and policies which manifest the ECB's deep engagement in the management of the fiscal

---

[80] 'Haircut' refers to reduction in the value of the collateral depending on its riskiness.

crisis in the Eurozone provoke the question of its possibly overstepping its primary monetary-policy mandate. With regard to individual measures, one can wonder what the constitutional basis for requiring policy-changes of individual states is, particularly if these fall outside the central-banking field. Of course, the ECB possessed no legal instruments to enforce for instance the demands in the letters in August 2011 addressed to Spain and Italy, but the Securities Markets Programme gave it other means to make them effective in countries dependent on ECB support. In turn, changes in collateral policy plus liquidity measures taken to combat the fiscal crisis could be assessed by the market-economy principle of Art. 127(1) TFEU and the collateral criterion of Art. 18(1) of the ECB Statute. Accepting Member State government bonds which financial markets and rating agencies have deemed unsafe can hardly be considered compliant with either the market-economy principle or the requirement of adequate collateral.

Art. 136 as the constitutional basis for a specific Eurozone regime

Diverging from rescue packages and mechanisms, European economic governance has mainly been strengthened within the legislative and institutional framework of the Union. This goes for the six- and two-pack legislation, which consists of EU Regulations and one Directive. Exceptions to the rule, though, exist. The EuroPlus Pact agreed on in March 2011 is a political commitment without immediate legal significance. By contrast, the Treaty on Stability, Coordination and Governance (TSCG) is an agreement under international law, which brought intergovernmentalism into reinforcing economic governance as well. We will discuss the TSCG in the next section.

Secondary legislation on economic governance is not devoid of constitutional issues either; legal innovation and experimentation has extended to this field, too. The post-Lehman Brothers financial crisis, with the consequent economic instabilities, did not spare non-euro states, either. Financial assistance under Art. 143 TFEU for balance-of-payments difficulties was activated for three non-euro states: Hungary, Latvia and Romania. But the fiscal and sovereign debt predicament, which worsened in 2010, hit the Eurozone in particular. The multilateral surveillance and excessive deficit procedures under Arts. 121 and 126 TFEU address all Member States. However, the crisis was seen to require stricter fiscal discipline especially in euro states. Furthermore, Arts. 121 and 126 TFEU rely mainly on soft-law methods, such as peer review and legally non-binding recommendations. Only Art. 126(11) allows the Council as a last resort to impose fines on recalcitrant Member States in the excessive deficit procedure. By contrast, fines are not included in the arsenal available in the multilateral surveillance procedure under Art. 121. Moreover, in both the preventive arm under Art. 121 and the corrective arm under Art. 126, the Commission can only submit non-binding recommendations and proposals to the Council, which takes the final decisions on recommendations, warnings and notices addressed to a Member State.

Art. 136(1) TFEU has provided the constitutional basis for a specific Eurozone regime:

In order to ensure the proper functioning of economic and monetary union, and in accordance with the relevant provisions of the Treaties, the Council shall, in accordance with the relevant procedure from among those referred to in Articles 121 and 126, with the exception of the procedure set out in Article 126(14), adopt measures specific to those Member States whose currency is the euro:

    (a)   to strengthen the coordination and surveillance of their budgetary discipline;

    (b)   to set out economic policy guidelines for them, while ensuring that they are compatible with those adopted for the whole of the Union and are kept under surveillance.

The six-pack and two-pack Regulations, which are applicable only in the euro area, have been issued on the basis of Art. 136(1), together with Art. 121(6) TFEU. The latter provision contains a legislative delegation for Regulations, which provide detailed rules for the multilateral surveillance procedure. This competence basis has been indicated, first, for the six-pack Regulation 1173/2011 on the effective enforcement of budgetary surveillance in the euro area. This Regulation introduced depositions as sanctions even into the preventive arm of monitoring under Art. 121 TFEU, that is, the multilateral surveillance procedure. Furthermore, it raised the level of deposits and fines available in the corrective arm; that is, the excessive deficit procedure under Art. 126 TFEU. It also enhanced the position of the Commission by adopting so-called reversed majority voting in decision-making on sanctions in both multilateral surveillance and excessive deficit procedures. The Council can only overturn Commission recommendations concerning deposits or fines by a qualified majority. Thus, an exception was made to the Treaty-level decision-making rules applicable to both multilateral surveillance and excessive deficit procedures.[81]

Second, Regulation 1174/2011, which instituted fines and reversed majority voting in the new procedure of excessive macroeconomic imbalances for Eurozone states, was also issued under Arts. 136(1) and 121(6) TFEU. Finally, this competence basis was indicated for the two-pack Regulations, which have effect solely in the euro area. Regulation (472/2013) inter alia obliges Eurozone states to present their draft budgets to the Commission annually by 15 October. The Commission has the right to assess and issue an opinion on draft budgets, and even ask them to be revised. Yet, Art. 121 TFEU does not provide a legal basis for monitoring Member States' annual budgets. Furthermore, Chapter V of the Regulation (*Ensuring the Correction of Excessive Deficit*) addresses issues which concern the excessive deficit procedure and fall under Art. 126, rather than Art. 121. This is true for the other two-pack Regulation (473/2013), too, which includes provisions on, e.g., the macroeconomic adjustment programme which Member States requesting financial assistance are obliged to prepare, as well as the relationship of this programme and the ensuing monitoring to the excessive deficit procedure.

The Eurozone Regulations provoke fundamental questions on the reach of delegation in Art. 136(1) TFEU. Does the delegation warrant establishing new competences for EU institutions with regard to Eurozone states, such as power to impose deposits and fines or to monitor annual budgets in procedures under Art. 121 TFEU? The wording of Art. 136(1) intimates a negative answer. The wording appears to imply that the specific measures adopted for euro states must respect not only the procedures established in Arts. 121 and 126 TFEU but also the substance of the relevant Treaty articles. A reading of Art. 136(1) which rejects its use in establishing new powers for EU institutions finds support in the explicit requirement of Art. 13(2) TFEU that each EU institution must act within the limits of the powers conferred on it in the Treaties. If, however, creating new competences for EU institutions for strengthening coordination and surveillance of euro states' budgetary discipline were allowed, it is difficult to see how the limits of such competences should be defined. How would extensive encroachments on euro states' sovereignty in fiscal and economic policy be possible? And

---

[81] Art. 16(3) TEU lays down the requirement of a qualified majority. For counting such a majority in cases where the state at issue is precluded from voting, Arts. 121(4) and 126(13) TFEU refer to Art. 238(3)(a) TFEU.

then, what about the procedural rules issued under Art. 136(1) TFEU? May these deviate from those laid down in the Treaties? Here a negative answer is warranted by both the wording of Art. 136(1) and the hierarchical supremacy of Treaty provisions over secondary legislation. Secondary legislation, such as Regulations, may not contradict Treaty provisions if these do not explicitly allow for exceptions. Art. 16(3) TEU expressly lays down that exceptions to the rules on qualified-majority voting in the Council must be made at Treaty level.

Not only Art. 136(1) but Art. 121(6) TFEU, too, has been interpreted in a way which seems difficult to justify in the light of its wording and scope. In the context of Regulation 1173/2011 on the effective enforcement of budgetary surveillance in the euro area as well as the two-pack Regulations, Art. 121(6) has been invoked as a competence basis for provisions which deal not only with the preventive arm consisting of the multilateral surveillance procedure, but also the corrective arm of the excessive deficit procedure. Obviously, the reason for such innovative interpretation lies in the explicit prohibition in Art. 136(1) to take recourse to Art. 126(14) which establishes the Council's power to issue complementing rules on the excessive deficit procedure.

Pringle examined European economic governance solely with regard to its implications for the constitutionality of intergovernmental stability funds, such as the ESM. In neither *Pringle* nor any other ruling has the ECJ taken a position on the reach of Art. 136(1) TFEU and thereby clarified the existing constitutional possibilities of erecting a specific regime of economic governance for the Eurozone. Yet the liberal reading by the EU (Eurozone) legislator of Art. 136(1) TFEU hints at an ongoing constitutional mutation in this field, too; a mutation aimed at removing obstacles to a further differentiation of the Eurozone from the rest of the Union.

Constitutionality of the TSCG

The Treaty on Stability, Coordination and Governance must also be regarded as an essentially Eurozone project, although it is partially open to non-euro states, too. The history of the project demonstrates that Art. 136(1) TFEU was not seen to justify unlimited intrusions in Member State sovereignty for the sake of budgetary discipline. In Spring 2010, Germany started to push other Member States to adopt debt brakes in their constitutions, as Germany itself had done in 2009. Imposing a legal obligation on the Member States was considered to require a

Treaty amendment. Discussions on such an amendment at the European Council meeting in December 2011 ran into rejection by the UK. In this situation, the Eurozone states decided to proceed by way of an inter-governmental agreement, soon to be called the Fiscal Compact. This Compact would oblige the Signatory States to adopt national measures guaranteeing respect for the reference values of budget deficit and sovereign debt defined in Art. 126 TFEU and the Protocol on the excessive deficit procedure. Hence, recourse was taken to the intergovernmental option in a field of Union action after a failed effort to initiate a Treaty amendment. Now the question is whether Member States are free to resort to agreements under international law in subject matters of the Treaties after adopting primary or secondary EU legislation has proven to be politically impossible.

The situation under discussion now is fundamentally different from the one we examined above: the canalisation of financial assistance from other Member States to a Member State in fiscal distress. Financial stability mechanisms, such as the EFSF or the ESM, have coordinated Member State action outside the Treaty framework. The Founding Treaties have not included any specific competence basis which would facilitate EU legislation for such purposes, nor has the amendment to Art. 136, expressly justifying establishment of an intergovernmental stability mechanism, created one. The financial justification for the intergovernmental option is obvious, too. The European Union, which lacks the power of taxation and whose budget resources are limited, does not possess the fiscal capacity needed for maintaining financial stability and buttressing the common currency. Recourse to intergovernmental assistance appears to be not only legally justified but even financially necessary.[82] By contrast, the TSCG addresses issues of Union action which clearly belong to the scope of the Founding Treaties and which have already been submitted to quite dense secondary legislation. Here the reason for picking the intergovernmentalist way was simply the veto by the UK – and later the Czech Republic – which blocked the Union way.

The gravest constitutional doubts concerning intergovernmental agreements within the scope of the Founding Treaties relate to side-stepping the procedural requirements which have to be respected in

---

[82] The establishment of the EFSM through Regulation 407/2010, though, shows that the Union framework allows for quite flexible arrangements, including credit-market financing. However, involving only the euro states in a stability mechanism functioning under the EU budget might have been constitutionally difficult.

amending the Treaties or in drafting and adopting secondary legislation. These requirements aim to engage all the major EU institutions, including the European Parliament, and grant a voice to all Member States. In the post-Lisbon era, national parliaments, too, have a right to intervene in the legislative procedure. By contrast, drafting, adopting and implementing intergovernmental agreements involves merely the contracting parties. These, in turn, are represented primarily by governments, while parliamentary input depends on the provisions of the national constitution.

The TSCG is not the first instance where a group of Member States have resorted to an intergovernmental agreement in order to proceed further in Treaty-related cooperation than other Member States, more jealous of their national sovereignty, have been willing to accept. The Schengen Agreement and Convention are the precedents most often invoked.[83] Their relevance as precedents can, though, be questioned. At the time, the Treaty on the EC did not include provisions on police and criminal law cooperation. The Treaty of Maastricht altered the constitutional situation with its provisions on the third Pillar of Justice and Home Affairs. But note that Art. K.7 of the Maastricht Treaty explicitly authorised intergovernmental cooperation and, by the same token, justified continuing the Schengen regime.[84] The Treaty of Amsterdam again changed the law through provisions on enhanced cooperation in situations where unanimity among Member States on further integration had proven impossible to reach. The Amsterdam Treaty also repealed former Art. K 7. Still, this did not put an end to recourse to intergovernmental agreements in third-pillar issues, as is shown by the Prüm Convention, concluded in 2005.[85] It is, though, doubtful whether Prüm, either, can be invoked as a precedent for assessing the TSCG. Its compatibility with EU law was never tested in the ECJ. In legal literature, it was criticised, not only for producing a political rift in the EU

---

[83] See, e.g., B. de Witte (2001). Reference can also be made to the Rome Treaty provision (Art. 233, presently Art. 350 TFEU) on Benelux cooperation, as well as to the 1994 Accession Act provision on Nordic cooperation (Final Act, Pt III, Joint Declaration 28).

[84] "The provisions of this Title shall not prevent the establishment or development of closer cooperation between two or more Member States in so far as such cooperation does not conflict with, or impede, that provided in this Title." See B. de Witte (2001), p. 40.

[85] Convention between the Kingdom of Belgium, the Federal Republic of Germany, the French Republic, the Grand Duchy of Luxembourg and the Republic of Austria on the stepping-up of cross-border cooperation, particularly in combating terrorism, cross-border crime and illegal immigration, 6 December 2006, Council of European Union Doc. 16382/06.

Area of Freedom, Security and Justice, but also for circumventing the Treaty-based procedures which give a voice to all principal EU institutions and all Member States.[86] These procedures include what after Nice is called enhanced cooperation.

The viewpoints evoked in the criticism of the Prüm Convention are equally pertinent in assessing use of intergovernmental agreements in European economic governance. If political negotiations aiming at consensus among all Member States fail, should not the Member States who still want to push ahead rely on the procedure the Treaties have expressly reserved for such a situation; namely, enhanced cooperation within the EU?[87] We shall approach the issue by examining, first, the arguments presented in the literature for the continuing availability of the intergovernmental option even where enhanced cooperation is constitutionally possible; and, second, the scope of enhanced cooperation, as it emerges in the light of *Pringle*.

Bruno de Witte's main argument in support of his view that the intergovernmental way is legally open after Amsterdam, too, is that to exclude this option would be "a drastic curtailment of the Member States' treaty-making competences that cannot be assumed to have taken place in the absence of any clear indication in the founding treaties".[88] Because of the Treaty provisions on enhanced cooperation, this argument is not as convincing in the post- as it perhaps was in the pre-Amsterdam era. De Witte clearly perceives the main reasons for the continuing allure of the intergovernmental way: "i) the legal conditions for taking the 'outside' route are less onerous than the conditions set for intra-EU closer cooperation and ii) Member States preserve, when acting under international law, complete control over the negotiation process and almost complete control over the implementation and enforcement of the obligations which they accept in the agreement".[89] But he does not seem to accept the circumvention argument. He explains the severity of the conditions for enhanced cooperation as follows: "as the closer cooperation delivers the keys of the powerful EU/EC engine to a group of Member States, such a move should be allowed less liberally than 'old-fashioned' recourse to the more modest instruments of international law".[90] But if a group of Member States through an intergovernmental agreement entrust EU institutions with implementation tasks, as is the

---

[86] T. Balzacq *et al.* (2006); J. Ziller (2006).
[87] Cf. the questions posed by P. Craig (2012).
[88] B. de Witte (2001), p. 40.   [89] *Ibid.*, p. 33.   [90] *Ibid.*, p. 57.

case with the TSCG, they endeavour to have the best of both worlds: recourse to the 'powerful EU engine' within a regime established under the less onerous conditions of public international law.

In sum, a powerful case can be made for Member States not being allowed to resort to intergovernmental agreements where enhanced cooperation is legally possible. The available scope of enhanced cooperation is defined in Arts. 20(1) TEU and 329(1) TFEU. The provisions are not entirely unambiguous; at least at first glance, the definition in Art. 20(1) TEU is narrower than that in Art. 329(1) TFEU. According to the former provision, "Member States which wish to establish enhanced cooperation between themselves within the framework of the Union's non-exclusive competences may make use of its institutions and exercise those competences by applying the relevant provisions of the Treaties". In turn, Art. 329(1) TFEU lays down that enhanced cooperation can be established "in one of the areas covered by the Treaties, with the exception of fields of exclusive competence and the common foreign and security policy". In *Pringle*, the applicant had claimed that conferral of new tasks on EU institutions by Member States was possible only through enhanced cooperation. In that connection, the ECJ adopted a rather strict interpretation of the possible scope of enhanced cooperation. It argued that as the Founding Treaties do not create a specific competence for the Union to establish a permanent stability mechanism such as the ESM, enhanced cooperation was not available. Therefore Art. 20 TEU on enhanced cooperation does not preclude the conclusion or ratification by the Member States of an agreement such as the ESM Treaty. This reading means that for enhanced cooperation to be possible, it does not suffice that the matter for cooperation falls under an area of shared competence, as the wording of Art. 329(1) TFEU appears to imply. What is further required is that a specific competence basis for Union action can be identified.

The Court's definition of the scope of enhanced cooperation seems justified, although its application in Pringle can be criticised. As we have argued above, a combination of the emergency competence in Art. 122(1) and the auxiliary power under the flexibility clause of Art. 352 TFEU could well justify establishing a permanent Union stability mechanism; indeed, such a justification appears to be necessary for the constitutionality of Regulation 407/2010 on the EFSM. But the underlying principle is sound: if the Founding Treaties do not permit action by the Union as a whole, neither is action possible by a restricted number of Member States, employing the Union institutional and legislative framework. The principle entails an important conclusion which possesses direct relevance for assessing the TSCG as well. Enhanced cooperation is not available for transcending obstacles on the road of amendments to the Founding Treaties; it can only open political deadlocks hampering secondary legislation or other measures within the Treaty-based powers of the Union.

Enhanced cooperation does not lie at the centre of the Court's reasoning in *Pringle*. Still, it is interesting to note that the Court's reasoning can be read to support the view that the intergovernmental road is blocked if no legal obstacles to enhanced cooperation exist. The Court argued that because – on grounds with which we are not in total agreement – enhanced cooperation was excluded, Art. 20 TEU on enhanced cooperation did not preclude conclusion or ratification of an intergovernmental agreement such as the ESM Treaty.

But the case of the constitutionality of the TSCG is not yet closed. Originally, recourse to the intergovernmental way was taken as an alternative to an amendment to the Founding Treaties which had proven politically impossible. But as enhanced cooperation is available only in the field of secondary legislation, it was not an option here. Legal assessment is further complicated by the fact that in intergovernmental negotiations, the TSCG underwent several alterations. The need for Treaty amendment arose from the wish of some states – in the first place Germany – to oblige at least the euro states to enshrine in their constitutions a debt brake analogous to the one already adopted in Germany. The Founding Treaties were – rightly, in our view – seen not to allow for imposing such an obligation on Member States through secondary legislation. In the course of intergovernmental negotiations on the TSCG, the obligation was watered down, and in its final form the TSCG no longer implies an absolute obligation of constitutional enshrinement. According to Art. 3(2) of the Treaty, the rules articulating the debt brake "shall take effect in the national law of the Contracting Parties at the latest one year after the entry into force of this Treaty through provisions of binding force and permanent character, preferably constitutional, or otherwise guaranteed to be fully respected and adhered to throughout the national budgetary processes".

Without engaging in detailed discussion of the contents of the TSCG in its final form, we would contend that after the toning down of the central requirement of national guarantees for the debt break, the provisions could have been given a formulation which would have facilitated their adoption by way of enhanced cooperation. The concerns about bypassing enhanced cooperation are not removed by Art. 10 TSCG, where the Contracting Parties proclaim their readiness to comply with the Founding Treaties and "to make active use, whenever appropriate and necessary", of not only Art. 136 TFEU facilitating specific Eurozone measures but of enhanced cooperation as well. In the face of such readiness, one cannot help wondering why the Contracting Parties did not at the very beginning opt for the procedures available under the Treaties, but took recourse to an intergovernmental agreement, which the very procedures invoked in Art. 10 TSCG render legally suspect.

With regard to the TSCG, too, the viewpoints concerning Member States' duty of sincere cooperation and the supremacy of EU law are of pertinence. We have already discussed these principles in the context of intergovernmental agreements on fiscal rescue mechanisms, and there is no need to repeat that discussion here. Yet, the particular contents of the TSCG occasion some additional comments.

The TSCG includes provisions which are aimed to guarantee respect for the principles of sincere cooperation and supremacy of EU law. Art. 2(1) TSCG evokes the principle of sincere cooperation: "This Treaty shall be applied and interpreted by the Contracting Parties in conformity with the Treaties on which the European Union is founded, in particular Art 4(3) of the Treaty on European Union, and with European Union law, including procedural law whenever the adoption of secondary legislation is required." Furthermore, Art. 2(2) TSCG, in accordance with the supremacy of EU law, lays down that "the provisions of this Treaty shall apply insofar as they are compatible with the Treaties on which the Union is founded and with European Union law" and that "they shall not encroach upon the competences of the Union to act in the area of the economic union".[91]

Above, we came to the conclusion that the potential pre-emptive effect of EU legislation, based on Art. 2(2) TFEU and the Protocol on shared competence, is not confined to conflicting rules. It is wider than mere rule pre-emption but narrower than field pre-emption: it

[91] The TSCG includes a particular provision whose compatibility with Union law is questionable: Art. 7 where the euro states commit themselves to supporting proposals or recommendations by the Commission where it considers that a euro state in breach of the deficit criterion is in the framework of an excessive deficit procedure and adapting a reversed majority vote among themselves. It is difficult to see how such an obligation under international law, introducing a voting procedure in clear contradiction with Art. 126 TFEU, in combination with Art. 16(3) TEU, could permit the Contracting Parties to fully respect the procedural requirements of the Founding Treaties, as Art. 7 TSCG also implies.

precludes Member State action within the scope of EU legislation. Yet, we also argued that economic policy should not be examined within the dichotomy of exclusive and shared competences and that it is therefore questionable to apply the doctrine of pre-emption to economic policy. If, however, the doctrine were considered pertinent, the TSCG would have to be seen as a rather clear case of breach of pre-emption. The Fiscal Compact, which makes up Title III of the TSCG, addresses issues which lie in the focus of Art. 126 TFEU, the Protocol on the excessive deficit procedure and the respective secondary legislation under the Stability and Growth Pact. In turn, Title IV *Economic policy coordination and convergence* regulates issues within the scope of Art. 121 TFEU and complementary secondary legislation. But even if the doctrine of pre-emption did not apply, the constitutional problem arising from the primacy of enhanced cooperation would still remain.

The Preamble to the TSCG proclaims that when reviewing and monitoring budgetary commitments under the TSCG, the Commission will act within the framework of its Treaty-based powers, primarily those set out in Arts. 121, 126 and 136 TFEU. Yet, the TSCG confers on the Commission a particular monitoring task which has no correspondence in the TFEU or the complementing secondary legislation. Under Art. 8(1) TSCG, the Commission is expected to monitor whether the Contracting Parties have abided by their obligation to provide national guarantees for respecting the rules on government deficit and debt set out in Art. 3(1) TSCG. Still, the expanded doctrine on conferral of new tasks on EU institutions through Member States' *inter se* agreements, propounded in *Pringle*, appears to apply to this case as well. It is evident that the new monitoring task does not affect the essential character of the powers of the Commission and, hence, does not exceed the limit set in *Pringle*. As regards the new task conferred on the ECJ, Art. 8(3) TSCG declares itself to be a special agreement between the Contracting Parties within the meaning of Art. 273 TFEU; as may be recalled, this article allows Member States to establish Court jurisdiction for their mutual disputes in matters related to the Treaties. The legal significance of such self-interpretation of the TFEU can be questioned. Yet, the doctrine expounded in *Pringle* appears to justify the task conferred on the ECJ, too.

The TSCG not only confers new tasks on existing Union institutions, but even establishes new bodies, although only for the Eurozone. The Lisbon Treaty confirmed the institutional and legislative status of the Eurozone through the provisions in Chapter 4 Title VIII TFEU (*Provisions specific to Member States whose currency is the euro*), complemented by the Protocol on the Euro Group attached to the Treaty. This can be argued to have given expression to a constitutional principle: if particular institutional structures complementing or relating to the institutions enumerated in Art. 13(1) TEU are created for the euro area, this should take place through the Founding Treaties. This principle would hold even if these structures did not possess formal decision-making powers. Thus, provisions on the Euro Group and its President are included in Art. 137 TFEU and the related Protocol, although these bodies do not take legally binding decisions. In the light of this argument, the provisions in Title V of the TSCG (*Governance of the euro area*) on Euro Summit meetings and the President of these meetings appear constitutionally problematic. Euro Summit meetings are not convened merely for the purposes of implementing the TSCG but are supposed to discuss economic governance of the euro area in general.[92] Constitutional doubts can be extended to the provision on the conference of representatives of the relevant committees of the European Parliament and national parliaments.

These concerns evoked by the institutional provisions in Title V lead us to our final constitutional comment on the TSCG. This comment is of a principal nature and related to the initial purpose of the TSCG. Originally, the TSCG was intended to replace an amendment to the Founding Treaties. As we have argued, enhanced cooperation is not available for such a purpose so that the argument from the primacy of enhanced cooperation was not applicable to the first draft treaty involving a strict obligation to enshrine the rules on government deficit and debt in the national constitution. But if Member States are prohibited from circumventing the political blockage of secondary legislation through an agreement under international law, are they permitted such a procedure in case of an impasse of primary legislation; that is, a Treaty amendment? Supremacy of EU law precludes provisions in international agreements between Member States which conflict with the Founding Treaties. But is complementing the Founding Treaties

---

[92] According to Art. 12(2) TSCG,

> Euro Summit meetings shall take place when necessary, and at least twice a year, to discuss questions relating to the specific responsibilities which the Contracting Parties whose currency is the euro share with regard to the single currency, other issues concerning the governance of the euro area and the rules that apply to it, and strategic orientations for the conduct of economic policies to increase convergence in the euro area.

possible? Or are there issues which fall under the exclusive competence of the EU constitutional legislator? Do the Founding Treaties
exert a pre-emptive effect with regard to *inter se* agreements between
Member States, by reserving certain topics for EU constitutional law?
Together with the interpretation of the reach of enhanced cooperation and Art. 136 TFEU, the answers to these questions largely determine the leeway for a separate Eurozone regime; the possibility of
a two-speed Europe, with the Eurozone escaping to its own way of
deepened economic *and* political integration.

6 Realignment of the principles of the macroeconomic constitution

The Maastricht legacy

The new layer of the European economic constitution, introduced by the Maastricht Treaty and reinforced through the Stability and Growth Pact, was underpinned by certain fundamental principles. For Member States joining EMU, monetary policy was defined as an exclusive Union competence and assigned to the ECB. The ECB was seen as an expert body which was supposed to focus on pursuing the specific monetary-policy objective of price stability. Its position as an expert body was buttressed by an enhanced independence from external influence, whether from other Union institutions or from Member States. In contrast, in fiscal and economic policy Member States retained their sovereignty, while the Union was to possess merely coordinating functions. Yet, fiscal sovereignty was not absolute but circumscribed by constitutionally defined reference values on budget deficit and public debt. Restrictions on fiscal sovereignty reflected the primacy of the monetary-policy objective of price stability; they were expected to impose on Member States the budgetary discipline which a monetary policy focusing on price stability was seen to require. In addition, they addressed the probability that in a monetary union negative repercussions of reckless fiscal policy in one Member State would spill over to all the others. Hence, specific preventive safeguards were adopted to ensure prudent fiscal policy. Member States' fiscal sovereignty found its reverse in their fiscal liability, expressed by the no-bailout clause in Art. 125(1) TFEU. The EU in general and EMU in particular was supposed to be no 'transfer union', but only to allow for strictly limited financial transfers from the European level to Member States or from one Member State to another.

The Maastricht principles of the European macroeconomic constitution were informed by particular economic assumptions and expectations. Many of these have been proven to be mistaken by the Eurozone
crisis, if not earlier. The Eurozone did not develop to meet the criteria
of an optimal currency area where a 'one-size-fits-all' monetary policy
would be feasible. The importance of exchange-rate flexibility for rem-
edying structural shocks did not decline; quite the contrary. A unitary
monetary policy with unitary nominal interest rates for economically
divergent states deepened structural differences among euro states. The
policy led to lower real interest rates in countries which were experiencing cost pressures due, for example, to larger than average wage
increases. Adjusting national fiscal and economic policy to a changing
economic environment, including the impact of common monetary
policy, appeared to be much more difficult than euro-optimists had
hoped. To the nationally divergent impact of transnational monetary
policy were added the largely ignored externalities of national fiscal
and economic policies: Member States did not live up to their Treaty
obligation to consider their economic policies a common concern. As
a preventive safeguard against fiscal crisis, the disciplining effect of
credit markets was overestimated, despite warnings expressed by the
Delors Committee and several senior central bankers, among others.
The same goes for the efficiency of the monitoring procedures under
Arts. 121 and 126 TFEU, complemented by the Stability and Growth
Pact. On the other hand, the Maastricht Founding Fathers had largely
neglected the importance of financial-stability concerns in the face of
dramatically increased private and public debt. High debt levels and
cross-border ownership of debt certificates made financial system(s)
more vulnerable to shocks and even to self-fulfilling insolvency crises. Indeed, the danger of contagion and the impossibility of isolating
an insolvency crisis, as well as the interdependence between financial institutions and sovereigns, were hardly discussed outside central
banks, even though the Asian crisis in 1997–8 gave a fresh warning just
before the start of the final phase of EMU.

Mistaken economic premises could explain why the Maastricht
macroeconomic constitution did not include any crisis resolution mechanism which could have been activated at the outbreak of the crisis.
The legal and institutional experimentation characterising European
responses to the crisis launched a constitutional mutation which is
not confined to an innovative and liberal interpretation of individual

Treaty provisions but has shaken central Maastricht principles as well. It is to these principles that we now turn our attention.

Financial stability as a new overriding objective

In the Maastricht macroeconomic constitution, stability was a major economic objective. However, it was explicitly expressed in terms of price stability. Art. 3(3) TEU sets out that the Union "shall work for the sustainable development of Europe based on balanced economic growth and price stability, a highly competitive social market economy, aiming at full employment and social progress, and a high level of protection and improvement of the quality of the environment". In Arts. 119(2) and 127(1) TFEU, price stability is specified as the primary objective of monetary policy, entrusted to the ECB. Yet, it would be erroneous to restrict the significance of price stability merely to narrowly defined monetary policy. As the Stability and Growth Pact made clear, fiscal constraints for the purpose of sound public finances were also designed to serve the higher-order objective of price stability.[1] Restrictions on national fiscal sovereignty, imposing fiscal discipline and securing sound public finances were expected to create in national fiscal policy the presuppositions that common, transnational, monetary policy aiming at price stability required.

Arguably, the euro-area crisis has replaced price stability with financial stability as the overriding objective which European economic policies, including the monetary policy of the ECB, are expected to serve. The objective of the financial stability of the euro area as a whole has been the main justification invoked in the context of rescue packages and stability mechanisms, and it has also played a major role in the operations of the ECB in the financial and fiscal crises. It is true, though, that Art. 127(5) TFEU, in the context of the definition of the ECB's and the ESCB's competences, makes reference to the stability of the financial system. This provision lays down that "the ESCB shall contribute to the smooth conduct of policies pursued by the competent authorities relating to the prudential supervision of credit institutions and the stability of the financial system". Yet the 'stability of the financial system' can hardly be equated with 'financial stability of the euro

---

[1] See Council Resolution (EC) of 17 June 1997 on the stability and growth pact Amsterdam, [1997] OJ C236/1.

area as a whole'. Rather, at issue is the stability of national financial systems, composed mainly of private financial institutions. Moreover, the stability of this system is defined mainly as a national objective, the Eurosystem playing only a complementary, contributory role.[2]

It can, though, be argued that the objective of financial stability was, even if not explicitly, at least implicitly present already in the Maastricht economic constitution. Monetary policy focusing on price stability, complemented by disciplined fiscal policy and national prudential supervision of financial institutions, was expected to secure financial stability, too. The economic assumptions of the Maastricht macroeconomic constitution on the relationship between price stability and financial stability have not passed the test of reality. For instance, the macroeconomic trends of increased debt levels and the growing importance of medium-term financial cycles have presumably altered the relationship between price stability and financial stability. Furthermore, the Maastricht macroeconomic constitution seems to have underestimated the intertwinement of public finances and private financial institutions, as well as the degree and type of cross-border financial integration due, inter alia, to the liberation of capital markets and the EMU framework.

In sum, the new position of financial stability as an overriding economic objective, explicitly confirmed in *Pringle* and the amendment to Art. 136 TFEU, is a central part of the constitutional mutation at the level of principles. In line with other mutations, it reacts to the at least partial failure of the economic theory underpinning the Maastricht macroeconomic constitution.

Shaking of the Maastricht principles of monetary policy

As explained in Chapter 2, the German Bundesbank served as a model for the provisions in the Treaty of Maastricht on the ECB and the common monetary policy. Yet, the primarily ordoliberal view of monetary policy has never been as uncontested as is often intimated; divergent notions of the objectives of monetary policy, and of the optimal relationship between the central bank and the political branches of government have always existed as well. But it has clearly been the dominant

---

[2] It was most likely foreseen that supervisory activities would need to be centralised; it was, however, made clear that they should not become the task of the ECB.

position in post-war Germany, and it is doubtful whether Germany would ever have gone in for establishing EMU without its acceptance as one of the cornerstones of the Maastricht economic constitution. The German Constitutional Court has even declared that compliance with the independence of the European Central Bank and the primary objective of price stability are permanent constitutional prerequisites for Germany's participation in EMU.[3]

The main Maastricht monetary-policy principle is price stability as the overriding objective. In the ordoliberal perception, price stability is related not only to other parts of the economic constitution but also to other constitutional dimensions, as it is seen as one of the guarantors of basic individual freedoms. In the economic dimension, price stability was assumed to produce general economic stability, including financial stability.

Before EMU, monetary and fiscal policy had been in constant dialogue with labour-market policies in the nation-state setting, including Germany. The position of the parties to the dialogue, of course, varied from country to country, and in Germany the central bank had a stronger hand than in most other countries. In EMU, the dialogue came to an end or at least lost much of its importance. In its monetary policy, the ECB pays attention to current and expected fiscal- and labour-market policies, but it cannot fine-tune these to country-specific variations or engage in dialogue with national policy-makers or social partners. National actors have to take ECB decisions as given and adjust to them. On the other side, the country-specific implications of ECB monetary policy depend on national fiscal and labour-market policies. In this sense, their influence and responsibility have increased considerably.

The enhanced independence of the ECB was designed to safeguard the primacy of the monetary-policy objective of price stability. The ECB's independence comprised both goal and means independence: it was mandated to specify both the objective of price stability – permissible price fluctuation – and the policy means of achieving it. The specification of both goals and means were seen to derive from application of scientific economic expertise; this was the justification for the ECB's position as an independent expert institution.

---

[3] BVerfG, 2 BvR 987/10, 7 May 2010, para. 129; and BVerfG, 2 BvR 1390/12, 12 September 2012, para. 203.

Related to the constitutional principle of independence, the mandate of the ECB was defined narrowly and as exactly as possible. The ECB was expected to stay aloof from financial-stability or fiscal-policy considerations, which could engage it in discussion and action threatening its independence and the overriding objective of price stability. Furthermore, the limited and relatively clearly defined mandate of the ECB reduced the need for democratic inputs in defining or conducting its tasks.

During the financial and fiscal crises, the ECB has assumed tasks which have made all the central monetary-policy principles of Maastricht teeter: the primacy of the price-stability objective, the independence of the ECB and the narrow definition of its mandate. The Maastricht macroeconomic constitution retained the main responsibility for the stability of the financial system with national authorities. The ECB's active involvement in re-establishing financial stability has shaken this premise. By the same token, it has raised concerns of moral hazard, which may jeopardise both the primacy of the price-stability objective and the independence of the ECB. These concerns are further aggravated by plans to assign the ECB a major supervisory role in the future banking union. Given that the supervisory function can lead to liabilities for taxpayers, the enhanced independence of the supervisory agent is far from unproblematic from the democratic point of view.

The ECB Securities Markets Programme – replaced by Outright Monetary Transactions – has compromised on price stability as the primary objective of monetary policy, and the ECB's deep involvement in country-specific rescue operations and in the functioning of stability mechanisms in the Eurozone has problematised the principle of independence. In the Securities Markets Programme and Outright Monetary Transactions, the Maastricht relationship between European monetary policy and national fiscal policy has been reversed: the needs of the latter have determined the objectives pursued by the former.[4] By the same token, the ordoliberal tenets of monetary policy's non-political character and of the self-evident truth of price stability as the focus of that policy have suffered a severe blow. We have witnessed a tendency towards monetary policy's politicisation. What this means in terms of the legitimacy of the

---

[4] This has been the refrain particularly in German criticisms of the ECB. As a representative example, see A. Belke (2010).

ECB and the policy it pursues remains to be seen. If the legitimacy issue is considered relevant at all from ordoliberal premises, it is defined in terms of expert and output legitimacy, instead of democratic input legitimacy. The further away the ECB ventures from a monetary policy focused on price stability and the more active a role it adopts in fiscal rescue operations, the more the original justification for its present institutional status loses pertinence. We shall revert to this problem in Chapter 7.

Member States' fiscal responsibility

According to the doctrine the ECJ expounded in its *Pringle* ruling, the macroeconomic constitution provides not only for prevention but also for resolution of insolvency crises. The amendment to Art. 136 TFEU, which authorises euro states to establish an intergovernmental stability mechanism, articulates the same premise. Hence, these constitutional speech acts have confirmed the constitutional mutation which the European rescue packages and mechanisms of the past three years have implied.

Yet, it would be overhasty to declare that this constitutional mutation would have made the principle of Member States' fiscal responsibility moribund. The prohibition on bailouts in Art. 125(1) TFEU is still part of the macroeconomic constitution. However, through the constitutional complement of crisis prevention with crisis management, the scope of application of the prohibition has been restricted. It is only valid for good times but no longer for bad times. If, in spite of the preventive devices of the macroeconomic constitution, a euro state is hit by an insolvency crisis, other Member States are allowed to bail it out. However, two prerequisites must be met. First, the bailout must be necessary for maintaining the (financial) stability of the Eurozone (or the Union as whole) and, second, it must be accompanied by 'strict conditionality'.

The *Pringle* doctrine, confirmed by the amendment to Art. 136 TFEU, leaves the principle of Member State fiscal responsibility intact for other than crisis circumstances. Hence, more far-reaching proposals for debt mutualisation, such as introduction of Eurobonds – or stability bonds, as they are called in the Commission's Green Paper[5] – remain

---

[5] Commission (EU), 'Feasibility of introducing stability bonds' (Green Paper) COM (2011) 818 final, 23 November 2011.

constitutionally suspect.[6] All these proposals are premised on shared liability for the sovereign debt of individual euro states.

Fiscal and economic policy: sovereignty and coordination

The Maastricht model implied not only the principle of national fiscal liability but also its reverse: Member State fiscal and economic sovereignty. Sovereignty, though, was not absolute, but the Treaties, complemented by the Stability and Growth Pact, imposed restrictions, especially on national fiscal policy. These restrictions served the overriding objective of monetary stability. The starting-point, however, was that the Union would play a merely coordinating role in non-monetary economic policy. Accordingly, the means the Union had at its disposal to influence Member State policies consisted primarily of soft-law instruments, typical of what later came to be called the open method of coordination. The central role of the Ecofin Council emphasised the peer review character of monitoring procedures. Indeed, Art. 121(1) TFEU indicates the Member States as the subjects of coordination and the Council as the mere forum where Member States exercise it. The only exception from soft-law governance was adopted in Art. 126(11) as an *ultima ratio* means in the excessive deficit procedure. The Council could oblige a Member State which had failed to comply with a previous Council decision to make a non-interest-bearing deposit of an appropriate size with the Union and even impose a fine. The Union's coordinating role in principle covered economic policy as a whole, but as the Stability and Growth Pact made evident, its clear emphasis lay in fiscal policy; more precisely, in managing budget deficit and sovereign-debt rates.

Both rescue packages and funds, and the reinforcement of European economic governance have contributed to relativising Member States' sovereignty. Together they have unleashed a constitutional mutation at, not only the transnational, European, but also the national, Member State, level.

Most obvious is the curbing of the fiscal sovereignty and economic sovereignty of the crisis states. All forms of assistance, starting from the Greek loan facility and ending with stability support by the ESM, have been premised on 'strict conditionality'. The Memoranda of

---

[6] See the discussion in A. de Gregorio Merino (2012), pp. 1630–2.

Understanding or Programmes of Adjustment which the beneficiary countries have had to sign have contained not only general, aggregate, reference values on, say, public spending or the level of taxation, but also rather detailed provisions on how spending cuts should be allocated and deficits financed.[7] Moreover, every new imbursement of assistance has been made dependent on the recipient state's fulfilling its commitments, as assessed by transnational, Troika monitors. Demands have been raised for even tighter fiscal tutelage, a 'financial receivership'.[8] Two-pack legislation providing for enhanced surveillance of Eurozone states which experience severe financial difficulties or already receive financial assistance does not go as far as some discussants have suggested, but in any case entails further curbs on the fiscal sovereignty of crisis states. Austerity programmes have been flanked by commitments to typical supply-side structural reforms, such as general liberalisation, especially in the field of services, labour-market flexibilisation and reduction of tariff partners' autonomy in wage setting. These requirements have extended incursions in crisis states' sovereignty from fiscal to general economic policy. With their reference to strict conditionality, *Pringle* and the amendment to Art. 136 TFEU have made explicit the constitutional status of the curtailment of sovereignty which beneficiary states must accept as a price for financial assistance.

Rescue packages and mechanisms have had grave repercussions for the fiscal sovereignty of assisting states as well. Their financial liabilities, both taken separately for each instrument and in total,[9] are huge.

---

[7] This goes for Greece, Ireland, Portugal and Cyprus. Spain constitutes an exception, because the scope of its MoU is confined to the financial sector.

[8] In a discussion paper published by the ECB, Schuknecht *et al.* (2011), propose that 'a country requiring assistance under the ESM (be) placed in financial receivership if its adjustment programme fails to remain on track, with the planning and execution of budgets requiring the agreement of the appointed financial receiver' (p. 18). The authors clarify their proposal as follows: '… financial receivership is necessary where countries have no political consensus in support of reforms. Without such a provision, the moral hazard emanating from support programmes and the risk of countries failing to comply and/or defaulting would not be sufficiently mitigated. This is the ultimate step in a graduated process of increased monitoring and control over national budgetary policies' (p. 19).

[9] In Finland, the Constitutional Law Committee of Parliament has repeatedly emphasised that liabilities should be assessed as a whole, in order to appraise the encroachment on Parliament's fiscal powers and the possible endangerment of the state's ability to cope with its constitutional obligations. In addition, the risk connected to liabilities should also be taken into account. Indeed, such a holistic approach is needed, although it is difficult to execute, due to the different legal and economic nature of liabilities and the variation in the respective risks.

This has created constitutional problems in, for example, such Member States as Germany and Finland where the constitution enjoys high prestige in political and legal culture. The main constitutional issues relate to national sovereignty, the fiscal powers of Parliament and democratic legitimation of decision-making in fiscal policy. We shall return in a later section to Member State constitutional concerns which testify to the close intertwinement of European and national constitutional developments. Here it suffices to say that at the European level, the restrictions on assisting states' fiscal sovereignty are not explicitly constitutionally anchored as is the curtailment of beneficiary states' sovereignty.

Measures to tighten the European economic governance have addressed all Member States. Yet the crisis has led to the erection of a particular Eurozone regime, including specific treatment of the worst-hit states. In the preceding chapter, we have already discussed the constitutional doubts which some of the reforms raise in light of individual Treaty provisions. Such constitutionally suspect changes include introduction by way of secondary legislation of obligatory deposits and fines in monitoring procedures in the preventive arm under Art. 121 TFEU, as well as reversed majority voting in both the preventive arm and the corrective arm under Art. 126 TFEU. The changes have emphasised the role of formal sanctions and strengthened the position of the Commission in relation to the Council; due to the enhanced status of the Commission, it is difficult to conceive any longer of the Member States as the subjects of coordination. Thus, monitoring has moved away from peer review and soft-law mechanisms, typical of the open method of coordination.

Simultaneously, the scope of monitoring has been enlarged. The Stability and Growth Pact put the emphasis of the multilateral surveillance procedure under Art. 121 TFEU on fiscal policy. By contrast, the excessive imbalances procedure aims to cover all the main sources of economic imbalances and opens surveillance towards general economic policy. Establishment of the new procedure was a reaction to the fact that national discretion in maintaining competitiveness and more broadly avoiding explosive paths in national economies had failed in a number of cases. However, European discretion may not always fare much better, as the Greece rescue packages have demonstrated. The excessive imbalances procedure facilitates use of formal sanctions, but the criteria employed by the Commission are vague. A certain degree of indeterminacy is inevitable in defining yardsticks for macroeconomic surveillance, and the exact reference values for sovereign debt and budget deficit allow for exceptions, too. Yet, the combination of formal sanctions and vague criteria in the excessive imbalances procedure has given rise to severe criticism. Critics claim that a discretionary regime of economic policy governance has been established where the Commission can take individual Member States to account for macroeconomic developments for which they bear little responsibility and which they – after losing control over exchange and interest rates – possess but scarce means to influence.[10] Despite the vagueness of the criteria, the procedure can also be criticised for an effort to constitutionalise one particular, controversial approach to economic imbalances.

Economic governance under the original Stability and Growth Pact did not address annual budgetary processes; the focus was on medium-term fiscal planning. Nor was Member States' procedural budgetary autonomy affected; not only the content but the procedure for drafting and adopting the annual budget fell under Member State competence. The Protocol on the excessive deficit procedure, attached to the Treaty of Maastricht, though, set out a general duty of the Member States to ensure that national procedures in the budgetary area enable them to meet their Treaty obligations. Yet, before the Eurozone crisis, this general duty was not given any specific thrust through secondary legislation. The first intrusion into the procedural autonomy of Member States was effected by the Directive on requirements for Member State budgetary frameworks (2011/85), based on the delegation in Art. 126(14) TFEU and belonging to the six-pack.

The Directive retained the focus on multiannual budgetary planning. It aimed to secure that national procedures are consistent with the Stability and Growth Pact and promote compliance with the reference values on budget deficit and public debt. Regulation 1175/2011, which introduced the European semester, extended European monitoring from medium-term budget planning, focusing on aggregate objectives, to annual budgetary planning. Two-pack legislation goes still further and obliges euro-area Member States annually to submit a draft budgetary plan for the forthcoming year to the Commission and the Euro Group. Although the Commission has not the power to take legally binding decisions, its opinions are expected to put strong pressure on Member States. Moreover, opinions addressing a "particularly serious non-compliance" with European budgetary policy obligations will be made public.

[10] See F. Scharpf (2012), p. 28; M. Höpner and F. Rödl (2012).

The inroad into the procedural aspect of national budgetary autonomy opened by Directive 2011/85 was widened by two further instruments. First, the two-pack not only extended European monitoring to the annual budget process, but also includes provisions on, inter alia, the timeline of the national budget process. Second, the main thrust of the Treaty on Stability, Coordination and Governance (TSCG) is to create national guarantees to ensure that Member States respect the rules on balanced budget and limited sovereign debt. The TSCG also entrusts the Commission, other Member States and the Court with the task of monitoring the adequacy of these guarantees.

In sum, the ongoing constitutional mutation has altered the character of European economic governance, in particular in the Eurozone. Decisive steps have been taken from soft-law instruments to formal sanctions; the strengthening of the Commission's position, together with formal sanctions, has stripped governance of much of its peer review features; the scope of surveillance has been enlarged from fiscal to general macroeconomic policy; and in fiscal policy, monitoring has been extended from Member States' multiannual planning to both substantive and procedural aspects of annual budgetary processes. It is true, though, that Member States retain the final formal decision over their budgets. Still, European constraints have been considerably widened and deepened beyond those adopted in Maastricht. This has occurred in tandem with redefinition of the second-order objective of the Treaty provisions on economic policy; its reformulation as financial stability or simply stability, instead of price stability. In light of deepgoing country-specific restraints and monitoring as well as the new role of the Commission, it might be doubted whether European economic governance still corresponds to the characterisation in Arts. 5(1), 119(1) and 121(1) TFEU; namely, Member States' coordinating their economic policies within the Union.

The unity of the Union

The Maastricht Treaty still gave expression to the principle of the unity of the European Union. Member States were not only expected but even legally obliged to accede to EMU after meeting the convergence criteria. It is true, though, that two Member States particularly keen on retaining their sovereignty had negotiated opt-outs, which were authenticated in separate Protocols. Still, the opt-outs were generally assumed to be only temporary so that an economic and monetary union covering the whole Union lay on the horizon. Such a linear path of enlargement of the Eurozone has turned out to be an illusion. Not only have the UK and Denmark shown no serious sign of relinquishing their opt-outs, but Sweden has been granted a de facto, political opt-out, and the latest enlargements have brought in other states whose political will to accede is unsure. The Eurozone crisis has not exactly enhanced this will. In any case, the legal obligation to join must be considered desuetude.

Yet, the Maastricht Treaty's relation to the principle of unity within the macroeconomic constitution was ambivalent. It did construe accession to EMU as a legal obligation. But it also instigated differentiation of the regulatory framework: in addition to provisions concerning all the Member States, it included provisions addressed merely to EMU Members or Member States with a derogation. This differentiation was provided with a new constitutional basis by the Lisbon Treaty with the specific provisions on the Eurozone. The eruption of the crisis in Spring 2010 gave a decisive impetus to the wide and – as was shown in the preceding chapter – in some respects constitutionally suspect interpretation and application of the competence established by Art. 136(1) TFEU. A further instrument for a Eurozone *Sonderweg* has been found in intergovernmental agreements concluded among euro states, although in some cases at least partially open to other Member States as well. We shall not repeat here our discussion of the constitutional concerns raised by the Treaty on Stability, Coordination and Governance. What is important for discussing the principle of the unity of the EU is to point to the TSCG's contribution to, not only regulatory, but also institutional differentiation of the Eurozone. The default position of the Maastricht Treaty was that except for the ECB, EMU relied on existing EU-wide institutions. With Art. 137 TFEU and the complementary Protocol, the Lisbon Treaty formalised the position of the Eurogroup – that is, the Ecofin Council in its Eurozone composition – and its President. The TSCG added Euro Summit meetings and the Presidency of Euro Summits to this institutional parallelism, as well as the conference of representatives of the relevant committees of the European Parliament and national parliaments.

Moreover, *Pringle* adopted a wide interpretation of Member States' power to resort to intergovernmental agreements *inter se* even in matters which fall under the scope of Union legislation. The ruling also went beyond precedent case law in stating that Member States have the right to entrust to EU institutions tasks in the implementation of such agreements, provided that the new tasks do not alter the essential character of the powers conferred on the institutions by the Founding Treaties. Thus, *Pringle* confirmed intergovernmental agreements as the third option, alongside enhanced cooperation and use of Art. 136, which is available for establishing a particular Eurozone regime and retreating further from the principle of the unity of the Union.[11]

Changing the perspective: incursions in budget autonomy in light of national constitutions

The transnational, European constitution should always be examined in its interaction with national constitutions. The cultural sub-structure of national constitutions, that is, the constitutional traditions common to the Member States invoked in Art. 6(3) TEU, impact the cultural underpinnings of the European constitution.[12] Moreover, the EU constitutional legislator must heed the normative requirements of the constitutions of Member States which must ratify the Founding Treaties and their amendments in accordance with national provisions. In Germany, certain principles of the European macroeconomic constitution have been co-opted into the Basic Law, and the Federal Constitutional Court has confirmed that respect for these principles is a constitutional precondition for Germany's continuing EU membership. Ever since the Maastricht ruling in 1993, the Constitutional Court has repeatedly characterised monetary union as a 'stability union' and considered this as not only a normative principle of EU law but a requirement of German constitutional law, too. In turn, in 1992 the independence of the ECB and price stability as its primary policy objective were explicitly enshrined in Art. 88 of the Basic Law to pave the way for German ratification of the Maastricht Treaty.[13] This might be considered slightly surprising, taking into account that the independence of the Bundesbank was never constitutionally anchored.

---

[11] The legal and institutional automatisation of EMU, and the Eurozone within EMU, is one of the main constitutional implications of the crisis analysed by E. Chiti and P. Gustavo Teixeira (2013).

[12] See the discussion in J. E. Fossum and A. J. Menéndez (2011).

[13] "The Federation shall establish a note-issuing and currency bank as the Federal Bank. Within the framework of the European Union, its responsibilities and powers may be transferred to the European Central Bank, which is independent and committed to the overriding goal of assuring price stability" German Basic Law, Art. 88.

Still, as a rule national constitutional law does not include such comprehensive provisions on macroeconomic constitution as is the case in the EU. This reduces the possibility of outright contradictions between European law and national constitutional law. Until the Eurozone crisis, European law also refrained from posing normative requirements on Member States' constitutional regulation. In this respect, the history of the Treaty on Stability, Coordination and Governance possesses principal significance for the relationship between European law and national constitutional law. This history, it may be recalled, started from plans to amend, first secondary and then primary, EU legislation and ended up with conclusion of an intergovernmental agreement.

However, what national constitutions as a rule regulate are the competences of national parliaments. Fiscal competences, such as taxation and budgetary powers, have historically lain at the very core of the parliamentary regime and, together with legislative powers, constituted the vital pillars of representative democracy and parliamentary control over government. Accordingly, the arguably most important repercussions that constitutional mutation at the European level has had with regard to Member State constitutions concern the budgetary autonomy of the parliament. The extent to which these repercussions have been articulated and discussed in Member States depends, inter alia, on the particularities of constitutional review; for instance, the availability of *ex ante* review in general and in particular the possibility to subject EU legislation or international treaties to such review. In the following, we shall examine constitutional reactions in two Member States with *ex ante* review and a relatively high respect for the constitution: Finland and Germany. For us, the choice of Finland is of course natural, but we think objective reasons, too, favour our choice. In turn, Germany can hardly be ignored, due to its position as the biggest and most influential euro state and the status as *primus inter pares* of the Federal Constitutional Court, which has made of it the privileged interlocutor with the ECJ and a major player in the field of EU law, too.

In Finland, the Constitutional Law Committee of Parliament is the main constitutional review body. It is solely composed of MPs, representing both Government and Opposition parties. However, the Committee is supposed to exercise a quasi-judicial function in interpreting the Constitution. In its deliberations the Committee invariably consults constitutional experts, mainly constitutional law professors, who provide an important source of interpretive authority and legitimacy for the Committee. The Committee focuses exclusively on *ex ante* review where its opinions on the constitutionality of legislative bills and international agreements are binding on Parliament. If it finds a legislative bill or an international agreement to be unconstitutional, Parliament can still pass it with a qualified majority applicable to amendments of the Constitution. With regard to legislation, this possibility is now hardly ever resorted to but the usual procedure is to amend the bill in order to bring it into harmony with the Constitution. By contrast, approval by a qualified majority of international agreements and legislation incorporating them in the domestic legal order is not regarded as problematic. The Committee may assess in the light of the national constitution even draft EU legislation or draft intergovernmental agreements between Member States, such as the Treaty on the European Stability Mechanism or the Treaty on Stability, Coordination and Governance. The Government has a constitutional obligation to inform Parliament of draft European legal instruments, and Parliament can request the Constitutional Law Committee's opinion on their constitutionality.[14]

Ex ante review by the Constitutional Law Committee has covered the main legal instruments of both financial rescue facilities and economic governance. Its main constitutional worries, though, have concerned the fiscal liabilities deriving from rescue measures and mechanisms.[15] The Committee has worked under an exceptionally heavy time pressure but has still managed to capture the principal constitutional issues. The principal constitutional criteria it has employed are Parliament's budgetary power, combined with Finland's national sovereignty, and the state's fiscal ability to meet its constitutional obligations. In assessing possible infringement of these criteria, the Committee has examined the amount of potential liabilities, the risk of their realisation and Parliament's power to influence their future specification.

---

[14] Art. 96 provides that Parliament must be consulted on proposals for EU measures which otherwise, according to the Constitution, would fall within its competence. The proposals are discussed in the Grand Committee or the Foreign Affairs Committee, which may issue a statement to the Government. In addition, the Speaker's Council may decide that the matter be taken up for debate in plenary session, during which, however, no decision is made.

[15] The first Greek rescue package was deliberated in Parliament merely in the context of an amendment to the budget. Neither the Loan Facility Agreement nor the Inter-creditor Agreement was submitted to Parliament for approval. Clearly, this was due to the formalistic reason of the private-law nature of these intergovernmental agreements.

In the worst scenario, Finland's losses from its guarantee commitment under the EFSF Framework Agreement could amount to a sum which corresponds to more than half the annual budget. However, the Constitutional Law Committee has pointed to factors which softened the effect of the Framework Agreement on Parliament's budgetary power. All the major decisions in the EFSF affecting Member State guarantee liabilities required unanimity in the Board of Directors. Art. 96 of the Finnish Constitution, in turn, grants the Grand Committee of Parliament the right to pronounce on the position which Finland's representative will take. Moreover, the law incorporating the Framework Agreement obliged Government to seek Parliament's authorisation for every guarantee given under the Agreement. The Constitutional Law Committee considered such involvement of Parliament sufficient to guarantee that Parliament retains its budgetary power.[16]

Finland's total subscription to the authorised capital stock of the ESM equals more than a quarter of the annual government budget. If such a liability, to be paid in a single instalment, had flowed directly from the ESM Treaty, this would arguably have violated Parliament's constitutionally anchored budgetary power, as well as national sovereignty. Furthermore, the State's financial capability to meet its constitutional obligations could have been jeopardised. However, the ESM Treaty divides the authorised capital stock into paid-in and callable shares, and immediate liability of the Members covers merely the former. All major decisions affecting financial liability must be taken by mutual agreement, that is, unanimously, by the Board of Governors; these comprise calls for unpaid, callable capital. The requirement of mutual agreement also covers major decisions on the stability support the ESM provides. Consequently, individual Member States possess a veto power, and in Finland, Parliament (the Grand Committee) has the possibility to influence the Government's voting position. According to the judgment of the Constitutional Law Committee, this allays the Treaty's impact on Finland's sovereignty and Parliament's budgetary power.[17]

The ESM Treaty provides for an emergency procedure where decisions can be made by a qualified majority of 85 per cent of the votes cast. Under such a majority only the three largest Euro States – Germany, France and Italy – retain their veto power. Pursuant to Art. 4(4), the

---

[16] See the following Opinions of the Finnish Constitutional Law Committee: PeVL 5 and 14/2011.
[17] See Opinion PeVL 13/2012.

emergency procedure "shall be used where the Commission and the
ECB both conclude that a failure to adopt a decision to grant or implement financial assistance would threaten the economic and financial
stability of the euro-area". When the emergency procedure was first
introduced in treaty negotiations in late 2011, it would have comprised
not only decisions on granting assistance, but also decisions directly
affecting the liability of Member States, such as calls for authorised
unpaid capital. In December 2011, the Constitutional Law Committee
concluded that if the provision on the emergency procedure were
retained in its original form, the Treaty and the law on its incorporation would have to be accepted in Parliament by a qualified majority.[18]
Finland's constitutional concerns evidently contributed to amendment
of the controversial draft provision to the effect that decisions directly
affecting the liability of Member States were left outside the emergency
procedure. For the Constitutional Law Committee, this removed the
contradiction with the Constitution.

On several occasions, the Committee has emphasised that a quantitative assessment may not confine itself merely to the instrument under
examination but should cover all fiscal liabilities deriving from management of the Eurozone crisis. Moreover, attention should be paid to
the likelihood of the risks involved in each instrument. Of course, such
a comprehensive assessment is complicated, due to the different legal
and financial character of each instrument and the intricacy of risk
calculation. Furthermore, the Committee must, to a large extent, rely
on information provided by the Government. Even with regard to the
constitutional consequences of a quantitative analysis for Parliament's
budgetary power and the state's capability to meet its commitments, the
Committee has, for understandable reasons, granted the Government a
considerable margin of appreciation. The Committee has for instance
declined to define an exact quantitative ceiling for acceptable liabilities.
Such difficulties of constitutional review relativise the significance of
the major premise of the Committee: namely, that a parliamentary
majority may not, through the commitments it accepts, reduce future
parliaments' budgetary powers at will. In its final opinion on the ESM
Treaty in June 2012, the Committee considered the liabilities deriving
from this Treaty together with Finland's previous commitments under
the Greek loan facility and the EFSF Framework Agreement. Even in
such a comprehensive appraisal, the Committee did not find a breach

[18] PeVL 25/2011.

of the Constitution on the grounds of an infringement of Parliament's constitutional powers or national sovereignty. Nor did the Committee reckon that the commitments, even when taken as a whole, would jeopardise the State's capability to meet its constitutional obligations.[19]

The Committee's examination of draft six- or two-pack legislation or the TSCG has not come up with observations of contradictions with the Finnish constitution, either. The Committee's main argument has been that the changes in economic governance in comparison with the original provisions of the Maastricht Treaty do not essentially enlarge the restrictions on Finland's sovereignty and Parliament's fiscal powers which have already been accepted by a qualified majority with the Treaty of Accession and the law on its incorporation. Yet, the Opinion of the Constitutional Law Committee on the first draft of the TSCG intimates that the provisions on the Member States' obligation to incorporate the requirement of a balanced budget and debt brake in their constitutions would have been seen to touch upon the Constitution and presuppose a qualified majority in Parliament. The same goes for the monitoring role national courts and the ECJ would have had pursuant to the first draft.[20] Again, it is possible that Finland's constitutional doubts played a role in subsequent amendments to the draft treaty.

Evidently, the Opinions of the Finnish Constitutional Law Committee do not possess similar authority in the European playing field as the rulings of the German Constitutional Court. Still, they are not insignificant either, but testify for their part to the reciprocal character of the relations of influence between the transnational, European constitution and the national constitutions. Primarily, though, the Finnish constitution has been at the receiving end. Constitutional mutation at the European level has instigated changes to national constitutional doctrine which have allowed for unprecedented transnational substantive and procedural interference in the national budgetary process; articulated the criteria for assessing the constitutional acceptability of international or transnational fiscal liabilities; and consented to potentially significant cuts in future parliaments' budgetary powers.

During the Eurozone crisis, the German Constitutional Court has issued two important contributions to European constitutional discourse. The first ruling, in September 2011, focused on the Greek loan facility and

---

[19] See the following Opinions of the Finnish Constitutional Law Committee: PeVL 22 and 25/2011, and PeVL 13/2012.
[20] M. Poiares Maduro (2012); PeVL 24/2011.

the EFSF Framework Agreement, and the second one in September 2012 on the TESM, while touching on the amendment to Art. 136 TFEU and the TSCG, too. The latter ruling only decided on the issue of temporary injections; as we write, the ruling in the main issue is still to come. The main constitutional criteria the Court has applied have been national budget autonomy and the budgetary power of the democratically elected Parliament (the Bundestag). These criteria go back to the Court's probably most important and influential interventions in the European constitutional discourse: the Maastricht ruling of October 1993 and the Lisbon ruling of June 2009.[21]

In the Maastricht ruling, the Court defined EMU as primarily a monetary union, which the Treaty governs as "a community committed to long-term stability, in particular to monetary stability". The Court further stated that justifiable grounds may exist for suggesting that, "in political terms, the monetary union may be implemented practically only if it is supplemented immediately by an economic union which exceeds simple coordination of the economic policies of the Member States and of the Community". This would, however, require a Treaty amendment. The same goes for a political union. The Court also pointed out that assignment of most of the functions of monetary policy to an independent central bank restricts Member State sovereign rights and the democratic legitimation deriving from the electorate of Member States. The Court characterised monetary policy in rather ordoliberal terms as "a substantial political sphere which supports individual liberty by maintaining the value of currency, and influences public finances and those areas of politics dependent on them by controlling the money supply". Here the Court invoked the amendment to Art. 88 of the Basic Law which allowed for transferring the powers of the Bundesbank to a European Central Bank, provided that the independence of the Bank and the priority of monetary stability as its policy objective are guaranteed. The amendment modified the constitutional principle of democracy. Yet in the Court's view such a modification is justified not only by German experience but by a truth of economic science as well: "it takes account of the special factor, established in the German system and also scientifically proven, that an independent central bank is more likely to protect monetary value, and therefore the general economic basis for national budget policy and private planning and disposition, while maintaining economic liberty than are sovereign governmental institutions".

---

[21] BVerfGE 89, 155, 2 October 1993; BVerfG, 2 BvE 2/08, 30 June 2009.

The particular contribution of the Lisbon ruling lies in its elaborating the doctrine of the fundamental constitutional principles which define Germany's constitutional identity and which transfer of sovereignty to the Union in accordance with Art. 23 of the Basic Law may not encroach upon.[22] The main anchorage of this doctrine is the eternity clause in Art. 79(3) of the Basic Law which declares the principles laid down in Arts. 1 and 20 unamendable. These principles include democracy. In line with the Maastricht ruling, the Court argued that because of the weak democratic foundations of the Union, even under the Lisbon Treaty the necessary democratic legitimation for Union action derives mainly from national procedures. Hence, the principle of democracy requires safeguarding Member States' sovereignty so that "sufficient space is left to the Member States for the political formation of the economic, cultural and social living conditions". Areas of "democratic formative action" which must remain under Member State sovereignty comprise public revenue and expenditure. With regard to state expenditure, the Court especially emphasised the need to retain democratic decision-making over social policy. Furthermore, the Court pointed to the pivotal political role of the budgetary process and in particular parliamentary debate on the budget. The Court, though, conceded that the openness to European integration which the Basic Law calls for entails that the legislature responsible for approving the budget must respect European parameters and commitments. Yet, "what is decisive … is that the overall responsibility, with sufficient political discretion regarding revenue and expenditure, can still rest with the German Bundestag".

In its judgment of 7 September 2011, the Court assessed the Monetary Union Financial Stabilisation Act (*Währungsunion-Finanzstabilisierungsgesetz*), which authorised the loans granted to Greece, and the Act Concerning the Giving of Guarantees in the Framework

---

[22] Art. 23, which was amended in the context of the ratification of the Maastricht Treaty, provides, inter alia, that

> with a view to establishing a united Europe, the Federal Republic of Germany shall participate in the development of the European Union that is committed to democratic, social and federal principles, to the rule of law, and to the principle of subsidiarity, and that guarantees a level of protection of basic rights essentially comparable to that afforded by this Basic Law.

> To this end sovereign powers may be transferred by a law with the consent of the Bundesrat. However, the establishment of the EU, as well as changes in its treaty foundations and comparable regulations, that amend or supplement this Basic Law, or make such amendments or supplements possible, are subject to the eternity clause of Art. 79(2)-(3).

of a European Stabilisation Mechanism (*Gesetz zur Übernahme von Gewährleistungen im Rahmen eines europäischen Stabilisierungsmechanismus*), which authorised the guarantees under the EFSF Framework Agreement.[23] The second major ruling, issued on 12 September 2012, dealt with the ESM Treaty and the Act establishing the European Stability Mechanism (*Gesetz zu dem Vertrag vom 2. Februar 2012 zur Einrichtung des Europäischen Stabilitätsmechanismus*).[24] In both rulings the Court repeated the premise expounded in the Lisbon judgment: decision-making on public revenue and public expenditure is a fundamental part of the ability of a constitutional state to democratically shape itself. The Court also argued that democratic national budgetary procedures, which guarantee the democratic legitimation of EU action, are a requirement of not only national but even EU constitutional law:

> The provisions of the European treaties do not conflict with the understanding of national budget autonomy as an essential competence, which cannot be relinquished, of the parliaments of the Member States which enjoy direct democratic legitimation, but instead they presuppose it. Strict compliance with it guarantees that the acts of the bodies of the European Union in and for Germany have sufficient democratic legitimation.

The constitutional principle of democracy prohibits the Bundestag from relinquishing its budget responsibility so that it or a future Bundestag can no longer exercise the right to decide on the budget on its own responsibility. This would be the case if essential decisions on revenue and expenditure were taken without requiring the Bundestag's consent or if supranational legal obligations were created without such consent. The Bundestag may not commit itself to a financial mechanism which may lead without prior mandatory consent to such losses of revenue or expenses which cannot be calculated in advance. This imposes a constitutional ban on mutualisation of sovereign debt in the EU. The Court argues that under international treaties, no permanent mechanisms may be created which are tantamount to accepting liability for other states' decisions, above all if these entail consequences which are difficult to calculate. Similarly, open-ended guarantee commitments, too, are constitutionally prohibited.

The Court was very clear in its starting-points. Yet in applying them to the commitments under examination and in establishing whether a prohibited relinquishment of budget autonomy by Parliament existed,

---

[23] BVerfG, 2 BvR 987/10, 7 September 2011.
[24] BVerfG, 2 BvR 1390/12, 12 September 2012.

it displayed a high degree of judicial restraint and accorded the legislature a large discretion. It restricted itself to assessing 'manifest violations' of the prohibition when examining the amount of commitments, the risks of their being called on and the ensuing consequences for sustainability of the federal budget and the state's 'economic performance capacity'; i.e. criteria largely similar to those employed by the Finnish Constitutional Law Committee. In line with the Finnish Committee, the Court also specifically refused to define an absolute, justiciable quantitative limit for commitments. With regard to guarantees in the EFSF framework, it confined itself to stating that an upper limit could only be overstepped if "the guarantees took effect in such a way that budget autonomy, at least for an appreciable period of time, was not merely restricted but effectively failed".

As academic observers have remarked, both rulings adhere to the 'yes, but ...' formula, typical of the German Constitutional Court's EU-related judgments in general.[25] In neither ruling did the Court find that the examined statutes would have violated the principles of democracy and permanent budget autonomy. Yet it made its conclusion dependent on minor corrections or clarifications. In the first ruling, the Court only held the Act authorising the guarantees under the EFSF Framework Agreement compatible with the Basic Law provided that it be interpreted to the effect that the Federal Government is obliged to obtain prior approval by the Budget Committee of Parliament before giving guarantees. In the second ruling, the Court required as a condition for ratification of the ESM Treaty that under international law assurances be obtained that Art. 8(5) of the Treaty limits the amount of all Germany's payment obligations to the amount stipulated in Annex II so that higher obligations require the agreement of the German representative. A similar assurance was needed to warrant that provisions in the ESM Treaty on inviolability of documents, professional secrecy and immunity do not prevent comprehensive information to the German Parliament. The conditions the Court set for German ratification were met through a joint interpretive statement issued by the Contracting Parties on 27 September 2012.[26]

The latter ruling includes a preliminary discussion of the Treaty on Stability, Coherence and Governance, too. The Court pointed to the harmony of the provisions on balanced budgets and the debt brake

---

[25] K. Schneider (2013).
[26] TESM (2012), 'Declaration on the European Stability Mechanism', 27 September 2012.

with the amended Arts. 109 and 115 of the Basic Law. As another aspect which is important to constitutional assessment at national level, too, the Court invoked the fact that parts of the TSCG merely repeat provisions of European Union law or put them into more concrete terms. On the Court's summary view, the TSCG does not grant EU bodies powers which affect the overall budgetary responsibility of the German Bundestag, nor did such consequences derive from the provision on a national corrective mechanism to be activated in case of significant deviations from the medium-term objective of a balanced budget or the adjustment path towards it. Finally, in ratifying the TSCG Germany did not, in the Court's view, enter into an irreversible commitment to a particular budget policy.[27]

The reasoning of both the Finnish Constitutional Law Committee and the German Constitutional Court illustrates the tension between fiscal liabilities deriving from European rescue measures and national budgetary autonomy, backed up by the principle of democracy. By the same token, it also testifies to the difficulty of putting a brake on the largely incremental constitutional mutation occurring at the European level. As is shown by heeding national constitutional worries in (re)drafting the TSCG or the interpretative statement attached to the TESM in consequence of the German Constitutional Court's ruling, national constitutional concerns have had an impact at the European level. Still, they have not stopped the gradual process or changed its course. At least in the two Member States we have examined, European constitutional mutation has induced a mirror effect at the national level, instigating amendments to constitutional doctrine which national constitutional review has consecrated. National constitutional doctrine has had to bend and accept the diminution of substantive and procedural budget autonomy.

[27] In June 2013, the Court started the oral hearings in a third case with potential repercussions even for European constitutional discourse. In this case, the claimants dispute the constitutionality of the ECB's programme of Outright Monetary Transactions. The principal argument is that purchases of government bonds without any upper limit may entail fiscal liabilities for Germany without prior consent of the Bundestag. This would violate Parliament's budgetary autonomy and the democracy principle. See the Court's press release: German Federal Court (2012), 'ESM/Fiskalpakt – Anträge auf Erlass Einer Einstweiligen Anordnung', 2 July 2012.

7   Democracy and social rights

The constitutional principles of democracy and transparency

In the constitutional respect, the Eurozone crisis has not appeared only as a crisis of the macroeconomic constitution and entailed a significant change to the Maastricht principles. It has had important repercussions in other constitutional dimensions, too, primarily political and social. All the constitutional dimensions possess an institutional aspect. The institutional structure of the Union can be examined in the context of 'substantively' defined constitutional dimensions, and, indeed, analysing the status and mandate of the ECB has formed an integral part of our discussion of the macroeconomic constitution. But the institutional structure can and should also be explored as a whole; as a vital element of the political constitution, and in the light of the particular principles and values of this constitutional dimension. Evidently, the Eurozone crisis has lifted the macroeconomic constitution into a pacemaker position among the many constitutions of Europe. The economic constitution is clearly defining the agenda for the political dimension. Mutation of the macroeconomic constitution and expansion of the functions of expert institutions beyond their original role have consequences for the political constitution as well. The obvious danger is that the economic constitution also dictates the terms of development, so that insufficient attention is paid to specifically political constitutional values, such as democracy, transparency, legitimacy and accountability. This danger is enhanced by the sneaking, piecemeal mode in which the political constitution is being remoulded under the impact of the economic one.

In the Lisbon Treaty, the principles of democracy and transparency were accorded special attention. Already in Maastricht, in the Preamble to the Treaty on the European Union, the Member States confirmed "their attachment to the principles of liberty, democracy and respect for human rights and fundamental freedoms and of the rule of law", and expressed their desire "to enhance further the democratic and efficient functioning of the institutions so as to enable them better to carry out, within a single institutional framework, the tasks entrusted to them". In Lisbon, democracy was included in the values on which the Union is founded, which are shared by the Member States (Art. 2 TEU) and whose violation by a Member State can trigger off sanctions pursuant to Art. 7 TEU. For the German Constitutional Court, in turn, respect for democracy is a precondition for Germany's continuing participation in European integration.

Title II TEU contains more detailed provisions on the principle of democracy. It invokes EU citizens' equality; representative democracy as the foundation of the functioning of the Union; the role of citizens, representative associations and civil society; as well as National Parliaments' active contribution to the good functioning of the Union. Art. 15 TFEU sets out the implications of the principle of transparency. Union institutions, bodies, offices and agencies are obliged to conduct their work as openly as possible, in order to promote good governance and ensure the participation of civil society (Art. 15(1)). Union citizens, as well as any natural or legal person residing or having its registered office in a Member State are entitled to access to documents. This right covers the documents of Union institutions, bodies, offices and agencies, whatever the medium of the documents. It is, however, subject to principles and conditions to be defined in accordance with Treaty provisions.[1] In addition, the EU Charter of Fundamental Rights, to which the Lisbon Treaty gave legal effect, includes a provision on the right of access to the documents of the European Parliament, the Council and the Commission (Art. 42).

As the German Constitutional Court has repeatedly argued, in an assessment of the requirements and realisation of the principle of democracy, both the European and the Member State level must be involved. We start discussing issues of democracy from the division of competences between the European and the national level.

---

[1] The principles and conditions are defined in Parliament and Council Regulation (EC) No. 1049/2001 on public access to European Parliament, Council and Commission documents, [2001] OJ L145/43, Art. 15(3).

Division of competences

The division of competences between the national, Member State and transnational, European level is an issue not only of expediency but of democracy, too. Often enough, the default assumption is that transfer of competences from the national to transnational level signifies a defeat for democracy. Coverage of national democratic procedures is reduced in a manner which cannot be compensated for at the European level, due to the still largely lacking sociological and cultural prerequisites for transnational democracy. The standard position may grant an exception to 'non-political' policy fields, such as monetary or competition policy, or 'non-political' public functions, such as adjudication, which are considered more suitable for Europeanisation. These fields and functions are exempted from the requirement of democratic input legitimacy; if the legitimacy issue is considered at all relevant, it is conceived of in terms of output legitimacy, guaranteed by specific economic or juridical expertise.

Yet, things are not that simple. The standard view which brackets off expert fields and functions and claims the democracy argument for the side of national decision-making is open to contestation. We shall discuss the role of expert bodies in another section and focus now on the division of tasks between the national and transnational level. The basic idea of democracy is to give those concerned, that is, those affected by a decision, a possibility to have a say in its making. National sovereignty and democracy go together where the effects of decisions are confined within national boundaries. But the wider and deeper cross-border effects that decisions have, the more national sovereignty loses its privileged linkage to democracy. At a certain point, retaining decision-making under national sovereignty produces a democratic deficit by excluding from participation those affected by the externalities.

The cross-boundary consequences of national policies are a major reason and justification for the European project as a whole and for transnational developments in general.[2] Democratic arguments exist not only for defending national sovereignty but also for reducing its scope: transfer of competences from national to transnational level may be construable as a remedy for the democratic deficit which derives from the externalities of national policies. Still, another

---

[2] In his doctoral thesis, Poiares Maduro already invoked the externalities of national measures as a major justification for the ECJ's role as a constitutional court in the field of the microeconomic constitution. M. Poiares Maduro (1998).

solution to at least alleviate, if not resolve, the problem of externalities exists; namely, their inclusion in national decision-making, i.e.
the internalisation of the interests and viewpoints of other nation-
states and their peoples. By and large, this has been the preferred way
of the European economic constitution ever since the Treaty of Rome.[3]
It may be recalled that one of the principles underpinning the macroeconomic constitution introduced in Maastricht is Member States'
obligation to treat their economic policies as a common concern (Art.
121(1) TFEU). The reasoning underlying the Treaty provisions on economic policy appears to be that when Member States live up to this
obligation, the Union may confine itself to facilitating coordination
of national policies.

One of the lessons from the Eurozone crisis is that transcending a
narrow nationalistic perspective in economic policy-making and inter-
nalising the perspective of others has proved to be harder to achieve
than expected. This lesson has been a major background factor to
the efforts to tighten European economic governance and develop
it beyond the primarily soft methods of coordination set out in the
Maastricht constitution. The original approach left it mainly to national
discretion to ensure that national fiscal policy would not burden common monetary policy and fiscal policies of other Member States. This
discretion did not yield expected results, but in many cases failed to
heed even national medium-term considerations, let alone negative
externalities.

Moreover, privileging the intergovernmental way in rescue measures
and mechanisms appears to have further enhanced the nationalistic
perspective in Member States. Emphasis in national discussions often
enough seems to be on short-term national optimisation. Be that as it
may, our discussion has demonstrated that the assumption, inherent
in the standard view, that the democratic argument always weighs in
support of national decision-making is far too straightforward.

Above, we have often invoked the principle of conferral, which
applies to the competences of both the Union as a whole and each of its
institutions. This principle entails a presumption in favour of national
sovereignty: all the competences which have not been expressly
granted to the Union remain with the Member States.[4] In addition to

---

[3] Art. 103(1) obliged the Member States to regard their conjunctural policies as a matter
of common concern.
[4] It must, though, be recalled that the flexibility clause, at present in Art. 352 TFEU,
modifies the principle of conferral.

the principle of conferral, the relations of competence between the Union and the Member States are governed by subsidiarity. Art. 5(3) TEU lays down that

in areas which do not fall within its exclusive competence, the Union shall act only if and in so far as the objectives of the proposed action cannot be sufficiently achieved by the Member States, either at central level or at regional and local level, but can rather, by reason of the scale or effects of the proposed action, be better achieved at Union level.

As it is formulated in the TEU, subsidiarity relates to the use of shared competences under the present Treaties. But, of course, subsidiarity considerations are also relevant – though not legally binding – in discussing possible Treaty amendments and the need to adjust the current division of competences. The standard view sees subsidiarity, national decision-making and democracy as allies. We have tried to show that the argument from democracy may favour Union action and competences, as well. This point can be read into the very definition of subsidiarity in Art. 5(3) TEU, which enlists the effects of the proposed action as a factor favouring the use of Union competence.

It is probably needless to point out that the democratic deficit at the Member State level, related to the externalities of national policies, does not suffice to provide transnational decision-making with democratic justification. Meeting the externalities criterion can be deemed a necessary but not sufficient condition for such a justification. The problem remains how to ensure the necessary democratic input legitimation for Union policies and actions.

Narrowing the reach of national democratic legitimation

Democratic arguments played a part in determining the division of competences between the national and transnational level in the Maastricht macroeconomic constitution. A major reason for leaving the economic union incomplete, in spite of the probable majority opinion among economists, shared by the Delors Committee, was the perceived need for democratic input legitimation for fiscal and other economic policy; this need, in turn, could only be satisfied at the Member State level. This remains the principal line of reasoning of the German Constitutional Court, too, although the Court has consented to significant curtailing of national budget autonomy.

In the previous chapters, we have explored at both European and national level the constitutional mutation which has reduced Member States' sovereignty in fiscal and economic policy. This mutation has affected the democratic input legitimacy not only of national but even of European policies and actions. The German Constitutional Court has repeatedly pointed out that democratic national budgetary decision-making is a requirement not only of the Basic Law but of the Treaties as EU constitutional law, too; national democratic procedures are necessary for the democratic legitimation of Union action, as well. This normative argumentation has its sociological counterpart in Fritz Scharpf's observations on the two-level legitimation structure of the EU. The effects of European policies on European citizens have been mediated through Member States, and citizens have not confronted EU institutions, policies or the impacts of these policies in their daily lives directly, but indirectly, via Member State action.[5] Consequently, Member States have borne the burden of providing input legitimacy for the EU as well. This they have largely been able to accomplish, due to national democratic procedures and the controlling power of national parliaments, electorates and civil societies.

The discontent in both recipient and assisting states, finding expression in, for instance, the electoral success of populist parties riding on nationalistic and anti-European themes, testifies to increasing legitimation problems. This poses a grave danger for the future of the EU. European citizenry experiences the consequences of European policies without the dampening and legitimating mediation of national democratic procedures: "In the present euro crisis … the shield of legitimacy intermediation has been pushed aside as citizens are directly confronted with the massive impact of European policies – and with their manifest lack of democratic legitimacy."[6] In crisis states, governments and parliaments implement the austerity programmes agreed on by the Troika of the Commission, the ECB and the IMF, giving effect to the

---

[5]   … [t]he higher level of the European polity is generally beyond the horizon of citizens' expectations and political demands; it is not the target of public debates and party competition, and most importantly, it is not vulnerable to electoral sanctions … Citizens will not usually know the origin of the rules with which they are asked to comply, but they know that the only government which they might hold politically accountable is their own. In effect, therefore, national governments must generally bear the full burden of political accountability for unwelcome exercises of governing authority, regardless of how much European law may have contributed to these.F. Scharpf (2012), p. 19

[6]   *Ibid.*

strict conditionality of the assistance. National democratic institutions are widely conceived of as mere executors of policies imposed from the outside. In these circumstances, parliamentary and electoral mechanisms are hardly able to procure input legitimation even for national decision-making, not to speak of channelling such legitimation to the European level. In assisting Member States, too, the European level is increasingly held responsible for policies affecting citizens, and the national parliament is not seen to possess much leeway in their implementation. In addition to rescue measures and mechanisms, enhanced legitimation needs derive from tightened European economic governance, especially country-specific guidance buttressed by formal sanctions within both the preventive and corrective arms of the Stability and Growth Pact. In sum, in both recipient and assisting states the need for legitimation of European policies is growing while national democratic procedures are increasingly less capable of meeting it. Fritz Scharpf's assessment is dismal: "European responses to the euro crisis have disabled national democratic legitimacy, and at the same time, they have destroyed the possibility of legitimacy intermediation on which the European polity so far had depended."[7]

Two alternative responses exist to the legitimacy dilemma of fiscal and economic policy which has resulted from the gradual erosion of national sovereignty and the consequent shrinking of the legitimating power of national democratic procedures. The first of these is to redefine fiscal and economic policy and negate their need for democratic input legitimation. This strategy implies de-politicising fiscal and economic policy, labelling them fields of non-political expertise where decisions should be grounded in objectively given economic parameters. Thus, the model already applied to monetary policy would be extended to non-monetary economic policy as well. The door to redefinition was already opened ajar by the Maastricht macroeconomic constitution through its constraints on national fiscal policy, relying on quasi-objective, quantitative reference values. However, the reference values still left the content and size of the public sector at national discretion, as long as it was considered to be prudently financed. The expansion and deepening of European economic governance and the increasing substantive and procedural requirements imposed on national budgetary frameworks have widened the crack and enhanced the non-political

[7] *Ibid.*, p. 26.

features of fiscal policy. The new excessive imbalances procedure, with its scoreboard of macroeconomic parameters monitored by the Commission, has extended the tendency of de-politicisation to general macroeconomic policy. This tendency has taken institutional forms as well. Proposals for creating independent budget offices or councils at both the Member State and European level have abounded. With adoption of the two-pack, they have reaped their first practical results. Eurozone states are obliged to establish independent bodies monitoring compliance with fiscal rules. These must be structurally independent or "endowed with functional autonomy *vis-à-vis* the budgetary authorities of the Member State".[8] Schuknecht (and others) advocate a European Budget Office, which would be free from 'political interference'.[9] It would assess national policies within the euro area and proper implementation of governance procedures, as well as acting as the monitoring body and administrator for ESM programmes. The authors suggest that "it could potentially form the nucleus of what could become over time and in a step-wise manner a European Ministry of Finance". They argue that "it is clear from past experience that, at the euro-area level, only a strong and independent institution can compensate for member countries' tendency towards leniency in the implementation of fiscal rules".[10]

These calls for stricter control of fiscal (and social) policies tend to aggravate the tension between the two requirements imposed on national fiscal policy in EMU. After Europeanisation of monetary policy, fiscal policy is expected to assume greater responsibility for national economic policy, but enhanced requirements for fiscal prudence make this increasingly difficult. In an ideal world, the tension would be mastered by Member States' gaining sufficient room for manoeuvre through ensuring substantial fiscal surpluses during up-cycles. In that case, national fiscal discretion and national democratic procedures would not be subject to EU-level constraints that undermine legitimacy. De-politicisation of fiscal policy, as it is currently advocated, still

---

[8] European Parliament and Council Regulation (EU) No. 473/2013 of 21 May 2013 on common provisions for monitoring and assessing draft budgetary plans and ensuring the correction of excessive deficit of the Member States in the euro area, [2013] OJ L140/11, Arts. 2(1) and 5.

[9] L. Schuknecht *et al.* (2011).

[10] Other proponents of a European Ministry of Finance include Jean-Claude Trichet, former President of the ECB. L. Elliot (2011), 'EU Should Control Member States' Budget Says Bank Boss', 2 June 2011.

rests on a one-sided effort to control and prevent negative externalities, without sufficiently attending to national fiscal policy's general function in economic policy or the concomitant implications in terms of democratic legitimacy needs.

Hence, the strategy of de-politicisation has obvious limits. The need for legitimation arises from the impacts that policies have on citizens' lives. Democratic input legitimation has responded to the redistributive effects of fiscal and economic policy. European citizens have experienced these effects very profoundly during the Eurozone crisis. The need for legitimation has not disappeared; on the contrary, it has intensified. Redefinition of fiscal and economic policy signifies an effort to shift the emphasis from democratic input legitimation towards output legitimation, guaranteed by non-political, independent experts. But even if concrete results, testifying to the benefits of increasing the weight of non-political expertise, were to be seen, legitimacy expectations cannot be manipulated at will from above. Moreover, national budgetary processes are not only about the budget; they are about politics in general. In many nation-state democracies, the budgetary process lies at the very centre of political discourse and opinion formation, as the German Constitutional Court has repeatedly pointed out.

The obvious alternative to de-politicisation would be to try to remedy the notorious democracy deficit at the European level and to introduce or reinforce democratic federalist structures. In this respect, developments during the Eurozone crisis have not been very encouraging. The European Parliament and the national parliaments have been accorded but a peripheral position in both financial stability mechanisms and European economic governance. In rescue measures and mechanisms, intergovernmentalism has been the privileged option, and the amendment to Art. 136 TFEU and the establishment of the European Stability Mechanism have confirmed it as permanent, constitutionally anchored policy. Sidestepping the EU legislative and institutional framework has not conceded the European Parliament any role at all in either the designing or administrating and monitoring phase. In turn, the leeway and influence of national democratic procedures have depended, apart from pressures from the European level, on national constitutional arrangements.

Even in European economic governance, the European Parliament has, from the very installation of multilateral surveillance and

excessive deficit procedures, played but a minor role, restricted
mainly to the right to receive information.[11] The six- and two-pack
responded to criticism for lack of democracy with provisions on economic dialogue between EU institutions, in particular the Parliament,
the Council and the Commission. Dialogue takes place in the competent committee of Parliament, which may invite the President of
the Council, the Commission and, where appropriate, the President
of the European Council or the President of the Euro Group to discuss issues under consideration in the surveillance and monitoring procedures. The Member State concerned can also be allowed
to participate. Basic provisions on dialogue have been set out in
Regulation 1175/2011, which also formalised the European semester.[12]
In enhanced surveillance in the euro area, Parliament's role is more
prominent. In its Preamble, Regulation 1173/2011 on the effective
enforcement of budgetary surveillance in the euro area states that
"the strengthening of economic governance should include a closer
and a more timely involvement of the European Parliament and the
national parliament". The Preamble also provides for the possibility
of economic dialogue with the European Parliament which would
enable the Commission to make its analyses public and which could
involve the President of the Council, the Commission and, where
appropriate, the President of the European Council or the President of
the Euro Group. Moreover, the Preamble evokes the prospect of public debate on the spillover effects of national decisions, which could
engender public peer pressure to be brought to bear on the relevant

[11] According to Art. 121 TFEU, the Council informs the Parliament of its
    recommendation setting out the broad economic guidelines (Art. 121(2)), and the
    President of the Council and the Commission reports to the Parliament on the results
    of multilateral surveillance. Furthermore, the President of the Council may be invited
    to appear before the competent committee of the European Parliament. In turn,
    Art. 126 TFEU imposes on the President of the Council the obligation to inform the
    European Parliament of decisions taken with regard to a country submitted to the
    excessive deficit procedure.
[12] Regulation 1175/2011 focuses on the multilateral surveillance procedure under Art
    121. The other Regulations of the six-pack and the two-pack contain corresponding
    provisions on Economic Dialogue in the competent Committee of Parliament. In
    a uniform way, the provisions invoke the principle of transparency: the dialogue
    aims to ensure greater transparency and accountability. Parliament and Council
    Regulation (EU) of 16 November 2011 amending Council Regulation (EC) No. 1466/97
    on the strengthening of the surveillance of budgetary positions and the surveillance
    and coordination of economic policies, [2011] OJ L306/12.

actors. Still, involving national parliaments and civil society actors has largely remained at the level of programmatic statements.[13]

The rather modest efforts to engage the European Parliament and national parliaments in European economic governance, as well as to increase its transparency, are hardly able to affect the general picture. However, because of a potential institutional or – we could also say – democratic asymmetry, a more far-reaching involvement of the European Parliament is not unproblematic, either. Both stability mechanisms and deepening European economic governance focus in particular on the euro area. The increasing impact of the European Parliament, representing the citizenry of the EU as a whole, raises democratic worries about the congruence of influence on, and effects of, decision-making. Democracy requires that all those concerned be given a chance to participate. But, arguably, it also requires that those not concerned and not contributing be left without a voice.[14]

The weak formal position of the European Parliament in both financial stability mechanisms and European economic governance is not the only and perhaps not even the main obstacle to democracy at the European level. The major problems now as before concern sociological and cultural presuppositions: the still embryonic European civil society and public sphere, as well as the weak self-identity and frail mutual solidarity of the European citizenry. If the self-identity of European citizens is measured by electoral turnout, the development is rather discouraging: as the formal powers of the European Parliament have increased, electoral turnout has decreased. Consequently, the institution which is supposed to channel direct democratic legitimacy into the EU's institutional structure is suffering from a crisis of democratic

---

[13] Thus, the Preamble to Regulation 1175/2011 contains the following statement:

> In line with the legal and political arrangements of each Member State, national parliaments should be duly involved in the European Semester and in the preparation of stability programmes, convergence programmes and national reform programmes in order to increase the transparency and ownership of, and accountability for the decisions taken. Where appropriate, the Economic and Financial Committee, the Economic Policy Committee, the Employment Committee and the Social Protection Committee should be consulted within the framework of the European Semester. Relevant stakeholders, in particular the social partners, should be involved, within the framework of the European Semester, on the main policy issues where appropriate, in accordance with the provisions of the TFEU and national legal and political arrangements.(Recital 16)

[14] Currently, euro-area MEPs have less than two-thirds of the seats in Parliament.

legitimacy. However, no election for the European Parliament has been held since the eruption of the crisis, so that its impact on electoral activity is still untested.

If the Eurozone crisis has in general had positive consequences for democracy, one of these could be awakening a sense of European inter-connectedness both in the media and among the general public. For the first time in many Member States, European issues have occupied the forefront in national electoral campaigns. A sense of interconnect-edness is an indispensable prerequisite for a functioning European democracy. Unfortunately, this in itself positive development has been tainted by a nationalistic distortion: more often than not, events in other Member States and in Europe at large have been observed through the lenses of narrowly conceived national interests. On bal-ance, the crisis has probably done more to destroy than create socio-logical and cultural presuppositions for the emergence of a European demos; the subject of European democracy. One of the crucial issues for the future of European integration is how to end the inopportune mar-riage between rising European awareness and rising nationalism.

New intergovernmentalism

The rise of new intergovernmentalism, reliance on intergovernmen-tal legal and institutional structures, is especially conspicuous in the creation and administration of financial stability mechanisms.[15] Yet, it has left an imprint on the development of economic governance, too. The first Greek rescue package in May 2010 was based on a Loan Facility Agreement between Greece and the other euro-area states, set-tling the availability of credits in the form of pooled bilateral loans for Greece, and an Intercreditor Agreement among the creditor states; the European Financial Stability Facility (EFSF) was established as a limited liability company under Luxembourg law, and, subsequently, the euro-area states and the EFSF concluded a Framework Agreement, laying down the institutional structure of the EFSF, as well as the forms and conditionality of available assistance, and the procedure for granting it; and the European Stability Mechanism (ESM), replacing the EFSF, was founded through an Intergovernmental Agreement among the Member

---

[15] The rise of new intergovernmentalism is a central theme in E. Chiti and P. Gustavo Teixeira's discussion of the constitutional implications of European responses to the financial and public debate crisis. E. Chiti and P. Gustavo Teixeira (2013).

States. Furthermore, decision-making in both the EFSF and the ESM is entrusted to intergovernmental bodies outside the institutional structure of the EU. Only the rather insignificant EFSM (European Financial Stability Mechanism) has been established using the Union method, i.e. through secondary legislation (Regulation), and is administered by EU institutions.

Obvious reasons exist for opting for the intergovernmental way in financial assistance, the most important of these being lack of EU fiscal capacity. But the intergovernmental option was also adopted in strengthening European economic governance, where this justification does not apply. Efforts to amend the Founding Treaty in order to oblige Member States to introduce the debt brake and the balanced budget requirement ran into a veto by the UK and the Czech Republic. The way out was seen in the Treaty on Stability, Coordination and Governance, concluded without these two Member States. The intergovernmental way may be justified as an emergency policy, in particular in the field of financial assistance. Still, it also raises grave constitutional concerns. In Chapter 5, we have already discussed the major doctrinal issues; here we examine the implications for democracy.

The Eurozone crisis has spawned an abundance of new official, semi-official and unofficial bodies; some of them with formal decision-making powers, others without formal competence but still exercising considerable influence. Not only has the European Parliament been largely kept on a side-track but even the Commission and the Council have found rivals in novel organisational forms. Rescue measures and mechanisms, as well as tightening fiscal discipline, have been planned and negotiated not only within the institutions acknowledged by the Treaties but also in, for instance, a Working Group of the President of the European Council, the Working Group of the Eurogroup, the Euro Summit, 'Merkozy' meetings … The European Council, with its President, and the Euro Summit, both epitomising executive, intergovernmental federalism *par excellence*, clearly took the lead in determining the measures to be taken to overcome the crisis.

The federalist structures which the crisis has gradually engendered are largely based on intergovernmentalism, supported by expertise-based institutions, such as the Commission and the ECB. The sneaking federalism we see emerging has rightly been termed 'executive federalism'.[16] Given the two-level structure of legitimation in the EU and

---

[16] J. Habermas (2011), p. 43.

the formidable obstacles to an emergent European demos, intergovernmentalism might be seen as the institutional solution that democratic considerations call for. However, the two-level process of democratic legitimation can only function and contribute to the overall legitimacy of European policies on two conditions. First, executive participation in European policy-making should be subjected to constant supervision by national parliaments and civil societies. And second, bearing in mind the complementary nature of Europe-wide and national democratic procedures, intergovernmentalism and the related intermediated legitimation should contribute to rather than destroy the socio-cultural prerequisites for European democracy. Arguably, the new intergovernmentalism meets neither of these preconditions.

Stability mechanisms, such as the EFSF and the ESM, operate as separate financial institutions outside the Treaty framework, with their own intergovernmental decision-making bodies. They remain outside the scope of application of Treaty provisions on the principle of transparency and complementary secondary legislation, as well as the EU Charter of Fundamental rights.[17] Disregarding the promises of openness and the general right to access to documents, expressed by Art. 15 TFEU and Art. 42 of the Charter, stability mechanisms work behind the shield of far-going confidentiality and immunity. Moreover, the right of access to documents, enshrined in Art. 42 of the EU Charter of Fundamental rights, covers only documents of the Union institutions – the European Parliament, the Council and the Commission. Art. 34 TESM prohibits Members or former Members of the Board of Governors and of the Board of Directors as well as present or former functionaries of the ESM from disclosing information that is subject to professional secrecy; what professional secrecy comprises is not defined. Art. 35, in turn, establishes immunity from legal proceedings for acts they have performed in an official capacity. They also enjoy inviolability with regard to their official papers and documents. A separate provision ensures inviolability of the archives of the ESM and all documents belonging to the ESM or held by it (Art. 32(5)).

Such a wide confidentiality and immunity has raised concerns in Germany and Finland. Both the German Constitutional Court and the Finnish Constitutional Law Committee have underlined the necessity

---

[17] In addition to the provisions on democratic principles in Title II TEU-Lisbon, Art. 15 TFEU lays down in more detail the obligations of EU institutions and EU citizens' access to documents. The most important piece of secondary legislation is Regulation 1049/2001 (n. 1).

for parliamentary control, not only over establishment of the ESM, but its functioning, too, in particular decision-making affecting national liabilities. This control requires that adequate information be provided to Parliament. Accordingly, in its ruling on the TESM of September 2012, the German Constitutional Court presupposed as a condition for German ratification a guarantee that provisions on inviolability of documents, professional secrecy and immunity do not prevent comprehensive information to the German Parliament. The Finnish Constitutional Law Committee, in turn, has emphasised that the provision on immunity does not affect the possibility of realising legal ministerial responsibility pursuant to the national constitution.[18]

Perhaps even more detrimental to the possibility of democratic control than Treaty-based restrictions on transparency and accountability is the institutional fragmentation which has accompanied the new intergovernmentalism. Fragmentation has been further accentuated by differentiation of the Eurozone from the rest of the Union. Bodies such as the Euro Summit and Eurogroup, as well as the President and Working Group of the Eurogroup, have gained in importance and within the field of the macroeconomic constitution at least partially surpassed the corresponding bodies where all Member States are represented.[19] The hurdles to democratic supervision posed by institutional disintegration are further elevated by the mounting complexity of legislative instruments which determine the substance and procedures of European policies. The six- and two-pack, as well as intergovernmental agreements and complementary guidelines regulating the rescue mechanisms, have created an extremely complicated rulework; a dense and opaque jungle of rules where but few specialists are able to orient themselves. In these circumstances, control from the side of national parliaments and civil societies, implicit in the idea of two-level democratic legitimation, remains largely a fiction.

At the same time, the intergovernmental way of managing the sovereign debt crisis has taken the EU towards a 'transfer union' effected through financial transfers between Member States. By the same token, it has induced in Member States a very nationalistically determined view on European policies. It has put national democracies on a collision course, and re-enlivened old and spawned new prejudices among

---

[18] BVerfG, 2 BvR 1390/12, 12 September 2012; PeVL 13/2012.
[19] Such institutional parallelism may, though, be democratically justified by reference to the need to restore the symmetry of influence and effects in the decision-making of the Union.

European states and peoples. For European democracy, this is perhaps the most worrisome consequence of the crisis. Unfortunately, the crisis appears not to have brought European citizenry closer to but further distanced it from the kind of solidaristic civic community which could act as the subject of European democracy.

It is evident that a European stability fund is needed in the future as well. But what is not evident is the need to opt for an intergovernmental way which is apt to set Member States against each other and enhance nationalist sentiments among both general public and decision-makers. The alternative to intergovernmentalism would obviously require a considerable strengthening of the fiscal capacity of the EU (or the euro area), financed through, not increased payments from Member State budgets, but EU taxation, as has been proposed by, among others, Miguel Poiares Maduro and Mattias Kumm.[20] We shall resume discussion of these proposals in the final chapter.

In economic governance, the Council is the epitome of intergovernmentalism. In recent developments, the position of the Commission has been strengthened at the expense of the Council through, e.g., adoption of reversed qualified-majority voting. However, two-level legitimation can only function with regard to common European rules applicable to all (Eurozone) Member States. In two-level legitimation, each Government represented in the Council channels the consent of the national parliament and electorate to European policies and norms which concern the respective state, in the same way as other Member States. But, as Scharpf has observed, emphasis in economic governance has shifted away from common policies and rules to country-specific guidance and sanctions: "What needs to be legitimated, therefore, are European controls over national policy choices and national resources, rather than choices about common European policies and the allocation of European resources." Especially if country-specific measures cannot be based on clear rules, the two-level legitimation mechanism of intergovernmentalism runs short of its objective:

Concededly, the governments represented in the Council may be constitutionally and democratically legitimated to agree to common rules binding, and obligations burdening, their own polities. But there is no way in which German or Finnish voters and parliaments, or the voters and parliaments of most

---

[20] European Parliament, M. Kumm (2012), 'Democratic Challenges Arising from the Eurocrisis: What Kind of a Constitutional Crisis is Europe in and what Should be Done about it?', 4 October 2012.

member states, could authorize their governments to impose special sacrifices on the citizens of Greece or Portugal or of any other member state. In other words, intergovernmental input legitimacy may sustain general rules applying to all member states, but it cannot legitimate discretionary interventions in individual member states.[21]

The role of expert bodies

Expert bodies have played a central role in implementing and further elaborating the European economic constitution. Realisation and development of the microeconomic constitution has, to a great extent, relied on the Commission as the European Anti-Trust Authority and the ECJ as a constitutional court vis-à-vis both EC/EU institutions and – in the context of free movement, even primarily – Member State legislatures. In the field of the macroeconomic constitution, the ECJ's contribution has been rather peripheral. In contrast, the Commission has been assigned important functions in European economic governance – in monitoring and coordinating procedures under Arts. 121, 126 and 136 TFEU – as well as in recent rescue measures and mechanisms. Yet, the ECB is undoubtedly the most important expert body in the field of the macroeconomic constitution.

Independent expert bodies are exempted from the coverage of democratic input legitimation. This calls for both specific justification and a compensatory guarantee of legitimacy. We shall approach the democracy and legitimacy issues of EU expert bodies, primarily the ECB, through three ideal-typical roles of public bodies: expert, stakeholder and politician. Our hypothesis is simple: the more expert bodies acquire characteristics of a stakeholder or politician, the more the justification warranting their independence loses its pertinence.

The role of independent expert has two preconditions. First, a strong belief needs to exist that experts are best suited to perform a given task in a society. As a rule such a task is seen to require specific knowledge that is cumulative in the organisation. Performing the task involves applying scientific or quasi-scientific tools and information to specific cases. Modern societies abound in expert functions performed by publicly administered or funded expert organisations.

Second, experts are expected to perform their tasks independently from external, particularly political, influences. The input information

---

[21] F. Scharpf (2012), p. 29.

processed by experts is solely defined by the 'scientific' needs of their functions. The independence of an expert may be of a practical or formal (legal) nature. In the latter case, a perceived risk of harmful political interventions exists. Accordingly, a formally independent expert body should neither take orders or even advice from, nor be allowed to be given them by, political institutions. In a democratic constitutional state, a formally independent body exempt from democratic input legitimation always constitutes an exception, and particular reasoning is needed to justify such an exception. In its purest form, Jürgen Habermas characterises expertise-based decision-making as technocratic and contrasts it with the model of political decision-making. In the technocratic model, decisions are based on the most efficient way of applying available techniques to resolve problems at hand. As scientific rationalisation leaves only one available option, there is no longer any room or need for political decision-making.[22]

Courts of law are the classic example of an independent expert function. Their constitutionally protected independence is one of the cornerstones of the present understanding of the rule of law. Still, it is a fairly recent development. Competition (anti-trust) authorities are a later example. Their independent expert role is supported by theoretical and empirical economic analyses of the first half of the twentieth century. German ordoliberals, in particular, saw strictly applied competition rules as indispensable for the proper functioning of the economic system and a liberal society in general. Ordoliberals emphasised that in order for the competition authority to accomplish its important function, it needs strong expert knowledge and full independence. Without expert knowledge it is not able to apply competition rules to varying situations in a coherent manner. Independence must be guaranteed to prevent influence from particular economic interests, channelled through the political system and entailing detrimental consequences for not only the economic but the political system, too.[23]

The independent expert role of central banks is an even more recent phenomenon. Its underpinning intellectual foundation was only laid in the 1970s, when rational-expectations and game-theoretical economics started to impact design of an optimal economic policy framework. At the same time, empirical evidence suggested that the inflationary

---

[22] J. Habermas (1971), pp. 63–4.
[23] This refers to the ordoliberal nightmare of an interest group society that is well described for example in W. Eucken (1952).

tendencies of Western economies had negative implications for growth and economic stability. The German Bundesbank had gained practical, even if not constitutional, independence in conducting price-stability-oriented monetary policy even earlier, and offered an internationally recognised model. From the 1980s onwards, this has been the preferred form of organising the conduct of monetary policy.[24]

The most straightforward means to create a protected field of operation for an independent expert body is to enshrine it in the constitution. Yet, a protected independent expert position can also be achieved through popular support and prevailing political culture, as was largely the case with the German Bundesbank. Accordingly, without such backup, it will become increasingly difficult for an expert body to maintain its independence, irrespective of constitutional protection. In the nation-state context, even independent institutions functioning outside democratic legitimation mechanisms still continue to operate "in the shadow of democratic majorities" and embedded in the surrounding political and labour-market system.[25]

Guaranteeing the accountability of independent expert bodies creates particular problems. Control mechanisms should not endanger independence but should still guarantee that discretion is not misused. Judicial accountability is essential but difficult to arrange, at least outside failures to act or transgression of a legally defined mandate. Beyond this 'natural' scope of juridical control, judicial supervision presupposes that actions can be construed as based on application of legal rules. The more actions are presented as resulting from scientific knowledge, the more they escape juridical control. This accentuates the significance of transparency and openness to public discourse. Effective transparency is needed, even if expert functions do not always allow for full publicity.[26] Public discourse lives on sufficient information, and independent expert bodies cannot achieve public support for their actions without openly accounting for them. Transparency is necessary for expert bodies, such as courts, competition authorities or central banks, to achieve their objectives in a sustainable manner in democratic societies.

---

[24] One of the most influential examples is the practical non-inflationary independence given to the US Federal Reserve during the period of Paul Volcker in 1979–87.

[25] F. Scharpf (2007), p. 176. G. Majone (2012) has also emphasised that the ECB enjoys even greater independence than the Bundesbank as it is politically and socially 'disembedded'.

[26] O. Issing (2005).

Accountability contributes to the legitimacy of independent expert bodies. Still, in terms of the distinction between input and output legitimacy, the emphasis is on the latter. Independent courts are expected to guarantee individual rights and the rule of law in general; independent competition authorities are expected to guarantee economic freedoms and a liberal market economy; and independent central banks are expected to guarantee monetary stability and consequent economic prosperity. Furthermore, they are supposed to produce their expected outcome in virtue of their expertise; their knowledge of the juridical or scientific laws which govern their field of action and which they apply to individual cases. Here lies the justification for their independence: expert bodies must be shielded from all influence which would derail them from a rigorous and disinterested employment of their particular expertise.

A stakeholder is a party who is affected by the outcome of decisions or actions and who hence has something at stake in the process. A stakeholder should be distinguished from the owner of the process; that is, the core beneficiary or responsible body of the process. In constitutional- or administrative-law doctrine, the stakeholder role does not appear in a clear-cut way and lacks sharp definition. In economic governance, stakeholder influence is complementary to democratic legitimation,[27] opening a channel for interested parties. The owner is interested in identifying the parties whose support is required for the success of the project and who, hence, should be engaged as stakeholders. EU comitology is often approached from this perspective. Competition authorities, in turn, must keep the political branches of government satisfied, as well as the general public involved, by providing information on their actions and the positive impacts these entail. The ECB is the main, though not the only, owner of the issue of price stability in the euro area. The list of stakeholders is broad and includes social partners deciding on wages. Furthermore, the ECB must also keep the man in the street informed about its aims and successes. Here, too, the Bundesbank, which was very skilful in its stakeholder policy, offers a model. It managed to convince the German public of the central contribution which monetary stability, achieved by a strong and independent central bank, made to the post-war *Wirtschaftswunder*.

Yet, if stakeholder influences penetrate the decision-making process of an expert institution to fill the gaps in scientific rationality they

---

[27] F. Losada Fraga (2013).

may lead to a loss of practical independence. A different kind of danger to the expert role may arise if the expert body itself becomes a stakeholder in a process of which it is not the owner. This may happen particularly if the stakeholder position is not reflected in its mandate. Through a stakeholder role, other influences than science-based information force their way into decision-making. If an expert body, such as the ECB, attains traits of a stakeholder, this may jeopardise the justification for its independence.

This justification is threatened by a politician role, too. Politicians make political decisions. These imply value judgements on a broad range of issues which do not have one single 'scientifically' correct solution. In contemporary democracies, deciding on public revenues and expenditure lies at the core of politics, as the German Constitutional Court has kept on repeating. Democratic regimes are based on the assumption that the political role can be organised in a way which guarantees direct or indirect popular input, incorporates divergent views and is able to produce generally accepted results. Thus, the political role is premised on democratic input legitimacy. Consequently, in a constitutional democracy, it is highly problematic to delegate value judgements to independent authorities, insulated from political influence. Conversely, the justification for independence loses credence if an expert body is perceived to take political decisions.

Has the ECB, during the Eurozone crisis, assumed new functions which overstep its expert role? Have its policies been influenced by stakeholder interests? Or has it even acted in a political role? In Maastricht, safeguards were created for preventing the ECB from becoming a stakeholder in areas which are in potential contradiction with its primary tasks. First, the ECB was not to become a stakeholder in government finances. The ECB was precluded any responsibility for government finances through the prohibition on central-bank financing of governments and the requirement that all lending be based on adequate collateral, as well as by its extensive independence. By the same token, common monetary policy was protected against negative spillover effects from recklessly handled public finances. Nor was the ECB involved in the monitoring processes under Arts. 121 and 126 TFEU, so that it was again prevented from becoming a stakeholder in public finances.

Second, the ECB was supposed to keep itself aloof from the problems of the banking sector. After a massive increase in lending exposure and a simultaneous decline in collateral quality, the ECB would face significant losses if a large number of banks defaulted on their debts. The ECB possesses two main policy instruments whose use affects the profitability of the banking sector: provision of liquidity and determination of short-term interest rates. It is highly relevant whether it can treat financial difficulties of individual banks as primarily private-sector and secondarily Member State problems or whether it is itself one of their victims. Our assessment is that through changes in its lending and collateral policy the ECB has risked attaining a stakeholder position vis-à-vis the banking sector, which may cause complications for its role as an independent monetary expert.

A similar analysis applies to the fiscal problems of crisis states – in particular Greece. Through its involvement in rescue operations, the ECB has become a stakeholder in public finances as well. Because of the intertwinement of banking and fiscal problems, the two stakeholder positions are interlinked: banks have been induced to buy national bonds with loan funding from the ECB. However, reasons exist to claim that the ECB has actually played a political role in the fiscal crisis. The massive increase in its indirect and even direct lending to Member States is effectively analogous to spending taxpayers' money. Thus, from the debtors' perspective, the Securities Markets Programme and its successor, the programme of Outright Market Transactions, are similar in their effects to government financing. This is further emphasised by the fact that the ECB has started to act like a creditor towards the states at issue. The letters it sent to the Italian and Spanish Prime Ministers, presupposing fiscal- and economic-policy changes as a precondition of sovereign-bond purchases are a case in point. Against this background, it should not come as a major surprise that particularly the ECB's outright purchases of government bonds have faced fierce criticism from multiple fronts and led to the resignation of two senior German ECB officials: Bundesbank President and ECB Governing Council member Alex Weber and ECB Executive Board Member and Chief Economist Jürgen Stark.[28]

The constitutional position defined for the ECB in Maastricht relied heavily on the model of an apolitical expert. Three crucial assumptions underlie delegation of powers to an independent expert body such as the

[28] C. Vits and S. Kennedy (2011), 'Weber to Leave Bundesbank in April, Throwing Race of ECB Chief Wide Open', 11 February 2011; Spiegel International (2011), 'Merkel ECB Candidate: German Central Bank Head Axel Weber Resigns', 11 February 2011; and also P. Müller, C. Pauly and C. Reiermann (2011), 'ECB Chief Economist Quits: Jürgen Stark's Resignation is Setback for Merkel', 12 September 2011.

ECB. First, the delegated tasks are supposed to lend themselves to supervision through the dual means of juridical control and public accountability, the latter guaranteed by transparency. Second, the tasks do not imply value judgements or are pre-defined in a rule-based form so that their implementation can be assigned to an expert.[29] Third, delegated tasks are defined *ex ante* relatively precisely. The more protected the independence of the expert body is, the more pertinent these assumptions are. Because of the constitutional enshrinement of its independence, the ECB enjoys high protection in legal terms. In practical terms, its independence can be deemed even more enhanced than that of national expert bodies, which remain embedded in the democratic national political system.

In the case of the ECB, the assumption most crucial to warranting its position concerns elimination of value judgements. In designing EMU, the role of money and monetary policy was seen in a monetarist or German ordoliberal perspective. In the ordoliberal discourse, central banking with monetary stability as its sole objective has been defined as a main guarantor of the systemic choice for a free market economy and, ultimately, a free society.[30] When this choice had been made – as, according to the ordoliberal narrative, had already been done in Rome – central-banking policies could be 'objectively' derived from the framework conditions of the chosen economic model. As a result, the Eurozone monetary environment was closer to an enhanced gold standard than a field of activist policy-making. However, it is questionable whether all Member States realised or subscribed to this premise, even if it was quite clearly written into the provisions of the Maastricht Treaty. From the side of the ECB itself, the narrow role of central banking, implicit in the Maastricht macroeconomic constitution, presupposed considerable self-restraint in the border zones of its constitutional mandate.

A lot was also left to the new institution to meet the requirements of transparency and public accountability. Accountability through transparency only works if the institution reveals all its influences and aims, and does not mislead the public. The main risk in this respect is that the institution continues to describe its actions in accordance with the role of an independent expert, although its actions are at least partly determined by a stakeholder or politician role. This would effectively prevent exposure to public scrutiny of actions the importance of which

[29] Obviously this has been a contested perception of central banking.
[30] This is particularly well described in Walter Eucken's *Grundsätze* in which monetary stability is the first of the constituent principles of the economic order. W. Eucken (1952), p. 254.

is enhanced by implicit value judgements. In the unfortunate situation where accountability through transparency has become void, only judicial control mechanisms remain. With regard to the ECB, this is still mostly untested territory. Yet it is hardly conceivable that in an acute crisis, the ECJ would, for example, order the ECB to narrow down its collateral list or to sell all the government bonds whose possession it cannot justify on short-term liquidity grounds. In *Pringle*, the Court showed little willingness – or ability? – to engage in argumentation on issues related to monetary policy. Both *Pringle* and the 2004 *Commission* v. *Council* ruling on the application of the Stability and Growth Pact[31] testify to the narrow limits of judicial control over contested macroeconomic policy choices.

In sum, in Maastricht the ECB was constitutionally protected as an independent expert institution with a clear and restricted mandate. Instead of supervision and guidance by European or national political authorities, it was expected to maintain accountability through the transparency and trustworthiness of its actions. However, the picture has become blurred in the course of the financial and fiscal crisis, as the ECB has, arguably, started to act as a stakeholder and politician with regard to both banking-sector profitability and Member State fiscal positions. This compromises its position as an independent expert institution in two respects. First, control mechanisms based on accountability through transparency and public deliberation require sincerity and openness about the underlying objectives of policies and actions. This requirement is difficult to meet if the ECB is forced to frame its policies and actions to suit the limited mandate of an independent expert. Second, the decisions the ECB has taken in the new fields of action hardly live up to the technocratic model, which is based on rational application of scientific information and exclusion of value judgements. For example, the ECB's insistence that Greek government debt should not be restructured before the rescue measures in Spring 2010 has even been criticised by the fellow Troika member IMF for putting financial stability in the euro area before Greek recovery.[32]

---

[31] C-370/12 *Thomas Pringle* v. *Government of Ireland*, Judgment 27 November 2012, not yet reported; C-27/4 *Commission* v. *Council* [2004] ECR I-6649.

[32] IMF (2013b), 'Greece: Ex Post Evaluation of Exceptional Access under the 2010 Stand-By Arrangement', June 2013. Former Bundesbank President Karl Otto Pöhl was even blunter in his claim that restructuring of debt would have been a far better solution. He maintained that the rescue operation "was about protecting German banks, but especially the French banks, from debt write offs". Spiegel International (2010), 'Former Central Bank Head Karl Otto Pöhl: Bailout Plan is all about "Rescuing Banks and Rich Greeks" ', 18 May 2010.

The major issue, of course, is how sound the underlying premises justifying the position of independent expert bodies really are: how objective the objectives and means of the policy field at stake are. The more the premise of objectivity and the concomitant claim of the absence of alternatives are contested and the more value choices are perceived to play a role, the less convincing expert legitimacy becomes. Accusations of transgressing legitimate boundaries and of imposing value choices under the robe of neutral expertise are familiar from criticism of the judiciary, both national and transnational; the ECJ, the main institutional actor in implementing and elaborating the first layer of the European economic constitution, has not been saved from such accusations, either. It is inevitable that similar reproaches are directed at the ECB, too. It may be debated whether even the aim and policies of price stability live up to objectivist premises. But especially if the ECB ventures outside the framework of a monetary policy aiming at price stability, criticism for overstepping its mandate and including value judgements in its decision-making is inevitable. For the moment, however, the status of the ECB seems to be buttressed by a relatively high valued output legitimacy. The ECB has managed to position itself as the saviour of the Eurozone and questions about its mandate and the relation of its measures to basic constitutional principles are relegated to the background. But most likely, experiences from the Eurozone crisis will dominate future debates on the role and institutional position of the ECB.[33]

In addition to the ECB, the Commission, too, clearly emerges from the Eurozone crisis more powerful than ever. The Commission has been a central actor in country-specific rescue measures, and even the European Stability Mechanism relies not only on its own institutional structure but on the Commission, too. Along with the IMF and the ECB, the Commission is the third limb of the famous Troika, which drafts and monitors financial assistance programmes. Tightening, remodelling and expanding European economic governance, especially in the Eurozone, has increased the competences of the Commission and left the Council, the epitome of intergovernmentalism, in the shadow. At the same time, the focus of competences has shifted towards country-

---

[33] A central topic in Christopher Lord's discussion on the legitimacy of the monetary union consists of the consequences of the ECB's alleged moving from rule-based to discretionary decision-making. C. Lord (2012).

specific monitoring. In particular, the crisis has enhanced the position of the Commissioner for Economic and Monetary Affairs and the Directorate-General for Economic and Financial Affairs he is in charge of.

The institutional position of the Commission has always been marked by a fundamental ambivalence. From Rome to Lisbon, the Commission has been treated mainly as an expert body. Yet, the fact that the Member States have possessed the right to nominate the Commissioners has added a distinct intergovernmental flavour to it. But as the Commissioners are not, despite the procedure for nomination, supposed to act as representatives of the Member States, the characteristic of an expert body has prevailed. This is also how the present Founding Treaties portray the Commission. Art. 17(3) TEU lays down that "in carrying out its responsibilities, the Commission shall be completely independent" and that "the members of the Commission shall neither seek nor take instructions from any Government or other institution, body, office or entity". Furthermore, in Art. 245(1) TFEU, Member States pledge to respect the independence of the members of the Commission and to not seek to influence them in the performance of their tasks. A third, parliamentary feature has been introduced by the provisions on the election of the President of the Commission by the European Parliament; the vote of consent in the Parliament preceding the appointment of the Commission; the collective responsibility of the Commission before the Parliament; and the availability of a motion of censure of the Commission. Instead of an expert body, intergovernmental and parliamentary traits point to the role model of a politician. The peculiar constitutional combination of features of an expert, intergovernmental and parliamentary institution entails that in terms of legitimacy expectations, too, the Commission is a hybrid body. The role of independent expert evokes the expectation of outcome legitimacy, guaranteed by unbiased application of expertise, while the role of politician implies the need for democratic input legitimacy. The picture is further complicated by the multiplicity of functions of the Commission; different functions may imply different roles and legitimacy expectations. In competition policy, the role of independent expert has been particularly accentuated.

Great uncertainty seems to reign over how the Commission's increased tasks and powers in economic governance and fiscal crisis resolution should be defined. The six- and two-pack legislation have accentuated the expert role of the Commission in fiscal and economic surveillance procedures as a counterweight to the intergovernmental Council, fulfilling a politician role. On the other hand, open contestation of the economic theory underlying the conditionality of financial assistance and country-specific economic governance has undermined belief in objective, scientifically proved foundations of austerity programmes and supply-side reforms.[34] It is increasingly difficult to present the goals and means of fiscal and economic policy as objectively given, admitting of no alternatives and involving no value choices. Critics discern a politician making value judgements under the Commission's robe of an independent expert.

The proposals for developing the Commission reflect this vacillation between the expert and politician roles. On the one hand, proposals exist to assign the fiscal-policy function of the Commission to an independent European Budget Office, complementing and crowning the structure of independent national offices or councils. These proposals are countered by plans to develop the Directorate-General for Economic and Financial Affairs into a European Ministry of Finance, and to enhance the parliamentary accountability of the Commission and especially the Commissioner of Economy and Finance.

Social constitution – the eternal loser

Equally important to paying attention to political developments is to be aware of the implications the changes in the macroeconomic constitution entail within the fledgling European social constitution. From the very beginning, the subordination of the social to the economic constitution has been clear enough. In social policy, division of tasks and competences between the Community and the Member States followed the solution adopted in economic policy. In line with economic policy, social policy was retained under Member States' sovereignty. Building up the post-war welfare state was a national project, premised on the solidarity uniting the national demos. Social policy enjoyed legitimacy provided by state-level democratic procedures, as even ordoliberal discussants, in so far as they in general approved of social-policy measures, were prone to recall. The need for

---

[34] The interventions of such academic observers as Paul de Grauwe have been complemented by the self-criticism of the IMF for the Troika measures in Greece. See P. de Grauwe (2011) and (2013), and P. de Grauwe and Y. Ji (2013); IMF (2013b), 'Greece: Ex Post Evaluation of Exceptional Access under the 2010 Stand-By Arrangement', June 2013.

democratic legitimacy, which only national legislative procedures are able to engender, has remained a major objection to a social Europe, involving European-level redistributive measures or harmonising Member State welfare regimes. The general expectation in Rome was that the common market and the microeconomic constitution of free movement and competition law would produce socially beneficial results in the shape of increased general welfare and resources for the national welfare-state project. In the division of labour and competences between the Community/Union and Member States, guaranteeing a socially just (re)distribution of increased prosperity fell to the latter.

In many discussions, social and fiscal policy have been seen as inseparable. If one remains with the Member States, the other one should remain as well. And, correspondingly: if one were to be transferred to the European level, the other one should follow. But in figuring out which policy field should take the lead, positions have diverged. In the debates on EMU, the Economists – those who emphasised that monetary union was impossible without economic union – started from the need for Europeanised fiscal policy and argued that this would entail Europeanisation of social policy as well. Those who wanted to retain national welfare regimes under national sovereignty were well aware that this required fiscal policy sovereignty as well. The German Constitutional Court has approached the close relationship between fiscal and social policy from the perspective of the national constitution. In the Lisbon ruling, the Court pointed out that "particularly sensitive for the ability of a constitutional state to democratically shape itself" are, inter alia, "fundamental fiscal decisions on public revenue and public expenditure, the latter being particularly motivated, inter alia, by social policy considerations".[35]

Although such key fields of social policy as social security and healthcare have been – with some exceptions – reserved for Member States, social values and objectives have, ever since Rome, occupied a prominent place in the Treaties. In line with the Treaty of Rome, the Preamble to the TEU-Lisbon evokes promoting both economic and social progress, and assures that advances in economic integration will be accompanied by parallel progress in other fields. The value basis of the EU, as defined in Art. 2 TEU, comprises values relevant for social policy such as justice, solidarity and equality between men and women. Furthermore,

[35] BVerfG, 2 BvE 2/08, 30 June 2009, para. 252.

Art. 3 TEU includes social objectives and, in defining economic object-ives, refers to their social implications as well.[36] In the provisions of the TFEU on categories and areas of Union competence, social policy is included in shared competences, but only "for the aspects defined in this Treaty" (Art. 4(2)). Specific social policy competences of the Union have remained meagre. Their clear emphasis is on the social security of moving workers – and, more recently, European citizens in general – and harmonisation of labour law. For other aspects, Union competences are confined to coordinating Member State policies (Art. 5 TFEU).

Union social policy has suffered from a fundamental imbalance between Treaty provisions on social and economic issues. Unlike Treaty provisions on free movement and competition law – that is, the core of the (micro)economic constitution – provisions on social policy have not enjoyed direct effect. This imbalance has turned the social constitution into a constitutional underdog, which but very rarely has been able to assert itself in conflicts with the economic constitution. This disparity between economic and social constitutional law is a European-level phe-nomenon unknown to national constitutions, which accord economic and social considerations equal constitutional status in political dis-course and decision-making. It is also one of the reasons which have made some observers doubt whether it is in general justified to speak about a distinct social dimension in European constitutionalism. This doubt is reinforced by the fact that Union legislation and social policy initiatives hardly amount to a coherent European social model which would provide a social constitution with its underpinning cultural level. This holds especially for such core welfare areas as social security and healthcare, which have a strong redistributive character and which are closely linked to fiscal policy. If the Union has made any distinct con-tribution to social policy, it should be localised in what has come to be

---

[36] The Union has not only to establish an internal market but also to "work for the sustainable development of Europe based on balanced economic growth and price stability, a highly competitive social market economy, aiming at full employment and social progress, and a high level of protection and improvement of the quality of the environment". The Union "shall combat social exclusion and discrimination, and … promote social justice and protection, equality between women and men, solidarity between generations and protection of the rights of the child". It shall also "promote economic, social and territorial cohesion, and solidarity among Member States". Moreover, according to Art. 9 TFEU, "in defining and implementing its policies and activities, the Union shall take into account requirements linked to the promotion of a high level of employment, the guarantee of adequate social protection, the fight against social exclusion, and a high level of education, training and protection of human health".

called regulatory private law: labour law; consumer law; anti-discrimination law; and law on the so-called universal services. Yet, we venture, though somewhat hesitantly, to speak of, if not a social constitution, a social dimension in European constitutionalism, with its particular focus on the interrelations between European and national levels.

The clear emphasis in realising the European microeconomic constitution, with its crux in free movement and competition law, has lain in negative rather than positive integration: in removing national restrictions on a Union-wide market economy, based on undistorted competition. Indeed, the most important encroachments on Member State sovereignty in social policy have not resulted from legislative harmonisation, exemplifying positive integration, but from negative integration pursued by, first and foremost, the ECJ. The Court has not hesitated to strike down Member State social legislation which it has deemed to derogate from fundamental market freedoms and which has not passed its test of proportionality. Particularly since the SEA, the Court has been the driving force in subjecting services – including social security and healthcare – to internal market law. This has created pressures on Member States to adjust their welfare regimes accordingly, in particular on those where the fundamental choice has been for public provision of social security and healthcare.

The macroeconomic layer of the European economic constitution, introduced in Maastricht, has further curtailed Member States' leeway in social policy. Due to the close intertwinement of redistributive social policy with fiscal policy, the fiscal constraints of the Maastricht macroeconomic constitution Treaty reduced the latitude for national social policy, too. One of the economic assumptions underlying the Maastricht macroeconomic constitution was that Member States would create sufficient room for manoeuvre for their automatic stabilisers in economic downturns; thus they would give effect to the enhanced macroeconomic function which national fiscal policy possesses in EMU after Member States have lost control over monetary policy instruments. As automatic stabilisers on the public expenditure side are largely identical to legal entitlements to social benefits, fiscal leeway would have protected national social-security regimes, too. However, due to national failures or the exceptional features of the crisis, fiscal leeway seems to have been exhausted in the middle of the economic downturn. Instead of relying on the automatic-stabiliser function of social expenditure, Member States, especially those hit worst by the crisis, have resorted to cutting social benefits. This tends to transform social expenditure from automatic stabiliser to a 'discretionary de-stabiliser', most likely aggravating the crisis as well as its social and even economic effects.

A common currency in a non-optimal currency area calls for high labour-market flexibility. Because of limited labour mobility and intra-euro-area fiscal transfers, increasing labour-market and wage flexibility has been deemed necessary to manage adverse country-specific developments which common monetary policy could not address. Yet, imposing such measures on countries caught up by the crisis has jeopardised national labour-market arrangements and their ability to find adequate policy solutions. The measures have implied a general tendency of shrinking the freedom of social partners and tariff agreements in wage-setting and putting pressure on social, especially unemployment benefits. If in general it has been justified to evoke a European social model, informing Community/Union positions on social policy, labour orientation and a central role for social partners have certainly been its essential elements. Even before the outbreak of the Eurozone crisis, the Maastricht macroeconomic constitution had instigated a significant change in the Union's labour-law and labour-market orientation. This change is an important aspect of the shift in emphasis between liberal and social market economies towards the former.[37]

The crisis has provided new impetus to the market-liberal tenets of marketisation and flexibilisation as central premises of European macroeconomic governance.[38] Simultaneously, the mode of governance has undergone a fundamental alteration: peer review and open method of coordination have yielded to legal obligations and formal sanctions. This is most conspicuous in the crisis states: in the Memoranda of Understanding, drafted and monitored by the Troika, reforms aiming at flexibilisation of labour market and wage setting, as well as reduction of the public sector, occupy a central place.[39] They

---

[37] F. Scharpf (2010).

[38] For example, tax and social contribution systems are to be reformed in order to boost incentives to seek employment. Public spending on older people in the areas of pensions and health care is to be cut and retirement ages raised in order to safeguard the sustainability of the financial system. The active labour market policies advocated are aimed, first and foremost, at establishing an obligation on the unemployed to reintegrate themselves in the labour market. Education is viewed functionally and in economic terms, primarily as a means of obtaining qualifications to enable participation in the labour market.B. Hacker and T. van Treeck (2010), p. 7

[39] K. Busch et al. (2013). As an analysis of Greek measures see A. Koukiadaki and L. Kretsos (2012).

also figured prominently in the ECB letters in August 2012 to the Prime Ministers of Spain and Italy. The effects of official market liberalism are not confined to the crisis states but extend to the Eurozone as a whole. The scoreboard indicators on which the Commission bases its sanction-backed monitoring within the macroeconomic imbalance procedure, include, inter alia, a three-year percentage change in nominal unit labour cost, with thresholds set at +9 per cent for euro-area countries.[40]

In addition to requirements of labour-market and wage-setting liberalisation and flexibilisation, austerity programmes have curbed crisis states' social-policy sovereignty through detailed and focused obligations to cut social expenditure and public-sector wages. Indeed, social spending has been a major target in measures aiming to reduce the budget deficit and public debt. The massive impact of European measures on the labour and welfare regime of, especially, the crisis states raises the question of the protective role of social rights.

In addition to provisions on, first, Union objectives and values and, second, Union competences, social rights represent the third limb of socially oriented Treaty law. Social rights are a latecomer in EU constitutional law. During the activism of the Delors era, efforts to strengthen the rights element in the feeble European social constitution led to adoption of the Community Charter of the Fundamental Social Rights of Workers in 1989. In the Maastricht Treaty, an explicit reference to both this Charter and the European Social Charter of the Council of Europe was included in Art. 136 TEC (now Art. 151 TFEU).[41] In addition, in the Preamble to the TEU the Member States confirm their attachment to fundamental social rights as defined in the two Charters. Furthermore, social rights are devoted a particular Chapter in the Charter of the Fundamental Rights of the European Union under the heading *Solidarity*. However, a distinction between principles and rights was adopted in the Preamble to and in Art. 52(5) of the Charter,

---

[40] European Commission website (2013), 'MIP Scoreboard', last updated 20 March 2013.
[41] The Union and the Member States, having in mind fundamental social rights such as those set out in the European Social Charter signed at Turin on 18 October 1961 and in the 1989 Community Charter of the Fundamental Social Rights of Workers, shall have as their objectives the promotion of employment, improved living and working conditions, so as to make possible their harmonization while the improvement is being maintained, proper social protection, dialogue between management and labour, the development of human resources with a view to lasting high employment and the combating of exclusion.

with the obvious intent of lowering the status of social rights to mere principles and watering down their legal significance.[42] In its case law, the ECJ has acknowledged the European Social Charter as one of the sources of inspiration of the common European tradition which defines fundamental rights as general legal principles of EU law. Yet the Court has been wary of basing its rulings on a provision of this Charter (or the solidarity provisions in the EU Charter of Fundamental Rights). In sum, the position of social rights in EU law remains rather weak. In such notorious cases as *Laval*[43] and *Viking*[44] where social rights have clashed with rights emanating from fundamental freedoms, the social dimension has rested on Member State law. Yet, these rulings are important for EU-level social rights, too, as they for instance explicitly acknowledged – even before the entry into force of the Lisbon Treaty – the right to strike as a principle of EU law.

It would denigrate the position of social rights in EU law to label them merely as constitutional soft law. The renewed European Charter of Social Rights belongs to the common constitutional heritage which in accordance with Art. 6(3) TEU determines the contents of fundamental rights as general principles of EU law. What is even more important is that the provisions on solidarity rights of the EU Charter of Fundamental Rights, along with other Charter provisions, were given explicit legal effect by the Lisbon Treaty, and, again similarly to other Charter provisions, they too are "addressed to the institutions, bodies, offices and agencies of the Union" so that these shall "respect the rights, observe the principles and promote the application thereof in accordance with their respective powers" (Art. 51(1)). The relevance of the Charter for the austerity programmes imposed on the crisis states through the Memoranda of Understanding, drafted and monitored by the Troika, might be questioned on the ground that the Commission and the ECB have not acted under their Treaty powers but under those conferred on them by intergovernmental agreements. However, the main contents of the MoUs have been repeated in Council decisions under Arts. 126 or

---

[42] According to the distinction, (subjective) rights must be respected and principles observed (Art. 51(1)). Principles may be implemented through legislative or executive acts. They become significant for courts only when these interpret or review such acts. They do not give rise to direct claims for positive action by Union institutions or Member States authorities.

[43] C-341/05 *Laval un Partneri* [2007] ECR I-11767.

[44] C-438/05 *International Transport Workers' Federation and Finnish Seamen's Union* [2007] ECR I-10779.

136 TFEU, which the Charter clearly covers. *Pringle* includes a position on the Charter's significance for the European Stability Mechanism, but only in relation to the Member States. The Court stated that in establishing a stability mechanism like the ESM Member States do not implement EU law and that pursuant to Art. 51(1), the Charter is not applicable (paras 179–80).[45] No conclusions can be drawn from *Pringle* on the pertinence of the Charter to EU institutions' action within or in relation to the stability mechanisms.

Nor does *Pringle* say anything on the Charter's relevance for the Member States implementing the MoUs. At least, after the MoU has been confirmed by a Council Decision taken under EU law, a Member State can be claimed to be implementing EU law in the meaning of Art. 51(1) of the Charter when giving effect to the MoU. This would entail the relevance of the solidarity rights for Member State measures. The ECJ has yet to take a position on the issue.[46]

According to the prevalent view of social rights, manifest in, e.g., the so-called Limburg principles, in times of austerity social rights function as criteria of prioritisation in the allocation of spending cuts.[47] Yet, we have found no reference to either the Solidarity Chapter of the EU Charter on Fundamental Rights or the renewed European Social Charter in the legal documents the Eurozone crisis has produced or in the conclusions of European bodies, except for one mention of the right to collective bargaining and action in the two-pack.[48] Here market-liberal economic reason has conspicuously overruled the European social constitution. With the constitutionalisation of strict conditionality and its

---

[45] It should also be noted that *Pringle* was issued before the entry into force of the amendment to Art. 136 TFEU. The amendment explicitly provides for Member States' right to establish a stability mechanism. It remains an open issue whether the Court would in the present legal situation still consider that in establishing a stability mechanism, such as the ESM, Member States do not implement EU law in the meaning of Art. 51(1) of the Charter.

[46] Future financial assistance will involve applying the two-pack provisions on the macroeconomic adjustment programme which Member States requesting assistance must prepare and which the Council approves. This will make the connection of the MoUs to EU law even clearer.

[47] Limburg Principles on the Implementation of the International Covenant on Economic, Social and Cultural Rights (1987), UN Doc. E/CN.4/1987/17, available in Human Rights Quarterly (1987).

[48] The two-pack Regulation 473/2013, which inter alia introduces economic partnership programmes for Member States in the excessive deficit procedure, evokes the social partners' role in wage setting. According to Art. 1(2) of the Regulation, its application must be in full compliance with Art. 152 TFEU, where the role of the social partners is recognised. Recommendations issued under the Regulation must respect national practice and institutions for wage formation. Here an explicit reference is made

interpretation in a market-liberal spirit, the social constitution has once more proved to be the loser, now in relation to the macroeconomic constitution. In face of the total failure of fundamental-rights monitoring within the EU, other trans- or international supervisory bodies have had to step in. These, however, possess less influence and have no jurisdiction over Union action or intergovernmental stability mechanisms. All they can do is to criticise national authorities which have had but little latitude in implementing the strict conditionality imposed on them.

The European Committee of Social Rights, which monitors Signatory States' observance of the renewed European Charter of Social Rights, has been perhaps the most active supervisory body. It has issued several decisions on complaints submitted by Greek trade unions and other NGOs, and included critical observations in its assessments of country-specific reports. In its decisions on collective complaints, the Committee has found several violations of the Charter. As a central premise for its judgments, the Committee has invoked its principal stance on the impact of economic crises on the obligations under the Charter. The Committee concedes that increased unemployment poses a challenge to social security and social assistance systems as the number of beneficiaries increases while tax and social security contribution revenues decline. Yet, it recalls that by acceding to the 1961 Charter, the Parties have accepted to pursue "conditions in which inter alia the right to health, the right to social security, the right to social and medical assistance and the right to benefit from social welfare services may be effectively realised". Economic crisis should not lead to reducing the protection of Charter rights. As a conclusion the Committee underlines that "governments are bound to take all necessary steps to ensure that the rights of the Charter are effectively guaranteed at a period of time when beneficiaries most need the protection". In labour law, limiting public expenditure or relieving constraints on business activity "should not excessively destabilise the situation of those who enjoy the rights enshrined in the Charter". In particular, encouraging employment flexibility should not deprive employees of their fundamental labour-law rights.[49]

to Art. 28 of the Charter, where the right of collective bargaining and action is enshrined. In turn, the other two-pack Regulation sets out that when preparing their draft macroeconomic adjustment programmes, Member States must seek the views of social partners as well as relevant civil society organisations.

[49] European Committee of Social Rights (2012), 'Decision on the Merits General Federation of Employees of the National Electric Power Corporation and Confederation of Greek Civil Servants' Trade Unions', 23 May 2012. See International Labour Office (2011), 'Report on the High Level Mission to Greece', 19–23 September 2011.

The International Labour Organization (ILO) has been another ener-
getic actor in the field of labour-market reforms and tariff autonomy.
In its major decision on a complaint submitted by Greek trade unions,[50]
the Committee on Freedom of Association found several violations
of trade-union and collective-bargaining rights enshrined in ILO conventions. The Committee declared itself to be "deeply aware that the
measures giving rise to this complaint have been taken within a context qualified as grave and exceptional, provoked by a financial and
economic crisis", but this awareness did not annul the criticism. The
Committee also expressed its expectation that

the social partners will be fully implicated in the determination of any further
alterations within the framework of the agreements with the European
Commission, the IMF and the European Central Bank (ECB) that touch upon
matters core to the human rights of freedom of association and collective
bargaining and which are fundamental to the very basis of democracy and
social peace.[51]

Within the crisis states, austerity measures and labour-market reforms
have led to litigation before national courts. In general, the results
have been meagre. The Courts have exercised judicial restraint and displayed far-going understanding of government defences invoking economic emergency and the strict conditionality of financial assistance.
The most important exception consists of the ruling by the Portuguese
Constitutional Court in April 2013, which struck down major parts of
the 2013 austerity budget as violating constitutionally protected social
rights. The parts the Court found unconstitutional included a drop in
holiday pay for civil servants, pension payment reductions and cuts in
unemployment and sickness benefits.[52]

In sum, social rights have proved to be rather toothless in resist-
ing or redirecting spending cuts or structural labour-market reforms
affecting the position of social partners and collective bargaining. This

[50] See Complaint No. 2820 (Greece) in International Labour Office, '365th Report of the
Committee on Freedom of Association', 1–16 November 2012.
[51] Critical observations especially on Greece have also been presented by the UN
human-rights bodies such as the Committee on the Elimination of Discrimination
against Women (2011), ('Seventh Periodic Report Greece', 14 March 2011) and the
Office of the United Nations High Commissioner for Human Rights (OHCHR) (2011),
Independent Expert on the effects of foreign debt and other related international
financial obligations of States on the full enjoyment of all human rights, particularly
economic, social and cultural rights (Greek crisis: 'Keep in mind the people's basic
human rights', 30 June 2011).
[52] Acórdão No. 187/2013.

general conclusion covers all levels of social-rights protection, whether European, international or national. With regard to the conditionality of European financial stability assistance, the primary deficiency is the lack of a Union-level monitoring mechanism and the non-existent commitment of key Union institutions.

Still a community based on the rule of law?

A discussion of the EU in terms of the rule of law or a community of law is riddled with conceptual difficulties. This is due not only to the well-known polyvalence of 'the rule of law' but, more profoundly, the collusion of two traditions whose interrelationship is not easy to grasp. Indeed, the German expressions *Rechtsgemeinschaft* and *Rechtsstaat* are more instructive than their English counterparts. Often enough both German terms are translated into 'the rule of law', thus obliterating their conceptual difference. On the other hand, 'community of law' as a translation for *Rechtsgemeinschaft* is not very informative either, because it lacks any established conceptual content. In *Les Verts*, the ECJ introduced a veritable terminological mishmash, 'a community based on the rule of law', obviously trying to capture something of the conceptual contents of both *Rechtsgemeinschaft* and *Rechtsstaat*.[53]

The Treaties do not employ the term 'community of law' or 'a community based on the rule of law'. In contrast, ever since Maastricht explicit reference has been made to the rule of law or, in the German version, *Rechtsstaatlichkeit*. In the Preamble to the Treaty on the European Union, the Member States declare that they draw "inspiration from the cultural, religious and humanist inheritance of Europe, from which have developed the universal values of the inviolable and inalienable rights

---

[53]   It must ... be emphasized ... that the European Economic Community is a Community based on the rule of law, inasmuch as neither its Member States nor its institutions can avoid a review of the question whether the measures adopted by them are in conformity with the basic constitutional charter, the Treaty. In particular, in Articles 173 [now 263 TFEU] and 184 [now 277 TFEU], on the one hand, and in Article 177 [now 267 TFEU], on the other, the Treaty established a complete system of legal remedies and procedures designed to permit the Court of Justice to review the legality of measures adopted by the institutions. Natural and legal persons are thus protected against the application to them of general measures which they cannot contest directly before the Court by reason of the special conditions of admissibility laid down in the second paragraph of Article 173 of the Treaty.Case C-294/83 *Les Verts* v. *Parliament* [1986] ECR 1339, para. 23.

of the human person, freedom, democracy, equality and the rule of law", and confirm "their attachment to the principles of liberty, democracy and respect for human rights and fundamental freedoms and of the rule of law". In Art. 2 TEU, the rule of law is included in the values on which the Union is founded and which are common to all Member States. These values are referred to in several other Treaty provisions, and a commitment to their promotion is a condition for accession to the Union (Art. 49 TEU). Art. 7 TEU sets out the procedure to be followed in case of a clear risk of a serious breach of those values by a Member State. The preamble to the Charter of Fundamental Rights, in turn, proclaims that "the Union is founded on the indivisible, universal values of human dignity, freedom, equality and solidarity", and "based on the principles of democracy and the rule of law". All in all, Treaty provisions and value proclamations, complemented by the case law of the ECJ repeatedly reconfirming the principle, leave no doubt as to the status of the rule of law as an overarching constitutional principle which pertains to all the constitutional dimensions, including the economic one.

The German notion of *Rechtsstaat* and the English (Anglo-American) principle of the rule of law have different roots which still, despite a rapprochement during the twentieth century, influence their understanding in the respective legal cultures. Yet, they share a common core: they both aim at preventing arbitrary use of power.[54] And it is this common core which also facilitates a conceptual synthesis in EU law, acceptable to different legal cultures. However, the rule of law is not the same as *Rechtsgemeinschaft*. It really makes a difference whether we discuss the EU in terms of *Rechtsgemeinschaft* or *Rechtsstaat(lichkeit)*.

The portrayal of the Community as a *Rechtsgemeinschaft* goes back to Walter Hallstein, the first President of the Commission. For Hallstein, the Community was a *Rechtsgemeinschaft* in three senses. It was a creation of law (*Rechtsschöpfung*), it was a source of law and it was a legal order.[55] The foremost of these connotations was the first one: the Community as a creation of law. Here Hallstein evoked the central role of law as the means and object of integration; the reason why European integration has so often been characterised as a legal project, in spite of its basic economic orientation. *Rechtsgemeinschaft* refers, first, to the community of states: instead of being simple relations of power, the mutual relations of the Member States and their relations to the Community are

---

[54] See Ch. 7 in K. Tuori (2011).   [55] See I. Pernice (2001).

governed by law. But, second, the connotation of *Rechtsgemeinschaft* possesses a societal aspect, too, and bears an echo of the ordoliberal conception of the marriage of economy and law. *Ordoliberals* read into the European economic constitution a *Gesamtentscheidung* in favour of a market economy based on undistorted competition. The *ordo* which such an economic model required was supposed to be provided by law, guaranteeing market freedoms and free competition. In this wider, societal connotation Hallstein's *Rechtsgemeinschaft* comes close to Franz Böhm's *Privatrechtsgesellschaft*.[56] One could perhaps say that *Rechtsgemeinschaft* has both a public and private aspect, referring to the peculiar character of the Community/Union as having as its constituent elements both European states and citizens (peoples).

In Chapter 2, we have already pointed to the differences between the micro- and macroeconomic constitutions in their relation to law and the courts. Because of its focus on economic activities of individual subjects, the microeconomic constitution could offer the law and the courts a crucial role and earn the community the label of *Rechtsgemeinschaft*. By contrast, the macroeconomic constitution is not about the activities of individual economic subjects but about macroeconomic objectives and aggregate values, as well as actions of Member States and EU institutions. What is missing in the context of the macroeconomic constitution is the societal or private aspect of the *Rechtsgemeinschaft*. But even in what we have termed public relations, the Maastricht macroeconomic constitution granted the law but a minor role. Non-monetary economic policy at the European level was supposed to be about coordination, and the instruments the Treaties indicated for this purpose were mainly of the character of peer review and soft law. Accordingly, it is hard to label the economic community of Member States which the Treaty provisions on EMU envisioned as a *Rechtsgemeinschaft*. Hence, with the prominence of the macroeconomic constitution the Union lost much of its quality of a *Rechtsgemeinschaft*.

In its original, Hallsteinian sense, *Rechtsgemeinschaft* is a descriptive rather than a normative notion. The rule of law (*Rechtsstaatlichkeit*), by contrast, is undoubtedly a normative principle, even in the EU. The rule of law, as developed in the Anglo-Saxon and Continental, mainly German, tradition, aims to prevent arbitrary power, and – as is often added – to safeguard rights of the individual. In the EU context,

---

[56] See Böhm (1966).

however, the rule of law must be examined in the tripartite relations between the Union, Member States and individual subjects. Even in the EU, the implications of the rule of law are most often discussed from the perspective of individual subjects. For these, the rule of law provides protection against arbitrary use of power by both the Union and Member States (when these are implementing EU law). This is the main perspective from which the ECJ has elaborated on the contents of the rule of law. As Laurent Pech has summarised the case law, "the Court essentially equates the rule of law, as a constitutional principle ... with judicial review (as it gives effect to the rule of law) and judicial protection of individual rights and in particular, the individual's fundamental rights".[57] But protection of individuals does not exhaust the significance of the principle in the EU. It is also relevant for relations between the Union and Member States, although its content cannot remain exactly the same as in discussing safeguards for individuals.[58] Thus, fundamental rights – the substantive element in the rule-of-law notion employed by the ECJ – lose relevance and must be replaced – so we suggest – with the competences or sovereignty rights of Member States.

Within the field of the macroeconomic constitution, the emphasis in the implications of the rule-of-law principle lies in Union–Member State relations. For the sake of analysing the repercussions of recent developments, we propose to unpack the principle into three main normative elements:

- protection of Member State competences,
- the principle of legality; and
- accountability.

The principle of conferral is the primary constitutional safeguard for Member State competences. It applies to both the Union as a whole and to each Union institution. Under Art. 5(2) TEU, "the Union shall act only within the limits of the competences conferred upon it by the Member States in the Treaties to attain the objectives set out therein", while "competences not conferred upon the Union in the Treaties remain with the Member States". Correspondingly, Art. 13(2) TEU lays down that "each institution shall act within the limits of the powers conferred on it in the Treaties". The principle of conferral is complemented

---

[57] L. Pech (2010), p. 380.
[58] A further relevant dimension consists of relations among EU institutions.

by subsidiarity which is supposed to govern Union action in areas outside Member States' exclusive competence.[59]

The principle of conferral has not been able to prevent erosion of Member State sovereignty in non-monetary economic policy or reduction of national latitude in core fields of social policy. The edge of the principle of conferral can be blunted through a liberal reading of Treaty provisions on Union and institution competences; as we have argued, this is what has largely occurred in the application of Arts. 121, 126 and 136 TFEU for the purpose of tightening European economic governance, as well as in interpreting the mandate of the ECB (Art. 127 TFEU). Furthermore, the principle of conferral can be rendered ineffective by recourse to the intergovernmental way, which has been the dominant option in rescue packages and stability mechanisms. The strict conditionality of financial assistance, whereby recipient states 'voluntarily' accept restrictions on their sovereignty, tends to undermine the principle of conferral as well. Even in economic governance, the efficacy of *ultra vires* review, focusing on transgressions of competence, can be doubted. Treaty provisions on economic policy competences tend to be vague while efficient *ultra vires* review would presuppose clearly defined competences.

Judicial control in the shape of *ultra vires* review is a necessary guarantee of respect for the principle of conferral. In economic governance within the institutional and legal framework of the EU, Member States can bring an action before the ECJ pursuant to and within the limits set out by Art. 263 TFEU.[60] As regards rescue mechanisms, both the EFSF Framework Agreement and the Treaty on the ESM include provisions on dispute settlement and access to justice. Yet, especially in financial assistance, judicial control can be deemed quite illusory, due to the duress under which the states receiving financial assistance find themselves and which leaves them little choice but to accept the conditionality of assistance.

---

[59] "Under the principle of subsidiarity, in areas which do not fall within its exclusive competence, the Union shall act only if and in so far as the objectives of the proposed action cannot be sufficiently achieved by the Member States, either at central level or at regional and local level, but can rather, by reason of the scale or effects of the proposed action, be better achieved at Union level" (Art. 5(3) TEU).

[60] The ECJ possesses jurisdiction over the legality of, inter alia, acts of the Council, of the Commission and of the European Central Bank, other than recommendations and opinions. In addition to EU institutions, actions can be brought by Member States "on grounds of lack of competence, infringement of an essential procedural requirement, infringement of the Treaties or of any rule of law relating to their application, or misuse of powers" (Art. 263 TFEU).

The principle of conferral also specifies the principle of legality with regard to the competences of the Union and its institutions. Yet the latter principle is not exhausted by the requirement of a competence basis in the Treaties but has a wider scope. As can be read from Art. 13(2) TEU, the principle of legality addresses even the procedures, conditions and objectives of action.[61] In addition, as has been emphasised in both the Anglo-Saxon and the German tradition, the principle implies particular qualities of the rules which are supposed to govern administrative action. In a highly influential article, Joseph Raz, clearly taking his cue from Lon Fuller's account of the 'internal morality of law',[62] has argued that legal norms must be prospective, adequately publicised, clear, relatively stable and that lawmaking, too, should be guided by open, stable, clear and general rules.[63] It easy to agree with Raz' criteria: only such rules can accomplish the two purposes of providing reliable *ex ante* guidance and facilitating *ex post* control of legality. We would, however, propose an additional requirement: the addressees must have a factual possibility to adjust their behaviour to the rules.

Due to the extreme complexity of the rule-work emerging from the Eurozone crisis, it can hardly be deemed to meet the rule-of-law requirement of clarity. Often enough, the rules are characterised by a peculiar combination of apparent exactness and great ambiguity. This applies, for instance, to provisions on budget deficits and sovereign debt: exact reference values are accompanied by vaguely formulated exceptions. Provisions on the procedure of economic imbalances follow the same pattern: the scoreboard the Commission is supposed to employ in its monitoring activities involves exact parameters but their application allows for wide discretion. What makes this discretion particularly worrying from a rule-of-law perspective is that it is backed by formal sanctions. Doubts can also be raised as to whether euro states with their essentially reduced macroeconomic arsenal can do much to improve the situation and to adjust their behaviour to rules and decisions.

The principle of legality implies access to justice, and, indeed, this is the crucial rule-of-law requirement the ECJ has emphasised in its case law. The jurisprudence of the ECJ is mostly related to individual subjects, but access to justice is also vital in controlling rules and decisions addressed to Member States. We have already commented

---

[61] Each institution must act within the limits of the powers conferred on it in the Treaties, and in conformity with the procedures, conditions and objectives set out in them.

[62] L. Fuller (1969).   [63] J. Raz (1979), pp. 214–15.

on problems affecting *ultra vires* judicial review. Substantive review, in turn, requires that decisions can be conceived of as resulting from the application of legal rules. Even if based primarily on non-legal, say, economic considerations, they should also be accessible to analysis in terms of legal rationality. In the field of the macroeconomic constitution this is but very rarely the case, and for easily understandable reasons. Both monetary and non-monetary policy must react to rapidly changing economic situations and heed a wide range of economic variables. This makes it extremely difficult – and, many observers would add, economically even irrational – to try to govern it with legal rules. It lies in the very nature of independent expert bodies, such as the ECB and the Commission, that the rules they employ in their decision-making are not supposed to be so much legal as scientific by nature. Even when these bodies overstep their expert role and adopt the features of a politician, the value judgements they make within their mandate are often not judicially controllable. The same, of course, holds for institutions which possess a primarily political character even under constitutional law, such as the Council. At both the transnational, European and national, Member State level, Courts have no choice but to leave a wide margin of appreciation to politicians and experts. This is a potential source of severe tensions, if expert institutions deviate far from the justified, rule-of-law-based expectations of Member States and their constituents. If these tensions do not find other than judicial means to dissolve, the legitimacy of the whole macroeconomic constitution may be jeopardised.

So, to arrive at the third component we have discerned in the rule of law, the reach of judicial accountability in the field of the macroeconomic constitution is necessarily limited. This makes the functioning of other forms of accountability, such as public and political accountability, important even from a rule-of-law perspective. Unfortunately, here one again confronts the hurdles to accountability raised by the complexity of the issues, the fragmented rule-work and institutional structure, as well as deficient transparency.

PART III

What next?

8   Initiatives on the table

Since the second half of 2012, financial markets have calmed down at least temporarily and the worst financial and fiscal crisis appears to be over. In the relative tranquillity, European institutions could focus on reflecting on the lessons of the crisis, as well as the need to develop EMU and to prevent future crises. Yet with the crisis easing, the enthusiasm for reforms appeared to decrease, too. Thus, despite the quite far-reaching reform plans on the table, the results of the subsequent meetings of the European Council have been meagre.

In June 2012, a Working Group consisting of the Presidents of the European Council, the Commission, the Eurogroup and the ECB, headed by Van Rompuy, put forth a scheme for a comprehensive reform of the EU. The scheme was further elaborated in the following months and received its final shape on the eve of the December 2012 European Council meeting.[1] A more ambitious initiative for "launching a European debate" – 'A blueprint for a deep and genuine economic and monetary union' – was produced by the Commission and published on 30 November 2012.[2] The European Parliament's major contribution to the discussion is a Resolution of 20 November 2012 on the report of the four Presidents. Furthermore, the Commission has produced documents on individual parts of reform packages, in particular the proposed banking union.

Our discussion of the future of the European economic constitution will mainly be based on the official initiatives. These do not, of course,

[1] European Council (2012b), 'Towards a Genuine Economic and Monetary Union', 5 December 2012.
[2] European Commission (2012a), 'A Blueprint for a Deep and Genuine Economic and Monetary Union: Launching a European Debate – Communication from the Commission', 30 November 2012.

exhaust the spectrum of interventions, and where we find it appropriate we shall also comment on proposals advanced by unofficial working groups[3] or individual commentators.

Realising the economic union

Proposals for completing the economic dimension of EMU are premised on the perceived weaknesses of the Maastricht construction which have been highlighted by the Eurozone crisis. Substantially, the proposals fall into three groups. The first group reacts to the financial crisis and aims to share its burdens; the objective is a banking – or financial-market – union and at least a partial mutualisation of sovereign debt. The banking union would respond to deepened financial integration, manage cross-border spillover effects of banking crises and break the vicious circle interlinking banking and sovereign debt. The second set of proposals aims to promote the transformation of EMU into an optimal currency area, through, for instance, completing the single market, and increasing price and wage flexibility, as well as labour mobility. The most ambitious plans concern a fiscal union, which would not content itself with European supervision and coordination of national fiscal policies. A fiscal union would dispose of a fiscal capacity which could respond to macroeconomic shocks, support structural reforms and facilitate incorporating the intergovernmental European Stability Mechanism (ESM) into the EU framework.

Of all the proposals on the table, the banking union – or the financial-market union, as the Van Rompuy Working Group calls it – has made most progress. The banking union received new impetus when the Euro Summit decided on 29 June 2012 – in the midst of the Spanish banking crisis – to make direct recapitalisation of banks by the ESM dependent on establishing a single supervision mechanism.[4] The Commission has been able to build its plans on the already partially realised substantive regulatory reform; the so-called single rulebook. The Commission's proposal includes assigning the ECB specific tasks relating to the prudential supervision of credit institutions.

---

[3] Of particular interest is the Report of the Tommaso Padoa-Schioppa Group (2012), 'Completing the Euro: A Road Map towards Fiscal Union in Europe'. This report, published in June 2012, contains many elements similar to the proposals of the Van Rompuy Working Group and the Commission.
[4] Euro Area (2012), 'Summit Statement', 29 June 2012.

The single supervision mechanism would consist of a network of the ECB's supervisory function and national supervisory bodies. The ECB would cooperate with the European Banking Authority, established in 2010 and responsible for further developing the single rulebook and ensuring convergence and consistency of national supervisory practices. The Regulation conferring specific tasks on the European Central Bank concerning policies relating to the prudential supervision of credit institutions[5] would be based on Art. 127(6). This provision allows but a complementary role for the ECB, and presupposes that the main responsibility for prudential supervision remains with the Member States, facilitating a direct link to democratic decision-making and taxpayers.[6]

After the turn in the crisis for the better in September 2012, even the single supervision mechanism appears to have stuck on the negotiation table. Issues such as the scope of ECB supervision and the position of financial institutions functioning in non-euro states, too, have hampered progress. Separation of the ECB's supervisory role from its other functions is causing trouble as well. Especially among German officials and economists, fears of moral hazard ensuing from the ECB's supervisory function and doubts about its compatibility with the enhanced independence of the ECB are still widespread. The other two main elements of the envisioned banking union are a single resolution mechanism and a deposit guarantee scheme. Here the political obstacles to be overcome are perhaps even higher than on the way to a single supervision mechanism. The most modest proposals aim merely to harmonise national resolution mechanisms and deposit guarantee schemes through respective Directives. Much more controversial is the creation of a single resolution authority and a European Resolution Fund (ERF). The ERF would be financed through levies on banks which participate directly in the single supervision mechanism; backing up the fund by means of an ESM credit line has also been discussed. Much polemic surrounds ideas of a single European deposit guarantee fund,

---

[5] Proposal for a Regulation conferring specific tasks on the European Central Bank concerning policies relating to the prudential supervision of credit institutions COM(2012) 511 final.

[6] "The Council, acting by means of regulations in accordance with a special legislative procedure, may unanimously, and after consulting the European Parliament and the European Central Bank, confer specific tasks upon the European Central Bank concerning policies relating to the prudential supervision of credit institutions and other financial institutions with the exception of insurance undertakings."

too.[7] Critical observers discern in far-going banking-union plans new signs of a development towards a 'transfer union'. National banking sectors have varying degrees of undisclosed losses, and, hence, mutualisation of risks could easily lead to fiscal transfers.

In the field of general economic policy – in creating an economic union – many of the initiatives strive at advancing the emergence of an optimal currency area – an integrated economic area – which the Economist side already called for in pre-Maastricht debates, or at least alleviating the effects of the lack of it. In addition to completing the single market, as well as enhancing labour mobility and wage and price flexibility, proposals have been made for establishing an EMU-level stabilisation tool or a cyclical stabilisation insurance to support adjustment to asymmetrical, country-specific shocks. Moreover, structural imbalances and divergences within the Eurozone are targeted. The shock absorption function could provide support for structural reforms, too. Both the Van Rompuy Working Group and the Commission appear to place high expectations on the macroeconomic imbalances procedure, introduced by the six-pack, and the *ex-ante* coordination of structural reforms, evoked in Art. 11 of the Treaty on Stability, Coordination and Governance.[8] It is still too early to tell whether the expectations are justified or set too high. The *ex-ante* coordination of structural reforms even lacks a distinct framework; the Commission has announced that it will make a formal legislative proposal in the near future. A new procedure, intended for coordinating economic policies and suggested by the Commission, consists of a Convergence and Competitiveness Instrument. This Instrument would comprise country-specific contractual arrangements between a Member State and the Commission, as well as financial support from the EU budget for agreed reforms. The instrument would be established by secondary legislation, perhaps amending the Regulation on the macroeconomic imbalances procedure. Another legal option envisaged in the Commission blueprint is

---

[7] Such a fund "with functioning deposit guarantee schemes backed by appropriate levels of funding" was favoured by the European Parliament in its Resolution 20 November 2012.

[8] "With a view to benchmarking best practices and working towards a more closely coordinated economic policy, the Contracting Parties ensure that all major economic policy reforms that they plan to undertake will be discussed ex-ante and, where appropriate, coordinated among themselves. Such coordination shall involve the institutions of the European Union as required by European Union law."

recourse to the flexibility clause of Art. 352, if necessary by way of enhanced cooperation.[9]

Schemes for a banking or financial-market union have been adjusted to the present Treaty framework, and are intended to be realised through secondary legislation. The same goes for schemes intended to further progress towards an optimal currency area. In fiscal policy the proposals go for further European monitoring of national fiscal policies; incorporating the ESM into the EU framework, together with an at least partial mutualisation of sovereign debt; and developing EU or Eurozone fiscal capacity (budget). At least in some points, the proposals would clearly presuppose Treaty amendments. For instance, even a liberal reading of Arts. 121, 126 and 136 TFEU would hardly permit granting the Commission the power to oblige a Member State to amend its draft annual budget or to place states receiving financial assistance under 'financial receivership', bereaving them even of formal budget autonomy.[10] In turn, incorporating the ESM, which would give effect to the view expressed by the ECB and the European Parliament during the preparatory phase of the TESM, and creating a European Redemption Fund[11] would require circumventing the constitutional hurdle raised by the ECJ's *Pringle* ruling. As may be recalled, rejecting Union competence to establish a permanent stability mechanism, such as the ESM, was a central part of the Court's argumentation in *Pringle* (see Chapter 5).

In addition, mutualisation of sovereign debt in the form of euro bonds or stability bonds[12] would most likely conflict with the no-bail-out clause of Art. 125(1) TFEU which, under the *Pringle* doctrine, is still constitutionally valid for other than crisis times. Enhancing Union (EMU) fiscal capacity is required by many of the initiatives aiming at

---

[9] See also the Commission's Communication: European Commission (2013), 'Towards a Deep and Genuine Economic and Monetary Union: The Introduction of a Convergence and Competitiveness Instrument', 20 March 2013. In its final report, the Van Rompuy Working Group also evoked contractual arrangements.

[10] The Tommaso Padoa-Schioppa Group argues that "euro area countries should become subject to much stricter budgetary surveillance and be willing to give up some elements of their sovereignty when they are cut off from the market" and that "the core principle should be: sovereignty ends when solvency ends". The Group suggests the creation of a European Debt Agency (EDA) that would provide a flexible refinancing possibility in exchange for a stepwise transfer of sovereignty. The Report of the Tommaso Padoa-Schioppa Group (2012), pp. 38–41.

[11] The initial proposal was developed by the German Council of Economic Experts as part of a 'European Redemption Pact' (2012).

[12] The Commission's blueprint uses the term 'Eurobills'.

completing the fiscal and economic union, including incorporation of the ESM. However, present Treaty law sets limits on how fiscal capacity could be financed. Persuasive reasons exist for preferring direct taxation and the right to issue bonds over contributions from Member States, but both of these options could topple at constitutional hurdles. Even the flexibility clause of Art. 352 might not be flexible enough. All in all, during the Eurozone crisis the Treaty competences pertaining to fiscal policy have been stretched to such an extreme that even the most imaginative lawyers would find it difficult to discover more leeway in the present constitutional setting for further intensifying European monitoring of national policies or developing an independent EU or EMU fiscal capacity.

Patching up the democracy deficit

The Eurozone crisis has been, first of all, an economic crisis and, accordingly, its direct constitutional repercussions have been felt in the field of the (macro)economic constitution. Hence, it is no surprise that reform proposals, too, focus on the economic dimension. Still, all the major initiatives under examination pay at least lip service to the central values of the political constitution: democracy, legitimacy and accountability. In its resolution, the European Parliament is, as could be expected, especially concerned about its own position in stability mechanisms and the various procedures of European economic governance.

From the very beginning, the implications of an economic and monetary union for political integration have figured prominently on the agenda. Yet, the political decision-makers have always retreated from following up the implications to the very end. The Werner Group, which in 1970 produced the first outline for EMU, did not shy away from concluding that significant transfer of competences to the European level had political union as a logical consequence. Still, it refrained from detailed institutional design, except for suggesting creation of a 'centre of decision for economic policy', politically responsible to the European Parliament, and a Community system for central banks. Of the initiatives now under debate in the EU, the Commission's blueprint is most explicit in pondering the repercussions the completion of EMU would have in the political dimension. The Commission argues that a full fiscal and economic union would "involve a political union with adequate pooling of sovereignty with a central budget as its own fiscal capacity and a means of imposing budgetary and economic decisions on its members, under specific and well-defined circumstances". The Commission is also much more detailed than the Van Rompuy Working Group in its ideas for ensuring democratic legitimacy and accountability in the stage-by-stage development of a banking, fiscal and economic union.

The Working Group emphasises that democratic control and accountability should be ensured at the level where the decisions are taken. For the Working Group, at the European level this implies the involvement of the European Parliament. At the same time, the pivotal role of national parliaments should be maintained, where appropriate. The Working Group acknowledges the role of parliamentary decisions on national budgets with a formulation echoing the rhetoric of the German Constitutional Court: "Decisions on national budgets are at the heart of Member States' parliamentary democracies." Yet, the Working Group sees a problem in heeding the common interest of the Union, which national parliaments are not in the best position to take into account. Hence, the Working Group concludes that "further integration of policy making and a greater pooling of competences at the European level should first and foremost be accompanied with a commensurate involvement of the European Parliament in the integrated frameworks for a genuine EMU". The Working Group's more specific suggestions include:

- Accountability of the ECB as single supervisor and future single resolution authority should be realised at the European level. Yet strong mechanisms for information, reporting and transparency to national parliaments should be created as well.
- Member States should ensure appropriate involvement of national parliaments in the context of the European Semester, and new mechanisms for cooperation between national and European parliaments should be devised.
- The 'full democratic legitimacy and accountability' of EMU should be ensured.
- Intergovernmental arrangements, which "have been created as a result of the shortcomings of the previous architecture", need ultimately to be integrated into the Union framework, as already foreseen under the Treaty on Stability, Coordination and Governance.

In its 'blueprint for a deep and genuine economic and monetary union', the Commission sets out two basic principles for enhancing EMU's democratic legitimacy. First, accountability should be ensured at the level where decision is taken; due attention, though, should be paid to the (other) level where the decision has an impact. This principle entails a crucial position for the European Parliament in ensuring democratic accountability for decisions taken at the Union level, particularly by the Commission. Accordingly, many of the Commission's more detailed initiatives imply a deepened involvement of the Parliament. Yet the Commission points out that "the role of national parliaments will always remain crucial in ensuring legitimacy of Member States' action in the European Council and the Council but especially of the conduct of national budgetary and economic policies even if more closely coordinated by the EU". The Commission's second basic principle relates the need of democratic legitimacy at the European level to the degree of transfer of sovereignty from Member States to the Union. This leads the Commission to distinguish between implications of short-term action, realisable through secondary legislation, and further stages which involve Treaty amendments. As regards short-term reforms, the Commission is rather complacent with the mechanisms of democratic legitimacy under the Lisbon Treaty and seems to downplay the quite significant changes in the macroeconomic constitution initiated by European responses to the Eurozone crisis. These changes have not involved Treaty amendments, except for the new Art. 136(3) TFEU which has been declared to have been of a merely clarifying character. The Commission does, though, draw attention to issues raised by intergovernmental action, both with regard to compatibility with EU primary law and organisation of parliamentary accountability. The Commission underlines that in future reinforcement of governance structures in EMU, the Union's institutional framework and the Community method should be preferred.

The Commission's short-term proposals, focusing on 'practical measures', aim to foster parliamentary debate in the European Semester, building on the Economic Dialogue set up by the six-pack; involve the Parliament in the choice of the multiannual priorities of the Union as expressed by the Integrated Guidelines of the Council (Broad Economic Policy Guidelines and Employment Guidelines); and to inform the Parliament regularly of the preparation and implementation of adjustment programmes of the Member States receiving financial assistance. The Commission also advances the idea of establishing a special committee in the Parliament for euro matters. Finally, in the context of promoting the emergence of a 'genuine European political sphere', the Commission evokes the proposal of political parties nominating candidates for the office of Commission President before European elections.

Considering the profundity of the legitimacy crisis in the Union, in particular in the Eurozone, the Commission's short-term proposals appear fairly unpretentious. The Commission bypasses most of the critical developments to which we have pointed above. These relate to grave disturbances in the two-level legitimation mechanism and narrowing of the reach of the legitimacy coverage that Member States' democratic procedures can offer; the rise of nationalist sentiments due to the intergovernmental way of coping with the Eurozone crisis; and expert bodies, such as the ECB and the Commission, assuming stakeholder or politician roles. The Commission goes somewhat further in suggestions which address the mid-term situation where EMU is strengthened through Treaty amendments, but where a full fiscal and economic union is not yet established. The Commission proposes using co-decision to legitimise Union power to require revision of a national budget and advocates integrating the European Stability Mechanism into the EU framework. In an institutional respect, the euro committee of the Parliament could even be granted decision-making powers, and a specific relationship of confidence and scrutiny could be created between this committee and the Commission Vice President for Economic and Monetary Affairs. This would be part of a development towards "political direction and enhanced democratic accountability of a structure akin to an EMU Treasury within the Commission". The parliamentary supervision the Commission envisages for the ECB is confined to allowing normal budgetary control by the Parliament over the ECB's activity as a banking supervisor and falls short of any political responsibility.

Finally, the Commission discusses the implications for democracy and accountability of mutualising sovereign debt underpinned by a joint and several guarantee by all Eurozone states. Such mutualisation could lead to a "considerable financial burden for one individual Member State's finances, for which that Member State's parliament is accountable, although the burden is the result of policy decisions that have been made over time by one or several other Member States under the responsibility of their parliaments". This is exactly the situation which the German Constitutional Court has deemed to curtail the Bundestag's budget autonomy in a way which contradicts the democracy principle, protected by the Basic Law's eternity clause (see Chapter 6). The Commission notes that the problem cannot be effaced simply by entrusting management of mutualised sovereign debt to an EU executive even if this were accountable to the European Parliament.

What is further needed is far-reaching Union powers in economic policy in the Eurozone and a substantial Union budget for which the
European Parliament is responsible. In the Commission's view, the
problem would be resolved in a full fiscal and economic union where
Member States would not be jointly and severally liable for each other's
sovereign debt. Such a union would itself dispose of a substantial central budget, the resources for which would be derived from an autono-
mous power of taxation, complemented, if necessary, by the EU's own
sovereign debt. This would be concomitant with a large-scale pooling
of sovereignty over the conduct of economic policy at EU level. The
European Parliament would then have reinforced powers to co-legis-
late on Union taxation and provide the necessary democratic scrutiny
for all decisions taken by the EU executive. If issuance of eurobills were
allowed through a Treaty amendment before the final stage of a full
fiscal and economic union, the Commission calls for an accountability model resting both on the EU and national levels. The European
Parliament would provide accountability for decisions on management
of eurobills to be taken by an EMU Treasury within the Commission.
The mechanism would also include Council decisions, adopted by unanimity of the euro-area Member States with the consent of the European
Parliament, on the establishment and periodic renewal of the eurobills
scheme. Involvement of the Council would open the way for the impact
of national legitimation mechanisms. It would then be up to Member
States to provide the parliamentary accountability they deem necessary
for consenting to decisions to be taken by the Council. A European debt
redemption fund, in turn, would require a detailed legal basis. If this
could be ensured, the Commission foresees setting up the fund through
a decision of the Council, again adopted by unanimity of the euro-area
Member States with the consent of the European Parliament, and subject to ratification by Member States. The Commission, accountable to
the European Parliament, would then manage the fund pursuant to the
precise rules laid down by Council decision.

In its resolution of 20 November 2012, the European Parliament
focuses on its own role in banking, fiscal and economic unions, integrating intergovernmental treaties and stability mechanisms into the
legal and institutional framework of the Union, as well as respect for
the Community method in general. The Parliament reiterates many
of the initiatives already included in the report of the Van Rompuy
Working Group or the Commission communication, such as creating
specific means for democratic accountability for the Commissioner for

Economic and Monetary Affairs or a European Treasury Office. New openings are but few.

A perusal of the initiatives which European institutions and bodies have produced for strengthening democratic legitimacy and accountability, particularly in the Eurozone, leaves one somewhat perplexed. They do not really appear to grasp adequately either the roots or the gravity of the legitimacy crisis or the multifaceted nature of the democracy issues spawned by the Eurozone crisis. And if the diagnosis is deficient, the remedies cannot be appropriate, either. In Chapter 7, we presented our own analysis of the spillover effects which the crisis of the macroeconomic constitution has had in the field of the political constitution, especially with regard to democracy, legitimacy and accountability. We discussed the division of competences between the European and national level as a democracy issue; the implications of the narrowing of the reach of national democratic legitimation, due to reductions in Member State sovereignty in fiscal and economic policy, and the shrinking of national parliaments' budget autonomy; the repercussions of resort to the intergovernmental way; and the consequences of independent expert bodies, such as the ECB and the Commission, assuming features of a stakeholder or politician role.

Transfer of competences to the European level is discussed but not as a democracy issue. By contrast, Miguel Poiares Maduro, who has produced a report on 'a New Governance for the European Union and the Euro' for the European Parliament,[13] has grasped this perspective and, indeed, considers it the fundamental democracy issue in Europe. He is also more sensitive to the detrimental consequences for the legitimacy of the European project of the intergovernmental way of dealing with the Eurozone crisis. It is true, though, that official initiatives, too, call for incorporating intergovernmental agreements, including the TSCG, and intergovernmental mechanisms, such as the ESM, into the Union framework. But Poiares Maduro makes clear the contribution of intergovernmentalism to the rise of narrow nationalism in both assisting and recipient states. For him, this a central reason for strengthening Union (EMU) fiscal capacity and financing it through Union taxation, instead of transfers from national budgets. Moreover, Poiares Maduro is conscious of the social and cultural prerequisites of a functioning European democracy and does not confine his perspective merely to the interplay of European institutions among themselves or with their

[13] M. Poiares Maduro (2012).

national counterparts. Yet, in the end, his recipe for fostering European civil society and European belongingness among the citizenry is rather mild: it largely boils down to the suggestion that in order to raise interest and participation among the electorate, political parties should nominate their candidates for the Commission Presidency.

In our view, if progress is not made towards a civic European demos and if the damage caused by the unfortunate intergovernmental crisis resolution mechanisms is not undone, institutional solutions for patching up the democracy deficit cannot produce much result. Still, we would also caution against undervaluing the importance of such solutions. Thus, the interplay between the European Parliament and the national parliaments may increase awareness of the externalities of national policies and in this sense help to mend the democracy deficit. Moreover, enhancing the role of the European Parliament may also boost the general transparency of European economic governance, and foster discussion in the media and fledgling European civil society. But, of course, all proposals advocating a more prominent role for the European Parliament are overshadowed by the arguably weak democratic legitimacy of the Parliament itself.

Significant uncharted patches exist in attention to the institutional dimension, too. Official initiatives do address the reinforced need for democratic legitimacy of the Commission, in particular the Commissioner of Monetary and Financial Affairs, and embrace development towards a European Treasury, politically accountable to the European Parliament. This implies acknowledgement of the political element involved in fiscal and economic governance, as well as in the strict conditionality required from the states receiving financial assistance. But a major democratic issue remains untackled. Accountability to the European Parliament or involvement of the Council cannot provide sufficient legitimation for a quasi-commissarial fiscal and economic regime to which the crisis states, most notably Greece, have been subjected. Another vacuum surrounds the position of the ECB, which is hardly touched upon in the schemes under discussion in European fora. If the ECB has, even if for at least partially good reasons, exceeded the role of a technocratic expert body and if this is likely to recur in future crises, should not the necessity for democratic legitimation and accountability extend to the ECB, as well? As Fritz Scharpf has pointed out, national central banks in constitutional democracies, even when enjoying practical and even formal independence, are still embedded in a political and institutional system which guarantees interaction with the political branches of government, maybe the social partners, too, and which makes the central bank receptive to messages from the media and sentiments among the citizenry at large.[14] The ECB largely lacks such embeddedness. Here institutional innovations, facilitating regular communication of the ECB with other EU or EMU institutions, could perhaps initiate a healthy development, without jeopardising the formal independence.

Speeding up the two-speed Europe

The crisis has given new impetus to the differentiation of the Eurozone from the rest of the Union: a two-speed Europe is reality to a larger extent than ever before. Most of the proposals on the table for realising a banking, fiscal and economic union would entail further reinforcement of the specific Eurozone regime. The same goes for schemes intended to respond to the political and institutional implications of mutation of the (macro)economic constitution. Yet, at the same time a clear tendency towards preserving the unity of the Union as intact as possible also permeates official initiatives. In its blueprint, the Commission expresses two, at least on their face contradictory requirements as follows: "In order to secure the sustainability of the common currency, the EMU must have the possibility to deepen more quickly and more thoroughly than the EU as a whole, whilst preserving the integrity of the EU at large." For the Commission, accommodation of the two premises implies, first, that deepening EMU should build on the Treaty framework, so that intergovernmental solutions would only be resorted to in exceptional cases and transitionally, in anticipation of Treaty amendment. Such intergovernmental solutions must respect EU law and governance, and not raise new accountability problems.

Second, in deepening EMU preference should be given to EU-wide instruments, and specific euro-area measures should have merely a complementary role. The Commission invokes Art. 136 TFEU as a useful legal basis for deepening integration of the euro area. The Commission also advocates keeping, wherever legally possible, euro-area measures open for participation of other Member States, too. Third, priority should be given to the possibilities offered by the present Treaties, so that amendments to the Treaties should be contemplated only when indispensable

---

[14] F. Scharpf (2007), p. 176.

for improving the functioning of EMU. The Commission is cautious about institutional parallelism and opposes calls to strengthen the Eurogroup by making it responsible for decisions concerning the euro area and its Member States. The Commission argues that this would lead to a euro-area Council as a separate institution and exclusion of non-euro area Member States not only from voting – as Arts. 136 and 138 already allow – but also from deliberations and preparatory work preceding ministers' meetings. Neither the Commission nor the other official interlocutors have taken up the idea of a particular composition of the European Parliament for issues concerning only the Eurozone. The Commission is favourable to creating a euro committee in the Parliament but does not take an explicit position on its membership.

In public debates, most commentators have inferred from the crisis the need to deepen fiscal, economic and political integration, particularly in the Eurozone. Those who would like to keep open the option of a rolling back and a return to the pre-Maastricht time include prominent academics and public intellectuals – such as Giandomenico Majone and Fritz Scharpf.[15] Seizing this option would be based on the judgment that the flaws of EMU cannot be remedied, which is intellectually a defendable position. With regard to single Member States, it would be not only economically but also politically and morally questionable to demand their continuous membership in EMU or sanction exit by linking it to exit from the EU, too, if the common currency is causing them burdens which cannot be compensated by potential benefits. Yet, even a partial dissolution of EMU would imply that European leaders concede that a colossal mistake has been made and that, therefore, the direction of European integration should be reversed, at least for some Member States. And, as is well known, conceding mistakes is not easy.

If deepened integration is the chosen direction, we agree with those who prefer the Union legislative and institutional framework to intergovernmental agreements and mechanisms. Our reasons relate to considerations of democracy, legitimacy and transparency. If Treaty amendments are not needed, secondary legislation is the natural choice. Still, here we would propose caution in the interpretation of present Treaty provisions on competence, such as Arts. 121(6), 126(14) and 136(1) TFEU. An excessively liberal reading of Treaty provisions weakens confidence in the EU as a 'community based on the rule of

---

[15] See F. Scharpf (2012) and G. Majone (in press).

law' and further jeopardises its legitimacy. The liberal, and in our view constitutionally suspect, interpretation of Art. 136(1) TFEU has largely rendered enhanced cooperation obsolete in the field of European economic governance. And, in any case, enhanced cooperation is only available for use of competences already granted by the Treaties, but not for Treaty amendments.

Treaty amendments are always politically cumbersome, and with 28 Member States more so than ever. The more far-reaching amendments are and the more they touch on Member State competences, the higher are the political obstacles. In addition, European leaders have not yet fully recovered from the shock caused by the failure of the Constitutional Treaty. Finally, the obvious intention of the UK Prime Minister to profit from the plight of the Eurozone Member States and to charge a high price for Treaty amendments responding to the needs of the Eurozone does not make an exhaustive round of Treaty negotiations a particularly enticing option.

Against such a backdrop, it is not surprising that some discussants embrace the intergovernmental way in deepening integration in the Eurozone. The 'Padoa-Scioppa Group' concludes that the euro area will have to agree on a new institutional and legal structure, which can best be achieved through a new intergovernmental treaty. Even if formally external to the EU framework, it should be closely linked to it and involve EU institutions and bodies as much as possible. At a later stage, it could be integrated into the EU framework. This very much resembles the Treaty on Stability, Coordination and Governance, and reproduces all the constitutional problems linked to it.[16] For reasons we have already stated, we have serious doubts about the intergovernmental way as an alternative, not only to secondary EU legislation, but to Treaty amendments, as well. Politically, a separate Treaty for the Eurozone could be more feasible, but political hurdles are quite high on that road, too.

We find the constitutional constellation which the crisis has produced in an incremental way in many respects unsatisfactory. We are especially worried about the spillover effects of changes in the macroeconomic constitution in the political and social dimensions. Yet, with alleviation of the crisis the momentum for additional constitutional reforms has slackened. Both European leaders and citizens appear to be

---

[16] Jean-Claude Piris, too, advocates for the road of an intergovernmental agreement to arrive at a two-speed Europe in J.-C. Piris (2012), pp. 122–42.

fatigued by the hectic developments of the past three years. Prospects for a comprehensive reform of existing Treaties or a new Eurozone Treaty are bleak enough. Most likely, incrementalism, from which very few exceptions exist in the constitutional history of the Community/Union, will continue.

In sum, we are not very optimistic.

References

BOOKS AND ARTICLES

Amtenbrink, F. and de Haan, J. (2003) 'Economic Governance in the European Union – Fiscal Policy Discipline Versus Flexibility', 40 *Common Market Law Review*, 1057–106.

Antoniadis, A. (2011) 'Debt Crisis as a Global Emergency: The European Economic Constitution and Other Greek Fables', in A. Antoniadis, R. Schütze and E. Spaventa (eds.), *The European Union and Global Emergencies: A Law and Policy Analysis* (Oxford: Hart Publishing).

Balzacq, T., Bigo, D., Carrera, S. and Guild, E. (2006) *Security and the Two-Level Game: The Treaty of Prüm, the EU and the Management of Threats* (Brussels: Centre for European Policy Studies).

Baquero Cruz, J. (2002) *Between Competition and Free Movement: The Economic Constitutional Law of the European Community* (Oxford: Hart Publishing).

Barro, R. (1976) 'Rational Expectations and the Role of Monetary Policy', 2 *Journal of Monetary Economy* 1, 1–32.

Bean, C. (2010) *The Great Moderation, the Great Panic and the Great Contraction* (Fiesole: European University Institute).

Belke, A. (2010) *Driven by the Markets? ECB Sovereign Bond Purchases and the Securities Markets Programme* (Essen: Ruhr Economic Papers).

Benati, L. and Surico, P. (2008) *VAR Analysis and the Great Moderation* (Frankfurt: European Central Bank).

Bernanke, B. (2004) 'Remarks by Governor Ben S. Bernanke: Great Moderation', Meetings of the Eastern Economic Association, 20 February 2004.

Bernoth, K., von Hagen, J. and Schuknecht, L. (2004) *Sovereign Risk Premia in the European Government Bond Market* (Frankfurt: European Central Bank).

Blundell-Wignall, A. and Slovik, P. (2010) 'The EU Stress Test and Sovereign Debt Exposures', *OECD Working Papers on Finance, Insurance and Private Pensions*, 4 OECD Financial Affairs Division.

Böhm, F. (1928) 'Das Problem der Privaten Macht', *Die Justiz* 3, 324–45.

(1933) *Wettbewerb und Monopolkampf. Eine Untersuchung zur Frage des Wirtschaftlichen Kampfrechts und zur Frage der Rechtlichen Struktur der Geltenden Wirtschaftsordnung* (Berlin: Carl Heymanns Verlag).

(1966) 'Privatrechtsgesellschaft und Marktwirtschaft', 17 *ORDO*, 75–151.

Borger, V. (2013) 'The ESM and the European Court's Predicament in *Pringle*', 14 *German Law Review*, 113–40.

Busch, K., Hermann, C., Hinrichs, K. and Schulten, T. (2013) *Euro Crisis, Austerity Policy and the European Social Model: How Crisis Policies in Southern Europe Threaten the EU's Social Dimension* (Berlin: Friedrich Ebert Stiftung).

Calliess, C. (2011) 'Perspektiven des Euro Zwischen Solidarität und Recht – Eine Rechtliche Analyse der Griechenlandhilfe und des Rettungsschirms', 14 *Zeitschrift für Europäische Studien*, 213–82.

Calmfors, L. (Flam, H., Gottfries, N., Haaland Matlary, J., Jerneck, M., Lindahl, R., Nordh Berntsson, C., Rabinowicz, E. and Vredin, A.) (1997) *Calmforsraportten*, SOU 1996:158. Also published in English as *EMU – A Swedish Perspective* (Boston: Kluwer Academic Publishers).

Cappelletti, M., Seccombe, M. and Weiler, J. (eds.) (1985) *Integration through Law, European and the American Federal Experience* (Berlin: Walter de Gruyter).

Cecchetti, S., Mohanty, M. and Zampolli, F. (2011) *The Real Effects of Debt* (Basel: Bank for International Settlements).

Chen, R., Milesi-Ferretti, G. and Tressel, T. (2012) 'External Imbalances in the Euro Area', *IMF Working Papers*.

Chiti, E. and Gustavo Teixeira, P. (2013) 'The Constitutional Implications of the European Responses to the Financial and Public Debt Crisis', 50 *Common Market Law Review* 3, 683–708.

Chiti, E., Menéndez, A. and Teixeira, P. (2012) 'The European Rescue of the European Union', in E. Chiti, A. Menéndez and P. Teixeira (eds.), *The European Rescue of the European Union* (Oslo: ARENA Centre for European Studies), pp. 391–428.

Codogno, L., Favero, C. and Missale, A. (2003) 'Yield Spreads on EMU Government Bonds', 18 *Economic Policy* 37, 503–32.

Corriere della Sera (2010) 'Trichet e Draghi: Un'Azione Pressante per Ristabilire la Fiducia degli Investitori', *Corriere della Sera*, 6 August 2010, available at www.corriere.it/economia/11_settembre_29/trichet_draghi_inglese_304a5f1e-ea59–11e0-ae06–4da866778017.shtml.

Craig, P. (2012) 'The Stability, Coordination and Governance Treaty: Principle, Politics and Pragmatism', 37 *European Law Review*, 231–48.

Crouch, C. (2009) 'What Will Follow the Demise of Privatised Keynesianism?', 80 *The Political Quarterly* Issue Supplement s1, 302–15.

Davis, P. (1992) *Debt, Financial Fragility, and Systemic Risk* (Oxford: Clarendon Press).

de Grauwe, P. (2011) 'Who Cares About the Survival of the Eurozone?' *CEPS Commentary*, available at www.ceps.eu.

(2013) 'Design Failures in the Eurozone: Can They Be Fixed?' *LSE LEQS Paper No. 57*, available at www.lse.ac.uk/europeanInstitute/LEQS/LEQSPaper57.pdf.

de Grauwe, P. and Ji, Y. (2013) 'More Evidence that Financial Markets Imposed Excessive Austerity in the Eurozone', *CEPS Commentary*, available at www.ceps.eu.

de Gregorio Merino, A. (2012) 'Legal Developments in the Monetary and Economic Union During the Debt Crisis: The Mechanisms of Financial Assistance', 49 *Common Market Law Review* 5, 1613–46.

de Laroisière, J. (2009) *The High-Level Group on Financial Supervision in the EU Report*, 25 February, available at http://ec.europa.eu/internal_market/finances/docs/de_larosiere_report_en.pdf.

de Witte, B. (2001) 'Old-fashioned Flexibility: International Agreements between Member States of the European Union', in G. de Búrca and J. Scott (eds.), *Constitutional Change in the EU – From Uniformity to Flexibility* (Oxford: Hart Publishing).

(2011) 'The European Treaty Amendment for the Creation of a Financial Stability Mechanism', 6 *European Policy Analysis* 1, 1–8.

Drehmann, M., Borio, C. and Tsatsaronis, K. (2012) *Characterising the Financial Cycle: Don't Lose Sight of the Medium Term!* BIS Working Papers No. 380 (June 2012).

Dworkin, R. (1978) *Taking Rights Seriously* (London: Ducksworth).

Elliot, L. (2011) 'EU Should Control Member States' Budget Says Bank Boss', 2 June 2011, available at www.guardian.co.uk/business/2011/jun/02/trichet-wants-eu-central-finance-ministry.

Eucken, W. (1952) *Grundsätze der Wirtschaftspolitik* (Tübingen: JCB Mohr).

Fabbrini, F. (2013) 'The Fiscal Compact, the "Golden Rule", and the Paradox of European Federalism', 36 *Boston College International and Comparative Law Review* 1, 1–39.

Fassbender, K. (2010) 'Der Europäische "Stabilisierungsmechganismus" im Lichte von Unionsrecht und Deutschem Verfassungsrecht', 13 *Neue Zeitschrift für Verwaltungsrecht*, 799–803.

Faust, J., Rogers, J. and Wright, J. (2005) 'News and Noise in G-7 GDP Announcements', 37 *Journal of Money, Credit and Banking* 3, 403–19.

Fossum, J. E. and Menéndez, A. J. (2011) *The Constitution's Gift: A Constitutional Theory for a Democratic European Union* (Lanham, MD: Rowman & Littlefield).

Friedman, M. (1956) 'The Quantity Theory of Money: A Restatement', in *Studies in the Quantity Theory of Money*, reprinted in *The Optimum Quantity of Money* (Chicago: Aldine Transaction, 2005).

Fuller, L. L. (1969) *The Morality of Law* (New Haven, CT: Yale University Press).

Gaitanides, C. (2011) 'Intervention des IWF in der Eurozone – Mandatswidrig?', 14 *Neue Zeitschrift für Verwaltungsrecht*, 848–52.

Garriga, C., Gavin, W. and Schlagenhauf, D. (2006) 'Recent Trends in Homeownership', 88 *Federal Reserve Bank of St. Louis Review* 5, 397–411.

Gerber, D. (1994) 'Constitutionalizing the Economy: German Neo-liberalism, Competition Law and the "New Europe" ', 42 *American Journal of Comparative Law* 1, 25–84.

Giannone, D., Lenza, M. and Reichlin, L. (2008) *Explaining the Great Moderation: It is Not the Shock* (Frankfurt: European Central Bank).

Gilbert, M. (2012) *European Integration: A Concise History* (London: Rowman & Littlefield Publishers).

González Cabanillas, L. and Ruscher, E. (2008) *The Great Moderation in the Euro Area: What Role Have Macroeconomic Policies Played?* (Brussels: European Commission).

Habermas, J. (1971) *Toward a Rational Society: Student Protest, Science, and Politics* (London: Heinemann).

(2011) *Zur Verfassung Europas: Ein Essay* (Berlin: Suhrkamp).

Hacker, B. and van Treeck, T. (2010) *What Influence for European Governance? The Reformed Stability and Growth Pact* (Berlin: Friedrich Ebert Stiftung).

Häde, U. (2009) 'Haushaltsdisziplin und Solidarität im Zeichen der Finanzkrise', 12 *Europäische Zeitschrift für Wirtschaftsrecht*, 399–403.

Hänninen, S. (2010) 'Social Constitution in Historical Perspective: Hugo Sinzheimer in the Weimar Context', in K. Tuori and S. Sankari (eds.), *The Many Constitutions of Europe* (Aldershot: Ashgate), pp. 219–40.

Heipertz, M. and Verdun, A. (2010) *Ruling Europe: The Politics of the Stability and Growth Pact* (Cambridge University Press).

Höpner, M. and Rödl, F. (2012) 'Illegitim und Rechtswidrig: Das Neue Makroökonomische Regime im Euroraum', 92 *Wirtschaftsdienst* 4, 219–22.

Hufeld, U. (2011) 'Zwischen Notrettung und Rütlischwur: der Umbau der Wirtschaftsund Währungsunion in der Krise', 34 *Integration* 2, 117–31.

Issing, O. (2005) 'Communication, Transparency, Accountability: Monetary Policy in the Twenty-First Century', 87 *Federal Reserve Bank of St. Louis Review* 2 (Part 1), 65–83.

(2008) *The Birth of the Euro* (Cambridge University Press).

Issing, O., Gaspar, V., Angeloni, I. and Tristani, O. (2004) *Monetary Policy in the Euro Area Strategy and Decision Making at the European Central Bank* (Cambridge University Press).

James, H. (2012) *Making the European Monetary Union* (London: The Belknap Press).

Knopp, L. (2010) 'Griechenland – Nothilfe auf dem Verfassungsrechtlichen Prüfstand', 63 *Neue Juristische Wochenschrift*, 1777–82.

Koukiadaki, A. and Kretsos, L. (2012) 'Opening Pandora's Box: The Sovereign Debt Crisis and Labour Market Regulation in Greece', 41 *Industrial Law Journal* 3, 276–304.

Lord, C. (2012) *On the Legitimacy of Monetary Union* (Stockholm: Swedish Institute for European Policy Studies).

Losada Fraga, F. (2013) 'Exacerbated Economic Governance in the European Union – Or When Did We Forget About Democratic Legitimacy?', *Helsinki Legal Studies Research Paper No. 24*, available at SSRN.

Louis, J.-V. (2010) 'Guest Editorial: The No-bailout Clause and Rescue Packages', 47 *Common Market Law Review* 4, 971–86.

Luczak, J.-M. (2009) *Die Europäische Wirtschaftsverfassung als Legitimationselement europäischer Integration: Ein Beitrag zur wirtschaftsverfassungsrechtlichen Analyse des Unionsrechts durch den Vertrag von Lissabon* (Berlin: Duncker & Humblot).

Luhmann, N. (2004) *Law as a Social System* (Oxford University Press).

MacCormick, N. (2007) *Institutions of Law: An Essay in Legal Theory* (Oxford University Press).

MacCormick, N. and Weinberger, O. (1986) *An Institutional Theory of Law* (Dordrecht: Kluwer).

Majone, G. (2012) 'The Parable of EMU: Maastricht as the Decisive Constitutional Moment in EU History', presented at the conference *Constitutional Implications of the European Union Economic Crisis*, 28–29 March 2012, Helsinki.

(2013) 'The General Crisis of the European Union: A Genetic Approach', presented at the conference *Europe in Crisis: Implications for the EU and Norway*, 14–15 March 2013, Oslo.

(in press) 'Patterns of Post-National Europe: The Future Integration After the Crisis of the Monetary Union', in M. Fichera, S. Hänninen and K. Tuori (eds.), *Polity out of Crisis* (Aldershot: Ashgate).

Marsh, D. (2011) *The Euro: The Battle for the New Global Currency* (London: Yale University Press).

Mayer, T. (2012) *Europe's Unfinished Currency* (London: Anthem Press).

Mestmäcker, E.-W. (2003) *Wirtschaft und Verfassung in der Europäischen Union: Beiträge zur Rechtstheorie und Politik der Europäischen Integration* (Baden-Baden: Nomos).

Mosley, L. (2004) 'Government-Financial Market Relations after EMU', 5 *European Union Politics* 2, 181–209.

Müller, P., Pauly, C. and Reiermann, C. (2011) 'ECB Chief Economist Quits: Jürgen Stark's Resignation is Setback for Merkel', 12 September 2011, available at www.spiegel.de/international/europe/ecb-chief-economist-quits-juergen-stark-s-resignation-is-setback-for-merkel-a-785668.html.

Mundel, R. (1961) 'A Theory of Optimum Currency Areas', reprinted in M. Blejer, D. Cheney, J. Frenkel, L. Leiderman and A. Razin (eds.), *Optimum Currency Areas: New Analytical and Policy Developments* (Washington D.C.: International Monetary Fund, 1997).

Pattison, B., Diacon, D. and Vine, J. (2010) *Tenure Trends in the UK Housing System* (Leicester: Building and Social Housing Foundation).

Pech, L. (2010) ' "A Union Founded on the Rule of Law": Meaning and Reality of the Rule of Law as a Constitutional Principle of EU Law', 6 *European Constitutional Law Review*, 359–96.

Pernice, I. (2001) 'Der Beitrag Walter Hallsteins zur Zukunft Europas: Begründung und Konsolidierung der Europäischen Gemeinschaft als Rechtsgemeinschaft', *Walter Hallstein Institute Paper 9/01*.

Piris, J.-C. (2012) *The Future of Europe: Towards a Two-Speed EU* (Cambridge University Press).

Pisani-Ferry, J., Sapir, A. and Wolff, G. B. (2013) 'EU-IMF Assistance to Euro Area Countries: An Early Assessment', *Bruegel Blueprint*, available at www. bruegel.org/download/parent/779-eu-imf-assistance-to-euro-area-countries-an-early-assessment/file/1661-eu-imf-assistance-to-euro-area-countries-an-early-assessment/.

Poiares Maduro, M. (1998) *We the Court: The European Court of Justice and the European Economic Constitution* (Oxford: Hart Publishing).

(2012) *A New Governance for the European Union and the Euro: Democracy and Justice* (Florence: European University Institute).

Raz, J. (1979) *The Authority of Law: Essays in Law and Morality* (Oxford University Press).

Reinhart, C. M. and Rogoff, K. S. (2010) 'Growth in a Time of Debt', 100 *American Economic Review* 2, 573–8.

Ruffert, M. (2011) 'The European Debt Crisis and European Union Law', 48 *Common Market Law Review* 6, 1777–805.

Sauter, W. (1998) 'The Economic Constitution of the European Union', 4 *Columbia Journal of European Law* 1, 27–68.

Scharpf, F. W. (1999) *Governing in Europe: Effective and Democratic?* (Oxford University Press).

(2007) *Reflections on Multilevel Legitimacy* (Cologne: Max Planck Institute for the Study of Societies).

(2010) 'The Asymmetry of European Integration, or Why the EU Cannot Be a "Social Market Economy" ', 8 *Socio-Economic Review* 2, 211–50.

(2012) *Legitimacy Intermediation in the Multilevel European Polity and its Collapse in the Euro Crisis* (Cologne: Max Planck Institute for the Study of Societies).

Schneider, K. (2013) 'Yes, But … One More Thing: Karlsruhe's Ruling on the European Stability Mechanism', 14 *German Law Review*, 53–74.

Schorkopf, F. (2011) 'Gestaltung mit Recht – Prägekraft und Selbststand des Rechts in einer Rechtsgemeinschaft', 136 *Archiv des Öffentlichen Rechts*, 323–44.

Schuknecht, L., Moutot, P., Rother, P. and Stark, J. (2011) *The Stability and Growth Pact – Crisis and Reform* (Frankfurt: European Central Bank).

Schütze, R. (2006) 'Supremacy Without Pre-emption? The Very Slowly Emergent Doctrine of Community Pre-emption', 43 *Common Market Law Review* 4, 1023–48.

(2012) *European Constitutional Law* (Cambridge University Press).

Smits, R. (2005) 'The European Constitution and the EMU: An Appraisal', 42 *Common Market Law Review* 2, 425–68.

Spiegel International (2010) 'Former Central Bank Head Karl Otto Pöhl: Bailout Plan Is All About "Rescuing Banks and Rich Greeks" ', 18 May 2010, available at www.spiegel.de/international/germany/former-central-bank-head-karl-otto-poehl-bailout-plan-is-all-about-rescuing-banks-and-rich-greeks-a-695245.html.

(2011) 'Merkel ECB Candidate: German Central Bank Head Axel Weber Resigns', 11 February 2011, available at www.spiegel.de/international/germany/merkel-ecb-candidate-german-central-bank-head-axel-weber-resigns-a-745083.html.

Spiegel, P. (2013) 'EU's Olli Rehn Lashes out at IMF Criticism of Greek Bailout', *Financial Times*, 7 June 2013, available at www.ft.com/cms/s/0/ed72d2ac-cf4e-11e2-be7b-00144feab7de.html#axzz2Y3GjWyda.

Thym, D. (2011) 'Euro-Rettungsschirm: Zwischenstaatliche Rechtskonstruktion und Verfassungsgerichtliche Kontrolle', 5 *Europäische Zeitschrift für Wirtschaftsrecht*, 167–71.

Tomkin, J. (2013) 'Contradiction, Circumvention and Conceptual Gymnastics: The Impact of the Adoption of the ESM Treaty on the State of European Democracy', 14 *German Law Review*, 169–90.

Tridimas, T. (2006) *The General Principles of EU Law*, 2nd edn (Oxford University Press).

Tuori, K. (2002) *Critical Legal Positivism* (Aldershot: Ashgate).

(2010) 'The Many Constitutions of Europe', in K. Tuori and S. Sankari (eds.), *The Many Constitutions of Europe* (Aldershot: Ashgate), pp. 3–30.

(2011) *Ratio and Voluntas: The Tension between Reason and Will in Law* (Aldershot: Ashgate).

(2013) 'The Relationality of European Constitution(s)', in U. Neergaard and R. Nielsen (eds.), *European Legal Method: Towards a New European Legal Realism?* (Copenhagen: DJØF Publishing).

van Riet, A. (2010) *Euro Area Fiscal Policies and the Crisis No. 109* (Frankfurt am Main: ECB Occasional Paper Series).

Vits, C. and Kennedy, S. (2011) 'Weber to Leave Bundesbank in April, Throwing Race of ECB Chief Wide Open', 11 February 2011, available at www.bloomberg.com/news/2011-02–11/weber-to-leave-bundesbank-in-april-throwing-race-for-ecb-chief-wide-open.html.

Wegmann, M. (2002) *Früher Neoliberalismus und Europäische Integration; Interdependenz der Nationalen, Supranationalen und Internationalen Ordnung von Wirtschaft und Gesellschaft (1932–1965)* (Baden-Baden: Nomos).

(2008) *Der Einfluss des Neoliberalismus auf das Europäische Wettbewerbsrecht 1946–1965. Von den Wirtschaftswissenschaften zur Politik* (Baden-Baden: Nomos).

Weiler, J. (1999) *The Constitution of Europe* (Cambridge University Press).

Zilioli, C. and Selmayr, M. (2007) 'The Constitutional Status of the European Central Bank', 44 *Common Market Law Review* 2, 355–99.

Ziller, J. (2006) *Le Traité de Prüm: Une Vraie-Fausse Coopération Renforcée dans l'Espace de Sécurité de Liberté et de Justice* (Fiesole: European University Institute).

DOCUMENTS

BIS (2009) *Annual Report 2009* (Basel: Bank for International Settlements), available at www.bis.org/publ/arpdf/ar2009e.pdf.

CEBS (2009) 'Press Release on the Results of the EU-wide Stress Testing Exercise', 1 October 2009, available at http://eba.europa.eu/documents/10180/15977/CEBS-2009–180-Annex-2-%28Press-release-from-CEBS%29.pdf.

Committee for the Study of Economic and Monetary Union (Delors Committee) (1989) 'Report on an Economic and Monetary Union in the European Community', 17 April 1989, available at http://aei.pitt.edu/1007/1/monetary_delors.pdf.

Committee on the Elimination of Discrimination against Women (2011) 'Seventh Periodic Report Greece', 14 March 2011, available at www.un.org/ga/search/view_doc.asp?symbol=CEDAW/C/GRC/7.

Committee monitoring the UN Covenant on Economic, Social and Cultural Right (2004) 'Concluding Observations: Greece', 7 June 2004, available at www.refworld.org/publisher,CESCR,,GRC,42d26c904,0.html.

Council of the European Union (2010) 'Economic and Financial Affairs – Extraordinary Council Meeting Press Release', 9–10 May 2010, 9596/10, available at http://europa.eu/rapid/press-release_PRES-10–108_en.htm.

ECB (2007) 'Transcript of Press Briefing', 2 August 2007, available at www.ecb.int/press/pressconf/2007/html/is070802.en.html.

    (2008) 'Introductory Statement with Q&A with J.-C. Trichet', 2 October 2008, available at www.ecb.int/press/pressconf/2008/html/is081002.en.html.

    (2009a) 'Introductory Statement with Q&A with J.-C. Trichet', 7 May 2009, available at www.ecb.int/press/pressconf/2009/html/is090507.en.html.

    (2009b) 'Press Release', 4 June 2009, available at www.ecb.int/press/pr/date/2009/html/pr090604_1.en.html.

    (2010a) 'Introductory Statement with Q&A with J.-C. Trichet', 4 February 2010, available at www.ecb.int/press/pressconf/2010/html/is100204.en.html.

    (2010b) 'Introductory Statement with Q&A with J.-C. Trichet', 4 March 2010, available at www.ecb.int/press/pressconf/2010/html/is100304.en.html.

    (2010c) 'Introductory Statement with Q&A with J.-C. Trichet', 6 May 2010, available at www.ecb.int/press/pressconf/2010/html/is100506.en.html.

    (2010d) 'Statement by the ECB's Governing Council on the Additional Measures of the Greek Government', 3 March 2010, available at www.ecb.int/press/pr/date/2010/html/pr100303.en.html.

    (2011a) 'Press Release', 31 March 2011, available at www.ecb.europa.eu/press/pr/date/2011/html/pr110331_2.en.html.

    (2011b) 'Press Release', 7 July 2011, available at www.ecb.europa.eu/press/pr/date/2011/html/pr110707_1.en.html.

    (2012) 'Press Release', 6 September 2012, available at www.ecb.int/press/pr/date/2012/html/pr120906_1.en.html.

    (2013a) 'Intra-Euro Area Trade Linkages and External Adjustment', *Monthly Bulletin* 1, 2013, available at www.ecb.int/pub/pdf/other/art2_mb201301en_pp59–74en.pdf.

    (2013b) 'Press Release', 21 February 2013, available at www.ecb.int/press/pr/date/2013/html/pr130221_1.en.html.

    'The Definition of Price Stability', *Monetary Policy – Strategy*, available at www.ecb.europa.eu/mopo/strategy/pricestab/html/index.en.html.

ECB website, 'The Definition of Price Stability', available at www.ecb.europa.eu/mopo/strategy/pricestab/html/index.en.html.

EFSF Framework Agreement consolidated version, available at www.efsf.europa.eu/attachments/20111019_efsf_framework_agreement_en.pdf.

Euro Area (2011) 'Conclusions of the Heads of State or Government of the Euro Area', 11 March 2011, available at www.european-council.europa.eu/council-meetings/conclusions?lang=en.

(2012) 'Summit Statement', 29 June 2012, available at www.consilium.europa.eu/uedocs/cms_data/docs/pressdata/en/ec/131359.pdf.

Euro Area Loan Facility Bill (2010) Schedule 1, available through the Irish Parliament website at www.oireachtas.ie/documents/bills28/bills/2010/2210/b2210d.pdf.

Eurogroup (2010) 'Draft Statement', 2 May 2010, available at www.consilium.europa.eu/media/6977/100502-%20eurogroup_statement%20greece.pdf.

(2013a) 'Statement', 16 March 2013, available at http://eurozone.europa.eu/media/402209/Eurogroup%20statement%20CY_final__16%203%202013%20_2_.pdf.

(2013b) 'Statement', 25 March 2013, available at http://eurozone.europa.eu/media/404933/EG%20EG%20Statement%20on%20CY%2025%2003%202013.pdf.

European Commission (2004) 'External and Intra-European Union Trade', Statistical Yearbook 2004, available at http://epp.eurostat.ec.europa.eu/cache/ITY_OFFPUB/KS-CV-04-001/EN/KS-CV-04-001-EN.PDF.

(2011a) The Economic Adjustment Programme for Greece: Third Review – Winter 2011 (Brussels: Directorate-General for Economic and Financial Affairs).

(2011b) The Economic Adjustment Programme for Greece: Fifth Review – October 2011 (Brussels: Directorate-General for Economic and Financial Affairs).

(2011c) The Economic Adjustment Programme for Ireland: Spring 2011 Review (Brussels: Directorate-General for Economic and Financial Affairs).

(2011d) 'External and Intra-European Union Trade', Statistical Yearbook, 2011, available at http://epp.eurostat.ec.europa.eu/cache/ITY_OFFPUB/KS-GI-11-001/EN/KS-GI-11-001-EN.PDF.

(2012a) 'A Blueprint for a Deep and Genuine Economic and Monetary Union: Launching a European Debate – Communication from the Commission', 30 November 2012, COM(2012) 777 final/2, available at http://ec.europa.eu/commission_2010–2014/president/news/archives/2012/11/pdf/blueprint_en.pdf.

(2012b) The Economic Adjustment Programme for Portugal: Fifth Review – Summer 2012 (Brussels: Directorate-General for Economic and Financial Affairs).

(2013) 'Towards a Deep and Genuine Economic and Monetary Union: The Introduction of a Convergence and Competitiveness Instrument – Communication from the Commission', 20 March 2013, COM(2013) 165 final, available at http://ec.europa.eu/economy_finance/articles/governance/pdf/2039_165_final_en.pdf.

'Making it Happen – the European Semester', available at http://ec.europa.eu/europe2020/making-it-happen/index_en.htm.

European Commission, Spain (2012) 'Memorandum of Understanding on Financial-Sector Policy Conditionality', 20 July 2012, available at http://ec.europa.eu/economy_finance/eu_borrower/mou/2012–07–20-spain-mou_en.pdf.

European Commission website (2013) 'MIP Scoreboard', last updated 20 March 2013, available at http://ec.europa.eu/economy_finance/economic_governance/macroeconomic_imbalance_procedure/mip_scoreboard/index_en.htm.

European Committee of Social Rights (2012) 'Decision on the Merits General Federation of Employees of the National Electric Power Corporation and Confederation of Greek Civil Servants' Trade Unions', Complaint No. 66/2011, 23 May 2012, available at www.coe.int/T/DGHL/Monitoring/SocialCharter/Complaints/CC66Merits_en.pdf.

European Council (2010a) 'Conclusions', 28–29 October 2010, available at www.consilium.europa.eu/uedocs/cms_data/docs/pressdata/en/ec/137634.pdf.

(2010b) 'Conclusions', 16–17 December 2010, available at www.consilium.europa.eu/uedocs/cms_data/docs/pressdata/en/ec/118578.pdf.

(2010c) 'Statement by Heads of State and Government of the Euro Area', 25–26 March 2010, available at http://ec.europa.eu/economy_finance/focuson/crisis/2010-03_en.htm.

(2011) 'Conclusions', 24–25 March 2011, available at www.consilium.europa.eu/uedocs/cms_data/docs/pressdata/en/ec/120296.pdf.

(2012a) 'Conclusions', 1–2 March 2012, available at www.consilium.europa.eu/uedocs/cms_data/docs/pressdata/en/ec/128520.pdf.

(2012b) 'Towards a Genuine Economic and Monetary Union', 5 December 2012, available at www.consilium.europa.eu/uedocs/cms_data/docs/pressdata/en/ec/134069.pdf.

European Council the President H. van Rompuy (2012) 'Towards a Genuine Economic and Monetary Union Report', 26 June 2012, 120/12, available at http://ec.europa.eu/economy_finance/focuson/crisis/documents/131201_en.pdf.

European Monetary Institute (1998) *Convergence Report: Report Required by Article 109j of the Treaty establishing the European Community* (Frankfurt: European Monetary Institute).

European Parliament, M. Kumm (2012) 'Democratic Challenges Arising from the Eurocrisis: What Kind of a Constitutional Crisis is Europe in and What Should be Done About it?', presented at Challenges of Multi-Tier Governance in the EU Workshop, 4 October 2012, available at www.eui.eu/Events/download.jsp?FILE_ID=3543.

Finfacts team (2008) 'Government's Emergency Legislation to Provide €400 Billion Guarantee for Irish Banking System to be Passed by Oireachtas Today', *Finfacts Ireland*, 1 October 2008, available at www.finfacts.ie/irishfinancenews/article_1014861.shtml.

German Council of Economic Experts, 'European Redemption Pact', available at www.sachverstaendigenrat-wirtschaft.de/fileadmin/dateiablage/download/publikationen/working_paper_02_2012.pdf.

German Federal Court (2012) 'ESM/Fiskalpakt – Anträge auf Erlass Einer Einstweiligen Anordnung', Press Release, 2 July 2012, available at https://www.bundesverfassungsgericht.de/pressemitteilungen/bvg12-047.html.

Greek Financial Assistance Facility Agreement, available at www.efsf.europa.
    eu/attachments/efsf_greece_fafa.pdf.
IMF (2011) 'Changing Patterns of Global Trade', prepared by the Strategy,
    Policy, and Review Department and approved by Tamim Bayoumi (2011),
    available at www.imf.org/external/np/pp/eng/2011/061511.pdf.
    (2013a) 'Cyprus: Letter of Intent, Memorandum of Economic and Financial
    Policies, and Technical Memorandum of Understanding', 29 April 2013,
    available at www.imf.org/External/NP/LOI/2013/CYP/042913.pdf.
    (2013b) 'Greece: Ex Post Evaluation of Exceptional Access under the 2010
    Stand-By Arrangement', Country Report No. 13/156, June 2013, available
    at www.imf.org/external/pubs/ft/scr/2013/cr13156.pdf.
International Labour Office (2011) 'Report on the High Level Mission to
    Greece', 19–23 September 2011, available at www.ilo.org/global/standards/
    WCMS_170433/lang – nl/index.htm.
    (2012) '365th Report of the Committee on Freedom of Association, Case
    No. 2820 (Greece): Reports in which the Committee requests to be kept
    informed of developments', 784–1003. Available at www.ilo.org/wcmsp5/
    groups/public/---ed_norm/---relconf/documents/meetingdocument/
    wcms_193260.pdf.
Limburg Principles on the Implementation of the International Covenant
    on Economic, Social and Cultural Rights (1987) UN Doc. E/CN.4/1987/17,
    available in 9 *Human Rights Quarterly* (1987), 122–35.
Master Financial Assistance Agreement between European Financial Stability
    Facility, Kingdom of Spain as Beneficiary Member State, Fondo de
    Reestructuración Ordenada Bancaria as Guarantor and the Bank of Spain,
    available at www.efsf.europa.eu/attachments/efsf_spain_ffa.pdf.
Merkel, A. (2010) 'Regierungserklärung von Bundeskanzlerin Merkel zu
    den Euro-Stabilisierungsmaßnahmen', speech before the *Bundestag*,
    19 May 2010, available at www.bundesregierung.de/Content/DE/
    Regierungserklaerung/2010/2010–05–19-merkel-erklaerung-eu-
    stabilisierungsmassnahmen.html.
OECD (2013) 'Debt and Macroeconomic Stability', *OECD Economics Department
    Policy Notes* 16, 2013.
    'Strengthening Euro Area Banks', *Economic Outlook, Analysis and Forecasts*,
    available at www.oecd.org/eco/outlook/strengtheningeuroareabanks.htm.
Office of the United Nations High Commissioner for Human Rights (OHCHR)
    (2011) Independent Expert on the effects of foreign debt and other
    related international financial obligations of States on the full enjoyment
    of all human rights, particularly economic, social and cultural rights
    (Greek crisis: 'Keep in mind the people's basic human rights', 30 June
    2011), available at www.ohchr.org/EN/NewsEvents/Pages/DisplayNews.
    aspx?NewsID=11195&LangID=E.
TESM (2012) 'Declaration on the European Stability Mechanism', 27
    September 2012, available at www.consilium.europa.eu/uedocs/cms_data/
    docs/pressdata/en/ecofin/132615.pdf.

Tommaso Padoa-Schioppa Group (2012) 'Completing the Euro: A Road Map Towards Fiscal Union in Europe', June 2012, available at www.eng.notre-europe.eu/011–3317-Completing-the-EuroA-road-map-towards-fiscal-union-in-Europe.html.

UN Committee on Economic, Social and Cultural Rights (2004) 'Concluding Observations: Greece', 7 June 2004, available at www.refworld.org/publisher,CESCR,CONCOBSERVATIONS,GRC,42d26c904,0.html.

Werner Committee (1970) 'Report to the Council and the Commission on the Realization by Stages of Economic and Monetary Union in the Community (Werner Report)', (8 October 1970) available at http://ec.europa.eu/economy_finance/emu_history/documentation/chapter5/19701008en72realisationbystage.pdf.

Index